淮南市博物馆馆藏战国铜镜

Bronze Mirrors of the Warring States Period Collected in Huainan Museum

淮南市博物馆　编著

Edited by Huainan Museum

文物出版社

图书在版编目（CIP）数据

淮南市博物馆馆藏战国铜镜 : 汉英对照 / 淮南市博
物馆编著 . -- 北京 : 文物出版社 , 2022.11
ISBN 978-7-5010-7815-8

Ⅰ . ①淮… Ⅱ . ①淮… Ⅲ . ①古镜—战国铜器—淮南
—图集 Ⅳ . ① K875.22

中国版本图书馆 CIP 数据核字 (2022) 第 185954 号

# 淮南市博物馆馆藏战国铜镜

编　　著：淮南市博物馆

责任编辑：马晓雪　智　朴
责任印制：张道奇

出版发行：文物出版社
社　　址：北京市东城区东直门内北小街2号楼
邮　　编：100007
网　　址：http://www.wenwu.com
经　　销：新华书店
印　　刷：北京荣宝艺品印刷有限公司
开　　本：889mm×1194mm　1/16
印　　张：15.75
版　　次：2022年11月第1版
印　　次：2022年11月第1次印刷
书　　号：ISBN 978-7-5010-7815-8
定　　价：350.00元

# 目 录 Contents

# 淮南市博物馆馆藏战国铜镜综述

　　2010 年我馆出版的《淮南市博物馆藏镜》一书收录了馆藏铜镜 150 面。该书是在全面梳理了淮南市境内历年来经考古发掘、文物征集以及公安部门移交等入藏的铜镜后完成的。在出版该书的同时，开办了《鉴古照今——淮南市博物馆馆藏铜镜陈列》。在此过程中，我们研究了馆藏铜镜的构成并发现了其中的缺憾，其中最主要的是，虽然淮南是战国楚国最后都城所在地，地下战国墓葬丰富，但馆藏的战国铜镜收藏数量占比较小，仅 17 面。为此，我们确定了文物征集工作的方向和重点。十二年过去了，经过不懈努力，馆藏铜镜的构成比例和面貌有了很大变化，新增了一大批战国铜镜藏品。这样的结果归纳起来得益于三方面成果：其一是最近十多年来积极配合基本建设抢救发掘的战国墓葬中出土了一批战国铜镜；其二是加大了文物保护力度，配合公安部门破获了几起盗墓案件，获得收缴移交一批铜镜，其中有相当数量的战国铜镜；其三是主要方面，我馆调整了文物征集方向，坚持把散落在市域及周边地区的战国铜镜作为近十年的征集工作重点，但囿于征集经费等诸多因素，只能注重铜镜标本（残件）的征集，对能够修复完整的残件应收尽收，这样不仅增加了馆藏战国铜镜的品类，也抢救了一批流落民间的文物，通过修复使之在我们手里重新焕发其应有的价值。通过这三方面的努力，馆藏战国铜镜新增百余面，加上原有的馆藏，我馆战国铜镜总计有 120 余面。尽管这些铜镜的品类、质量还存在着许多不足，但从一座市级博物馆看，能有这样一批种类丰富的战国铜镜，也是令人欣慰的。

## 一　馆藏战国铜镜概述

　　本书收录的馆藏战国铜镜 110 面，其中多数为楚镜或楚式镜，也有少量具有典型特征的秦镜和中原、北方风格的战国铜镜。

　　110 面战国铜镜的主要类别有：素地及有简单纹饰的铜镜 23 面，其他地纹及有简单纹饰的铜镜 3 面，龙凤纹类铜镜包括虺纹镜等 45 面，山字纹铜镜 14 面，纯地纹铜镜 6 面，叶纹类铜镜 15 面，兽纹类铜镜 4 面。其中经考古发掘出土的约占 10%，本地公安部门打击盗墓收缴移交的约占 20%，征集入藏的约占 70%。现摘要叙述如下：

### 素地镜

　　23 面素地镜可分为全素镜、素地细弦纹镜、素地宽圈带纹镜、素地单线连弧纹镜、素地凹面宽带连弧纹镜等5个类别。

全素镜8面，一般尺寸较小，直径多在10厘米左右，镜钮有小三弦钮、弓形钮、小十字钮、粒状小钮，无钮座。镜体大都轻薄，镜缘斜平，镜的材质也大多粗糙，铸造工艺一般。全素镜是楚镜中最早出现的镜种，一般认为在春秋晚期至战国早期出现。《淅川下寺春秋墓》中的M3❶是春秋晚期前段的墓葬（公元前570～前521年），其中出土的素面镜，直径8.7厘米，厚0.1厘米。M3属高等级贵族墓葬，墓主人是一位女性，所使用的照面铜镜也仅是小而薄的素面镜，反映出在春秋晚期到战国早期时使用铜镜的人还很少，应是稀罕之物。

本书收录素地细弦纹镜2面（馆藏共5面），在此合并介绍。素地细弦纹镜，尺寸较小，直径一般不超过10厘米，最小的直径仅6厘米。有三弦钮、小粒状钮、小桥钮，铜质均较粗糙；弦纹有单弦纹和双弦纹两种。素地细弦纹镜流行的时间很长，从春秋晚期到战国晚期都有铸造，在河南南阳西汉早期墓葬中多有发现，所以素地细弦纹镜并非都属早期铜镜，而应根据其出土的墓葬年代和其材质、镜钮特征等综合断代。通过对馆藏铜镜的细微观察，我们发现在一些模制工艺较好的素面镜上，可以看到钮下有方形轮廓痕迹，似为将预先铸好的钮及钮座嵌入镜模中二次浇注成型，这类素面镜的时代可能在战国晚期至西汉。

素地宽圈带纹镜6面。此类镜尺寸稍大，一般直径都在10厘米以上，大者在20厘米以上。馆藏素地宽圈带纹铜镜有两个类型，一是单宽圈带纹，二是双宽圈带纹。高至喜先生在《论楚镜》❷中认为，有两道凸起的细弦纹和凹面宽带纹镜是战国时期秦镜，这在一些秦墓出土的铜镜中得以证实。

素地单线连弧纹镜5面。直径大都在15厘米左右，镜钮一般都是小三弦钮，镜的材质要明显好于素地弦纹镜和全素镜。这类铜镜都有一个共同特征，镜钮座饰一圈凹弧面宽带纹，绕钮座饰内向单线连弧纹，其中七连弧纹镜1面、十一连弧纹镜4面。连弧纹较小，不超过镜面中区，与宽带连弧纹相比，显得娇小秀气。

素地凹面宽带连弧纹镜2面。其流行的时间要晚于全素镜和素地细弦纹镜，它是在素地细弦纹镜的基础上演化而来的。这类铜镜的尺寸较大，一般直径在15～20厘米。素地凹面宽带连弧纹镜发现的较少，多见云雷地或加饰以龙纹、凤纹。我们判断，这种大尺寸的素地或有简单地纹的铜镜，在连弧纹间留有大片空白，疑为彩绘纹饰留下的空间。馆藏云雷地宽带连弧纹铜镜（馆藏编号2476），在云雷地上有厚厚的一层绿松石类颜色，疑为彩绘。除这2面素地凹面宽带连弧纹镜外，馆藏还有3面云雷地凹面宽带连弧纹铜镜。宽带连弧纹镜与宽圈带纹镜在纹样装饰风格及铸造工艺上很相近，且都属大尺寸铜镜，我们判断均属战国晚期秦镜风格。

## 龙凤纹类镜

龙凤纹类镜是战国晚期晚段主要流行的镜种，也是楚镜发展到高峰时期的代表性镜种，不仅种类繁多，且流行传播使用的区域广大。馆藏龙凤纹类镜包括单体写实龙纹、凤纹、变形龙纹、虺纹或尖形虺纹等铜镜，共 45 面，包括单体写实龙纹镜 3 面，六龙六菱镜 4 面，凤纹类镜 6 面，变形龙纹镜 22 面，变形虺纹镜 10 面。

其中 4 面六龙六菱镜是十分少见的镜种，直径都在 16 厘米以上，均为三弦钮，外饰凹弧面宽圈带纹，镜面龙纹华丽繁缛，龙的结构复杂，龙的形态两两相交为一组，龙身翻转舞动、矫健有力，是战国晚期晚段龙纹镜的代表作。凤纹类镜的纹饰也很少见，其中 4 面三凤三菱镜与龙纹类镜的风格相近，在菱纹和凤纹关系处理上与龙纹镜相近，不同的是龙纹遒劲有张力，而凤纹风格飘逸流畅，更显轻松自然。

馆藏凤纹类镜中，有 1 面直径在 14 厘米以上的三凤三龙镜，主纹是以三凤、三龙相间排列，这种装饰布局与三龙三菱镜相似，只是以三凤代替三菱，但纹饰的风格未变。凤单足立于钮座上，勾回首，小凤眼，短喙，凤口衔尾羽，两翼勾连两侧的龙羽；而龙的布局与凤相反，以头部顶托钮座，龙首硕大，回首，双目，大张口，口中有獠牙，足踏镜缘，前后翼与相邻的凤羽穿花勾连，龙凤的身躯呈蔓枝状缠绕。此镜中的主题纹饰以凤为主，凤的身体占据镜面中区，而龙的形态生动有趣，虽张口獠牙，但有笑面之容。从布局上观察，凤立上、龙居下，龙又呈呼唤凤的姿态，更有烘托凤的画面观感。此镜连同馆藏的另 4 面三凤三菱镜，装饰风格、模铸方法相近，都应是战国晚期晚段时期的产品。在这批三凤镜中还看到装饰方法的显著变化，其中有 3 面尺寸稍小的三凤三菱镜的纹饰，从平实的单线条开始向局部双勾线转化，这也反映出在战国晚期晚段时铜镜风格的变化。这面三凤三龙镜与上文所述的 4 面六龙六菱镜相比较，在时间上稍稍晚些，但都有可能是楚国迁都寿春以后的产品。

龙凤纹类镜中的虺纹镜占比较大，虺纹的演化过程在这批铜镜中得到集中体现。从盘曲错节的虺纹变成了简单的"S"形和"C"形，从实心宽线纹变为双勾线纹；铜质和铸造工艺也出现了由盛到衰的演变。双勾线纹装饰方法到西汉早中期时普遍用于博局镜和蟠螭纹镜上。

### 山字纹镜

本书收录的馆藏山字纹铜镜 14 面，有四山四叶、四山八叶、四山八叶四花、四山十二叶、四山十六叶、四山四鹿、五山镜等。

山字纹镜是铜镜研究者普遍关注的镜种，由于山字纹变化丰富、风格多样，研究者对其铸造地也有着不同的看法。20 世纪 30 年代末在河北易县曾出土 8 件山字纹镜的镜范，山西侯马出土过草叶纹镜的镜范，而战国镜出土较多的湖南长沙、河南南阳、安徽寿县等地，至今没有发现镜范。出土山字纹镜镜范的易县，无疑铸造过此类铜镜，而学术界普遍认为长沙作为楚镜的铸造中心，也理应铸造过山字纹镜，从已发现的山字纹镜的面貌上也可以辨别出其明显的地域特征。近年来在山东临淄齐国都城遗址出土的一批山字纹镜，有明显区别于楚镜的特征。其中永流战国墓 M198、M429[3] 出土的 2 件山字纹铜镜上的山是以四条平行单线组成，羽状地纹粗大、模铸不甚精细，但在范家墓地 M178[4] 出土的 1 件四山八叶镜的纹饰风格与楚式镜又很相近，只是地纹和叶纹相对粗大，缺少一点楚式镜的精细。临淄出土的这批山字纹镜的区域面貌特征明显，应是战国齐国都城所铸。这种差别是战国时期齐楚间的差异，如果区别楚地范围内的具体产地就十分困难了。

馆藏山字纹镜中有 3 面是值得重点关注的。其一是四山四鹿镜，该镜是 1987 年 12 月在淮南市西部与楚都寿春城遗址相邻的谢家集区红卫轮窑厂出土，直径 15.7 厘米，小三弦钮，双层方形钮座，四山左旋，羽状地上的四个山字之间饰鹿纹，鹿两足立地、两足弯曲，身饰鳞片纹，最生动的是鹿头高昂回首，整个姿态矫健有力。这是一面罕见的铜镜。除此镜外，国内已公开的资料上仅见上海博物馆收藏了 1 件四山四鹿镜，该镜双层圆钮座，直径 17.03 厘米，四山左旋，但鹿纹的铸造工艺不及本馆所藏，鹿纹与羽状地纹接缝不佳，山字中间竖笔向一侧倾斜，略显不对称。其二是羽状地四山四叶镜，品相极佳，是十分罕见的精细作品，其钮与钮座在楚镜中也是难得一见，钮下有一个稍稍大于钮径的小双层钮座，羽状地纹极为讲究，羽尾卷而凸起，极其细密。此镜地纹看不到接范痕迹，有可能是失蜡法所铸。上海博物馆陈佩芬先生在观察一些战国铜镜纹饰有明显的缩蜡痕迹后认为，这些铜镜确是用失蜡法铸造的❺。失蜡法在春秋早期开始使用，春秋晚期时已能铸造出复杂的铜器了，所以，用失蜡法铸造铜镜也在情理之中。其三是四山十二叶镜，此镜直径 15 厘米，小三弦钮，双层钮座，左旋四山字纹。其独特之处在叶纹。四山之间各有一由枝叶组成的如立人状的纹饰，在方钮座的四角各伸出一枝杆，枝杆顶端的叶片如人的头部，肩下两枝叶如人的手臂前后交叉，末端的叶片如人的手部，枝杆三层叠压，如站立的且手臂交叉的舞者，形象生动。这种山字纹镜很少见到，是否用失蜡法铸造有待研究。

上述 3 面山字纹镜都有战国晚期晚段特征，即镜体稍厚，尤其是镜缘的沿由尖变平，我们判断可能为楚迁都寿春后铸造的。

除以上 3 面重要的山字纹镜外，与我馆山字纹镜相关联的，也在此简要介绍。宿州市博物馆收藏的 2009 年出土的三山镜（图 1），直径 9.7 厘米，小三弦钮，双层圆钮座，三山右旋；2020 年在亳州市谯城万达 M23（该墓墓口 6.1 米 ×4.3 米，时代在战国中晚期）出土的六山镜，直径 17 厘米，小三弦钮，双层圆钮座，山左旋，羽状地

图 1　三山镜（宿州市博物馆藏）

纹非常精细；2011年在六安白鹭洲战国墓M566中出土的直径27厘米的六山镜❻，山中间竖划很长，顶托镜缘，山右旋，山山相接，内侧形成一个六角形，同墓还出土了1面直径17厘米的四山镜、1面直径8.1厘米的素地镜。六山镜存世量相对较多，据不完全统计，中国国家博物馆收藏2面，上海博物馆、广州西汉南越王博物馆、浙江私人藏家、日本东京国立博物馆、美国萨克勒博物馆各收藏1面，加上安徽出土的2面，总数应该在12面以上。这12面六山镜中，只有六安出土的是山右旋，其余均为山左旋。相比之下，三山镜发现的很少，从已公开的资料看，宿州市博物馆收藏1面、中国台湾私人收藏2面，另有瑞典东亚博物馆1面三山三鹿镜。瑞典东亚博物馆收藏的三山三鹿镜的地纹和鹿纹与我馆收藏的四山四鹿镜十分相近，应是同一地产品。传为洛阳金村大墓出土的直径14.6厘米的四山兽纹镜❼，其山字纹和兽纹的风格也与我馆收藏的四山四鹿镜相近，也同为少见镜种。

### 叶纹类镜

本书收录了叶纹类镜15面，其中四叶纹镜9面，八叶纹镜2面，八叶四花纹镜1面，十二叶纹镜3面。15面叶纹镜中，5面是云雷纹地，10面为羽状纹地。云雷地叶纹镜都较小，直径一般都在10厘米以下，镜体都很轻薄；羽状地叶纹镜直径多在10厘米以上，镜体相对厚实。

云雷纹地叶纹镜除直径较小外，还有个显著特征是纹饰铸造精细。其中的十二叶纹镜，小三弦钮，双层钮座，在钮座四角各伸出一枝杆，每枝杆饰两桃形叶片，在近缘处的四叶片间分别加饰一叶片。此镜虽然直径仅9厘米，但其地纹极为精细，粒状小点纹直径不到1毫米，细如发丝的卷云纹有5圈之多，层层都很清晰。云雷地叶纹镜的发现数量远少于羽状纹地叶纹镜，这类铜镜的流行时间要稍早于羽状地纹镜。馆藏的这批云雷地叶纹镜是其中佳品。

在叶纹镜上能够观察到战国铜镜装饰方法和基本规律，用一小片叶纹的变化如扁桃叶纹、长桃叶纹、柳叶纹，再结合以线、面的方法，就能演绎出千变万化的纹样来装饰铜镜，而羽状纹、山字纹等，都是截取某种纹样的局部并予以美化来进行装饰的。这其中的变化凝结着一代代铸镜工匠对美的追求和创造，也折射出那个时代人们的审美和思考。

### 兽纹类镜

本书收录了兽纹类铜镜4面，其中饕餮纹镜1面。此类镜发现较少，见于已公开材料的仅4面，有确切出土地点的是河北省邯郸市易县赵王陵周窑一号墓出土的1面，时代在战国晚期❽。饕餮纹镜的装饰风格、铸造技术与典型的楚式镜相比，有较大区别。其他变形兽纹镜以羽状纹为地，小三弦钮，圆钮座。变形的四兽纹十分特别，是将兽纹几乎变成方形或圆形的几何形状，这类铜镜在湖南楚墓中发现较多。从有首有眼、身躯圆胖、长尾翻转、形似灵长类动物，逐步演化成头部消失、身体变形成"C"形的几何状图案。湖南长沙楚墓中发现的这类铜镜，反映了兽纹变化过程中的不同时期的造型特点。除长沙外，河南南阳也有发现，但这类铜镜的产地可能在长沙。

## 二　对馆藏铜镜地纹的认识

战国时期是中国铜镜发展过程中第一个高峰期。战国铜镜大都有地纹，这也是战国铜镜的基本特征，地纹的作用是衬托各种主体纹饰。本书收录的这批战国铜镜中的地纹，可归纳成素地、云雷地纹和羽状地纹三大类。

战国铜镜的主体纹饰变化十分丰富，用作装饰的纹样也复杂多样。不同的时期，不同的主体纹饰会成为主流，从山字纹到龙纹、凤纹、虺纹、兽形纹等，它反映出当时审美的趋势。尤其是龙纹类装饰，形态各异、变化多样，有些龙纹的形态特征需要花些时间才能辨识出来。但是，地纹在战国时期的变化不如主纹，这也是重要的时代特征之一，不论主纹怎样变化，地纹都相对稳定，不仅变化不大，使用时间也相对较长，而且其细微的变化也反映出时代和地域特征。

云雷地纹和羽状地纹是战国铜镜地纹的主流，配以千变万化的主纹，共同构成战国铜镜变化多样的纹饰。如，山字纹镜大都以羽状纹为地，龙凤纹类镜大都以云雷纹为地，这种地纹与主纹相对固定的搭配，不仅在楚地使用，而且在北方各地也同样使用。这种固定搭配模式沿袭的时间跨度超过百年，不仅体现出一代代工匠的技艺传承，也反映出楚人审美的执着和情趣。同时，战国铜镜中也发现大量的仅有地纹、无主纹的铜镜，如云纹、云雷纹、羽状纹，用其满铺镜面；也发现罕有品类，本是用作地纹的纹样用作主纹，本书收录1面云雷地羽状纹镜（图2），十分罕见，这也是研究羽状纹变化的重要资料。

图2　云雷地羽状纹镜（淮南市博物馆藏）

## 三　对馆藏素地镜的认识

素地镜是指全素地镜或在素地上饰以单线弦纹、宽带纹、宽带纹加饰连弧纹等纹饰的铜镜。本书收录的馆藏素地镜23面，其中全素地镜8面，直径多在8～15厘米之间；素地宽圈带纹镜和素地宽带连弧纹镜镜体较大，最大的直径有23厘米，而素地单线弦纹镜大小居于全素镜和素地宽带纹镜之间，直径一般在15厘米左右。这其中应该蕴藏着素地镜演化过程中的某种规律。全素地镜不仅形制小、镜面平直，而且大多铸造相对粗糙；虽然无装饰，但也可以从镜钮上辨识其时代的不同。早期全素地镜有扁弓形钮，如馆藏编号2418、2481的2面全素地镜，而馆藏编号 2428 的三弦钮制作精细，明显有别于以上 2 面铜镜，有稍晚时代的特征。在一些素地镜镜钮下发现的方形模印痕，似是将预先模铸好的镜钮座嵌入镜模二次浇铸成型，这一类素地镜的时代可能要晚一些。

全素地镜最早出现于春秋晚期至战国早期，战国中期已经很流行了，也是楚式镜中最早出现的镜种，从其早中期的扁弓形钮逐渐演化到稍晚的三弦钮，使用时间的跨度很长，从河南南阳西汉墓葬中的出土的 15 面全素地镜 [9] 来推断，最迟可沿用到西汉中期。《长沙楚墓》[10] 所录出土的全素地镜 34 面，均出土于战国楚墓。通过以上比较可知，全素地镜在中原地区的流行使用时间比楚地中心区域包括长沙、荆州、寿春的时间要长久；另一方面，从制作工艺上看，全素镜的制作相对简单方便，这可能是其流行使用时间较长的原因之一。

素地细弦纹镜、素地宽圈带纹镜和素地弦纹加饰连弧纹镜，流行和使用时间跨度比全素镜更长。本书收录的 15 面素地弦纹镜，镜钮有扁弓形、三弦形、小桥形和小粒状等四种，饰单线凸弦纹、双线凸弦纹、双圈宽带连弧纹、三圈宽带连弧纹。从发展变化的顺序看，小素地镜产生在先，而后发展到单线连弧纹镜，到战国晚期晚段出现形制硕大的两圈宽带纹，直径在 20 厘米以上的大型铜镜。馆藏直径在 20 厘米左右宽圈带纹镜（馆藏编号 2541、2425、2426、2427），就是这一时期的产品。长沙出土的直径 17.8 厘米素地弦纹镜，是在白起拔郢之后的秦墓中出土的，南阳出土的直径 18.4 厘米宽带纹镜是在一座西汉早期墓葬中出土 [11]。这种直径硕大的宽带纹镜是素地镜发展到最后阶段的产品，有的还增饰彩绘。在馆藏编号 2541、2405 的 2 面镜上，还能看到彩绘的遗留物（馆藏编号 2541 镜上的彩绘疑是朱砂，馆藏编号 2405 镜上的彩绘疑是绿松石）。这可能是制镜工匠对这种形制硕大，纹样又相对简单、留有大片空白的铜镜的一种补充和美化。

馆藏素地弦纹镜中有 7 面属秦镜风格。一般认为素地镜中有一道弦纹的属楚镜，有两道凸起的细弦纹和凹弧面宽带纹的属秦镜，这在湖北云梦秦墓、陕西咸阳秦墓和四川涪陵秦墓中出土的铜镜上得到证实。这 7 面铜镜中有 5 面是双圈细线凸弦纹镜，尺寸不大，直径一般在 10 厘米左右，而双圈凹弧面宽带纹尺寸都较大，直径一般都在 20 厘米以上，比长沙市火车站邮电局秦墓 M7 出土的还要大一些（该墓的陶器组合及风格有典型的秦代风格）。

# 四　对馆藏龙纹镜的认识

龙纹镜是战国时期普遍流行的镜种之一。馆藏 120 余面战国镜中，龙纹类（包括凤纹、虺纹）铜镜 45 面，占比较高。龙纹镜的定名没有统一认识，同样的纹饰称谓不尽相同。客观原因是龙纹类铜镜纹饰复杂、变化丰富，大类就包括龙纹、变形龙纹等，具体来说，有称之为蟠螭纹、蟠龙纹、螭龙纹、虺纹、蟠虺纹等等。战国晚期铜镜上的龙纹大多是龙蛇复合体，又称之为蛇体龙，在这一点上认识基本相同，所以本书在铜镜定名上主要称之为龙纹或变形龙纹，无龙首特征的称之为虺纹。

馆藏龙纹类镜主要有：三龙镜、三龙三凤镜、三龙三叶镜、三龙三凤三叶镜、三龙三凤四叶镜、三龙三菱镜、四龙镜、四龙四叶镜、六龙六菱镜、三虺镜、三虺三菱镜、变形三虺三菱镜、四虺镜、四虺四菱镜、四虺四叶镜、四虺四叶四菱镜、八虺镜等等，约十余种纹饰类型。其中，三龙镜中的龙纹是最具象的。馆藏 2 面云雷纹地三龙镜（馆藏编号 2411、2467），三龙环列，龙首、龙翼、龙尾十分写实，与同期青铜器上的龙纹风格十分相近，也是人们普遍认知的龙的形象。这种形态的龙纹镜在长沙楚墓、江苏仪征都有出土，但数量不多。馆藏另 2 面三龙镜（馆藏编号 2463、2450）的龙纹布局变化不大，但身躯开始出现变化，近似一种菱形图案，龙的翼翅开始简化了。这类图案化的龙纹镜发现的也不多，在南阳出土的 1 面与本馆藏品十分相似。龙纹走向图案化是在三龙、四龙间加饰叶纹、菱形纹后开始的。在夸张的变形过程中，龙首的主要特征被保留下来，如馆藏的三龙三菱镜（馆藏编号 2443），龙首接近于正面形象，龙首上有少见的双圆目，一大一小，吐舌微卷；而龙的身体躯干已演变成图案形态，与菱形纹勾连穿插，成为一个整体。且这种图案化的龙纹变化得愈加复杂，逐渐演化为蔓枝缠绕，反复勾连，相互交错，以至于辨识起来都很困难。写实类龙纹镜数量、传播区域远不及变形图案化龙纹镜，这从一个侧面说明了写实龙纹镜流行的时间较短，而图案化的龙纹镜的存续时间较长、流行区域广泛。这种从简单的写实形象快速过渡到图案化形象，在已发现的龙纹镜中得到证实，在出土战国铜镜的湖南、湖北、安徽、河南、江苏、陕西、山东等地都有发现。其中，河南南阳出土了龙纹类镜约 60 面，其时代从战国晚期到西汉早期。而其中具象龙纹的龙纹镜也仅有 3 面。

龙纹镜上的纹饰最能反映楚人的审美观和文化特质。如楚人尚赤，这在楚墓出土的漆木器及丝织品的色彩中得以体现。但在单色的铜镜上是靠纹样的变化反映内心的精神世界。《楚辞》中记录了楚人充满幻想、神话、巫术的精神世界，将天、地、人、神融为一体。楚人尚凤尊龙，这在战国晚期的龙凤镜中表现得淋漓尽致。在奇幻多变的龙纹世界中，以繁缛、细腻、运动交错的龙纹展现出楚人的精神世界，营造出奇异诡谲的神秘之境。简化龙纹（包括凤纹、虺纹）镜是战国晚期晚段龙纹镜的基本面貌，从写实且简单的龙纹镜到奇异复杂多变的龙纹镜，再到简化的龙纹镜，楚国晚期的铜镜走过了由盛而衰的过程，这也是楚镜由辉煌走向衰落的缩影。细察这类简化的龙纹镜，还能看出铜镜的材质也发生了改变，模铸工艺水平也在下降，究其原因，其中最重要的是时代背景发生了重大变化。战国晚期晚段以后人口增多，尤其是汉初休养生息政策的实行，人口急剧增加，铜镜的使用愈加普及，需求扩大，产量随之增加，工艺水平也相应下降，这也为汉代铜镜风格的形成奠定了基础条件。

馆藏 2 面直径在 20 厘米左右的大尺寸龙纹镜，是这龙纹类铜镜的代表作。2 面龙纹镜的纹饰风格相近，都以云雷纹铺地，其中直径 24 厘米的龙纹镜为小连弧纹钮座，这种装饰手法比较少见，显露出其时代较晚的特征；另 1 面直径 19.8 厘米的四龙四叶镜（馆藏编号 2479）也比较少见，它以四个很小的叶片将龙纹分隔成四区，叶片分区的功能大于装饰作用。这一方面反映出龙纹纹饰变化的过程，另一方面能够借此观察到战国时期铜镜工匠在解决环列布局问题时的思考和做法。所以，我们今天看到的铜镜纹饰，不论是简单还是复杂，仔细查看后都能体会出其中的审美规律。

馆藏龙纹镜中有 4 面十分罕见的六龙六菱镜。这 4 面铜镜尺寸相近，均为 16 厘米左右（馆藏编号 2486、2543、1927、2478）。这 4 面铜镜都是以细密的云雷纹为地，主纹是变形龙纹。菱形纹的布局很有特点，在内区的镜钮外饰有三个很小的菱形纹，其上端靠近镜缘处也饰有三个很小的菱形纹，六个菱形纹上下交错安排的布局方法充分说明菱形纹分区功能大于装饰功能，在效果上起到凸显龙纹的作用，每个菱形纹与龙首上的角相连，融为一个整体。这 4 面铜镜的尺寸、纹饰、铸造工艺及装饰手法十分相近，应属同一产地。在湖南、湖北、河南等地楚墓中还尚未发现有类似纹饰的铜镜，有可能是楚国迁都寿春后铸造。

馆藏还有一批与龙纹镜装饰风格相同的凤纹镜。凤纹镜的流行是与龙纹镜同步的，一直延续使用至战国晚期晚段，并且同龙纹镜一样演化而成西汉早期铜镜的风格。馆藏 6 面凤纹镜可分为两大类：一是在地纹上沿钮座环列独立的凤纹，凤纹互不相连，凤的形象相对写实，凤与凤之间隔以花叶纹或菱形纹；这类凤纹镜在四川、湖南、河南等地都有出土，但数量不多。二是凤纹图案化，这类凤纹镜发现的更少，集中在淮南地区，在湖南等地有零星发现。

## 五　郢都寿春铸镜初探

战国时期楚国迁都寿春以后，有没有铸造铜镜？有学者提出，淮南出土的四山四鹿镜有明确的出土地点，所饰鹿纹与上海博物馆的四山四鹿镜的鹿纹完全一样，而这类山字镜在出土山字镜最多的湖南地区至今未发现此类鹿纹镜，推测其产于淮南地区的可能性要大些[12]。据统计，在淮南地区发现的特有纹饰的镜种不止如此。新中国成立以来，在淮南地区出土和征集的一大批战国铜镜中，有些镜种是十分少见且特殊的，是在其他地区未见或罕见的，如馆藏 4 面六龙六菱镜、三龙三凤四叶镜、三龙三凤镜、四山十二叶镜、十二花叶镜等等，这些纹样的铜镜在已公开发表的铜镜资料中很少见到，在寿春铸造的可能性很大。我们认为，寿春作为都城，手工业中的铸镜业是必不可少的，在楚国迁都寿春后，铸镜工匠应该会一同来到寿春，铜镜作为生活必需品，理应有铸造。甚至在迁都前，寿春作为楚国在北方的重要城市，可能就已经有铜镜铸造业了，只是不及迁都后的规模。

公元前 241 年（考烈王二十二年），楚国迁都寿春，改寿春为郢。20 世纪 80 年代，安徽省文物考古研究所丁邦均先生率队在寿县工作多年，通过实地调查、考古勘探和遥感勘测，基本确定了寿春城的位置和范围[13]。根据其研究成果，寿春城的地望在今寿县县城东南，其范围东至东津渡、西至瘦西湖西岸、南至十里头、北至淝河，总面积 26.35 平方公里。在淝河西岸发现的柏家台大型建筑遗址，面积 3000 多平方米，11 开间，进深 42 米。寿春城的面积超过纪南城、临淄城、侯马晋城、曲阜鲁城、邯郸赵城及郑州故城，寿春城的城市格局也是完备的，包括宫殿区、礼制高台建筑、水路交通、城门等，作为都城必需的手工业包括铸造铜镜在内的铸造业也应当是其重要的组成部分，1987 年在城北发现了制陶遗址，近年来在城东南牛尾岗又发现了为建造都城烧造建筑材料的陶作坊遗址。

新中国成立以来的 70 多年中，经过文物工作者长期不懈的努力，基本查明了淮南、寿县地区战国墓葬的分布状况。舜耕山南麓、瓦埠湖北岸、东淝河东岸的淮南市三和镇、杨公镇、望峰岗镇、李郢孜镇境内是楚国高等级墓葬区，这里密集分布着有高大封土堆的楚墓。在这一区域先后发现了李三孤堆楚幽王墓、蔡声侯产墓以及众多小型墓葬。2019 年以来，在淮南市三和镇徐洼村进行的武王墩墓抢救性发掘工作，现已完成封土揭取，正在发掘墓室。根据勘探结果，该墓为一座开口为 50 米 ×50 米的甲字形大墓，墓道长 42 米，墓西侧 60 米处有长 147 米的车马坑；经勘探还发现，以武王墩墓为中心，周边为大型陵园，是由围壕围成的近方形结构，占地面积 169 公顷，规模宏大、规制完备，在先秦王陵中十分罕见。武王墩墓正南方向 14.6 公里处的杨公镇朱家集李三孤堆墓，发现于 20 世纪 30 年代，1983 年安徽省文物考古研究所对该墓进行了勘探和清理，得知其墓口为 41 米 ×41 米，墓道长 22.4 米。1958 年和 1959 年在淮南市蔡家岗赵家孤堆发掘了 2 座春秋晚期墓，不少学者认为是蔡侯墓；1977~1982 年在淮南市杨公镇发掘了 11 座中型战国楚墓。近年来，在六安发掘了一大批战国楚墓，在安庆潜山、枞阳等地也都发掘了一批楚墓。在上述市县，包括阜阳、亳州的市县博物馆都收藏了一批战国铜镜，其中大部分是经考古发掘出土。

楚都寿春的周边，包括今天的淮南、六安、阜阳等地都出土了一批楚镜，这反映出战国晚期以后此地铜镜的需求量很大。1957 年在淮南市谢家集区唐山公社邱家岗战国墓中出土了四山四花四叶镜。1958 年在唐山公社九里大队 2 座战国墓中出土了 2 件羽状地草叶纹镜，其中 1 面是方形钮座小四叶镜，纹饰相对粗犷，另 1 面为小方座的十二叶纹镜，纹饰较为细腻。1972 年在离寿县邱家花园不远的谢家集区红卫轮窑厂战国墓中，出土的 1 面羽状地四叶镜，比九里大队出土的四叶镜时代应当更晚些，其羽状地更加细腻，圆钮座和四小叶片也更精细，这反映出四叶镜在淮南地区的发展变化。1982 年 8 月，在谢家集区赖山公社莲花大队战国墓中出土的 1 面龙纹镜，龙纹的形态和风格已从复杂细致转向简约。1986 年在谢家集区施家湖乡蒋成米家中收缴了 1 面刚刚出土于战国墓葬中的羽状地四叶镜，其四叶环绕钮座，叶的形状呈花苞状，这种绕镜钮布置小四叶纹是此类铜镜装饰的最后形态，此后就演变成多枚枝叶纹和变形叶纹的装饰手法。1987 年在谢家集区红卫轮窑厂战国墓中出土了 1 面羽状地四山四鹿镜，有明确的出土地点，是一面十分重要、难得一见的铜镜。2010 年在谢家集区李郢孜镇战国墓中出土了 1

面羽状地四叶镜，制作精美，纹饰清晰，层次分明，我们初步判断是用失蜡法铸造，其镜缘已明显变厚、变宽，有着显著的战国晚期晚段的特征。2020 年在淮南市高新区战国墓中出土了 1 面四龙四凤宽带连弧纹镜。近年来，安徽省文物考古研究所寿县中心工作站在淮南、寿县地区发掘了一批战国晚期墓葬，出土了铜镜 10 余面。相关著作中，《六安出土铜镜》收录战国铜镜 20 面，《寿县博物馆馆藏铜镜集粹》收录战国铜镜 12 面，《皖西博物馆文物撷珍》收录战国铜镜 5 面等。

成书于汉武帝时期的《淮南子》从另一个侧面记载了铜镜铸造的历史。《淮南子·修务训》："明镜之始下型，朦然未见形容，及其粉以玄锡，摩以白旃，鬓眉微豪可得而察"。这段记述详细记载了铜镜的使用方法，只有参与过铜镜铸造的，才有可能记录下这个过程。1974 年寿县板桥镇出土的"隆帝章和时淮南"铭龙虎纹镜，是一件反映本地东汉时期手工业制作水平的铜镜，极其难得。铜镜铭文首句写道："隆帝章和时淮南"，能够获知该镜铸造时间和产地，为东汉章帝章和元年时淮南寿春。《后汉书》中有章帝刘炟在章和元年（公元 87 年）南巡到九江郡治寿春的史实记载。寿春龙氏铸镜家族为纪念此事件铸造出了这面具有重要意义的纪年铜镜。这也反映出楚国虽亡，其手工业中的铜镜铸造在两汉时期的淮南地区，不仅没有衰落，而且仍在继续传承和发展。

淮南市博物馆馆长 汪茂东

❶ 河南省文物考古研究所、河南省丹江口库区考古发掘队、淅川县博物馆：《淅川下寺春秋墓》，文物出版社，1991 年。

❷ 高至喜：《论楚镜》，《文物》1991 年第 5 期。

❸ 淄博市临淄区文物管理局编：《山东临淄战国汉代墓葬与出土铜镜研究》，文物出版社，2017。

❹ 临淄区文物局：《山东淄博市临淄区范家墓地战国墓》，《考古》2016 年 2 期。

❺ 上海博物馆：《练形神冶 莹质良工——上海博物馆藏铜镜精品》，上海书画出版社，2005 年。

❻ 安徽省文物考古研究所、六安市文物管理局：《安徽六安市白鹭洲战国墓 M566 的发掘》，《考古》2012 年第 5 期。

❼ 霍宏伟、史家珍主编：《洛镜铜华——洛阳铜镜发现与研究》，科学出版社，2013年。

❽ 河北省文物管理处：《河北邯郸赵王陵》，《考古》1982年第6期。

❾ 南阳市文物考古研究所：《南阳出土铜镜》，文物出版社，2010年。

❿ 湖南省博物馆等：《长沙楚墓》，文物出版社，2010年。

⓫ 南阳市文物考古研究所：《南阳出土铜镜》，文物出版社，2010年。

⓬ 贺刚：《说山字纹铜镜》，楚文化研究会《楚文化研究论集（第六集）》，湖北教育出版社，2005年。

⓭ 丁邦均、李德文：《寿春城遗址遥感调查新收获》，楚文化研究会《楚文化研究论集（第二集）》，湖北人民出版社，1991年。

# An Overview of *Bronze Mirrors of the Warring States Period Collected in Huainan Museum*

The book *Bronze Mirrors Collected at Huainan Museum*, which includes 150 mirrors, was published in 2010 by the Huainan Museum. The book is based on the presentation of mirrors collected over the years from archaeological excavations, collecting and transfers by public security agencies. Meanwhile, the exhibition *Taking History as a Mirror and Learning Lessons from It: Exhibition of Bronze Mirrors Collected at Huainan Museum* has been opened to the public. In doing so, a number of problems have been revealed. The first is a minor percentage of bronze mirrors of the Warring States Period, including 17 mirrors. But we must not lose sight of the fact that Huainan City is the site of the last capital of the Chu State of the Warring States Period and contains a large number of tombs of the Warring States Period. For this reason, the direction and focus of collecting had been decided. As the number of mirrors of the Warring States Period increased through twelve years of tough work, the proportions and conditions of bronze mirrors collected have been considerably changed. Three results have emerged: The first is that the museum has collected mirrors of the Warring States Period unearthed by salvage excavations on tombs of the Warring States Period in the last decade of capital construction; the second is that some mirrors of the Warring States Period are given by public security institutions, which were seized in several cracked grave-robbing cases under the enhanced preservation of cultural relics; the third is that the emphasis on collecting cultural relics, as the primary importance, has changed in the last decade to the private collections of bronze mirrors of the Warring States Period in the city and its neighboring districts. Due to lack of funds and additional shortcomings, the museum has only the ability to collect fragments that could be properly repaired. Then the collections of bronze mirrors at the museum have grown in variety. Some cultural relics of private collections were rescued and have renewed their original value in the museum after being repaired. As a result of the efforts of all three, more than 100 new mirrors of the Warring States Period are collected at the museum. Now there are over 120 bronze mirrors of the Warring States Period in the museum, including the original collections. It is a fact that there are some problems with the variety and quality of the collections of bronze mirrors. But for a city-level museum, it is encouraging to have a diverse collection of bronze mirrors of the Warring States Period.

## I. A Summary of Bronze Mirrors of the Warring States Period Collected

This book contains 110 bronze mirrors, of which the largest number are mirrors of the Chu State or the Chu-style mirrors, the few mirrors of the Warring States Period with the typical styles of the Qin State, the Central Plains and the North.

Mirrors collected include: 23 mirrors with plain pattern as ground motif or simple motif, 3 mirrors with other pattern as ground motif and simple motif, 45 mirrors with motif of dragon and phoenix such as mirrors with motif of coiled serpent, 14 mirrors with inscription motif of "*shan* (mountain)" character, 21 mirrors with only ground motif or motif of simple leaves and 4 mirrors with motif of beasts. Of all the mirror collections of the Warring States Period, those collected from archaeological excavation account for 10 percent of the total, those from the transfer of cracked cases of grave-robbing by public security agencies account for 20 percent and those from collecting account for 70 percent. A brief introduction is now given as follows:

### Bronze Mirrors with plain pattern as ground motif

23 bronze mirrors with plain pattern as ground motif contain the mirrors without design, the mirrors with plain pattern as ground motif and design of slender bow string, the mirrors with plain pattern as ground motif and design of broad band, the mirrors with plain pattern as ground motif and design of linked arcs formed by single line and the mirrors with plain pattern as

ground motif and design of linked arcs formed by broad band with concave surface.

There are eight bronze mirrors without design, with a small size of about 10cm in diameter. Some mirrors do not have knob base. The knobs of mirrors are decorated with the design of three bow strings, or the shape of bow, the shape of a small cross and the shape of granule. Mirrors have a slim body and a slanting rim. The casting and material quality of the mirrors are poor. It is generally believed that the bronze mirror without design is the earliest style of the bronze mirror of the Chu State, appearing between the late Spring and Autumn Period and the early Warring States Period. The mirror without design, with a diameter of 8.7cm and a thickness of 0.1cm, was unearthed in the Tomb M3 of the book *Tombs of the Spring and Autumn Period at Xiasi Town, Xichuan County*[1]. The Tomb M3 is a high-class tomb of a nobleman of the early period of the late Spring and Autumn Period (570 BC – 521 BC). The owner of the tomb is a woman. The small and slim mirror without design unearthed shows that bronze mirrors were not in widespread use and were used by the wealthy.

The book records two bronze mirrors with plain pattern as ground motif and design of slender bow string. (The museum has a total of five bronze mirrors with plain pattern as ground motif and design of slender bow string in the collections. ) All introduce together here. The mirrors are in a small size with a diameter of no more than 10cm, and the smallest diameter of the mirrors is 6cm. The knobs of the mirrors are decorated with the design of three bow strings, or the shape of granule or the shape of bridge. The material quality of the mirrors is poor. The patterns of bow string contain the pattern of bow string formed by single line and the pattern of bow string formed by double lines. It had been cast for a long time between the late Spring and Autumn Period and the late Warring States Period. Some were unearthed in the tombs of the early Western Han Dynasty in Nanyang, Henan Province. So all mirrors can not be classified as the early style of bronze mirrors, and the distinguishing periods of the mirrors is by the quality of the material, the shape of the knob, and the time at which the tomb was excavated. On closer inspection, rectangular-shaped marks can be found under the knobs of the mirrors which are exquisitely technical, and can tell that the shape of the mirror could be formed in a second pour after the casted knob and knob base were embedded in the mirror mold. The bronze mirror with plain pattern as ground motif and design of slender bow string were in use from the late Warring States Period to the Western Han Dynasty.

There are six bronze mirrors with plain pattern as ground motif and design of broad band. These mirrors are in a big size with a diameter of over 10cm, and the bigger one has a diameter of over 20cm. On the mirrors of the museum, decorative patterns include the pattern of single broad band and the pattern of two broad bands. In the book *On the Bronze Mirror of the Chu*[2], Mr. Gao Zhixi makes the point that the mirrors with design of two raised slender bow strings or with the design of broad band with concave surface can be classified into the bronze mirrors of the Qin State in the Warring States Period. This view is confirmed by bronze mirrors unearthed in the tombs of the Qin State.

There are six bronze mirrors with plain pattern as ground motif and design of linked arcs formed by single line. They have a diameter of about 15cm. The knobs are decorated with the design of three small bow strings. The material quality of the mirrors is better than that of the mirrors with plain pattern as ground motif and design of bow string and the mirrors without design. These bronze mirrors are distinguished with the design of a broad band with concave surface on the knob base and the design of inward linked arcs formed by single line around the knob base. One of these mirrors is decorated with the design of seven linked arcs. Four of these mirrors are decorated with the design of eleven linked arcs. In contrast to the design of linked arcs formed by broad band, the design of linked arcs is delicate and smaller and is located at the space no more than the center of the mirror surface.

There are two bronze mirrors with plain pattern as ground motif and design of linked arcs formed by broad band with concave surface. These mirrors appeared later than the mirrors without design and the mirrors with plain pattern as ground motif and design of slender bow string, and evolved from the mirrors with plain pattern as ground motif and design of slender bow string. The mirrors are in a bigger size with a diameter of 15cm to 20cm. They are found in small numbers. The mirrors are mostly decorated with the ground motif of the design of cloud and thunder and occasionally decorated with the design of dragon and phoenix. It can be deduced that the space among the patterns of linked arcs on the mirrors without design in a big size or the mirrors with simple pattern as ground motif may be used for the decoration of coloured patterns. A bronze mirror with design of cloud and thunder as ground motif and design of linked arcs formed by broad band is in the collections of the museum, with the Collection No.2476. There is a thick layer of turquoise on the ground motif of the design of cloud and thunder. The layer is supposed to be a coloured pattern. There are three other bronze mirrors with design of cloud and thunder as ground motif and design of linked arcs formed by broad band with concave surface in the museum. The mirrors with design of linked arcs formed by broad band are similar to the mirrors with design of broad band in decorative style and casting technique, and they are both in a big size. It is deduced that the decorative style of the mirrors should be the style of the bronze mirrors of the Qin State in the late Warring States Period.

### Bronze Mirrors with motif of dragon and phoenix

The mirror with motif of dragon and phoenix was the dominant shape of the bronze mirrors in the late period of the late Warring States Period and is the representative shape at the peak of the development of the bronze mirrors of the Chu State. It has a wide variety of shapes and was used in a wide range of areas. The collections in the museum contain the mirrors with design of single realistic dragon, the mirrors with design of phoenix, the mirrors with design of stylized dragon, the mirrors with design of serpent and the mirrors with design of stylized serpent. There are 45 bronze mirrors in the museum, including 3 mirrors with design of single realistic dragon, 4 mirrors with design of six dragons and six rhombuses, 6 mirrors with design of phoenix, 22 mirrors with design of stylized dragon and 10 mirrors with design of stylized serpent.

The bronze mirrors with design of six dragons and six rhombuses are rarely seen. All four mirror collections of the museum are more than 16cm in diameter. They all have a knob with design of three bow strings. A broad band with concave surface adorns the outside of the knob. The dragon design is engraved overelaborately in the complicated shape of two powerful dragons dancing and intersecting as a group. The mirrors are the representative of the bronze mirrors with dragon design in the late period of the late Warring States Period. The bronze mirror with phoenix design is also rarely seen. In the composition of decorative patterns of rhombus pattern and phoenix pattern, the four mirrors with design of three phoenixes and three rhombuses are similar in style to the mirrors with dragon design. Unlike the vigorous and powerful dragon pattern, the phoenix pattern shows relaxation and nature with elegant and smooth lines.

Among the collections of the mirrors with phoenix design in the museum, there is a bronze mirror with design of three phoenixes and three dragons. It is over 14cm in diameter. The major motif is the design of three phoenixes and three dragons arranged alternately. Its decorative layout and style are similar to those of the mirrors with design of three dragons and three rhombuses, except that the pattern of three phoenixes is used instead of the pattern of three rhombuses. The decorative pattern of phoenix, with small eyes and short beak, stands on one foot at the knob base, turns its head and holds its tail in its mouth. In contrast to the phoenix motif, the dragon turns its head, carries the knob base on its head and treads on the rim of the mirror, with a big head, two eyes, an open mouth and buckteeth in its mouth. The bodies of phoenix and dragon intertwinded in a shape of branch and the wings of dragon are interlaced with the neighbouring feathers of phoenix. The pattern of phoenixes occupies the center of the mirror, as the major motif. The shape of dragon is vivid and interesting, showing a smiling face with an open mouth and buckteeth. The decorative arrangement of the phoenix pattern in the upper part and the dragon pattern in the lower part gives a picture of the phoenixes standing out and the phoenixes being called by dragons. There are other four mirrors with design of three phoenixes and three rhombuses in the museum, which are similar to the one above in terms of decorative style and casting technique. All mirrors can be dated from the late period of the late Warring States Period. The mirrors with design of three phoenixes show clearly a significant change in the decorative style. The three mirrors with design of three phoenixes and three rhombuses, with a small size, had been changed from using single simple line to using two curving lines in parts, reflecting the constant changes in style of the late period of the late Warring States Period. The mirror with design of three phoenixes and three dragons is later than the four mirrors with design of six dragons and six rhombuses above, but all mirrors are inferred to have been in use after the Chu State moved its capital to Shouchun town.

The mirror with design of serpent is in a larger proportion of the bronze mirrors with motif of dragon and phoenix. The evolution of the mirror with design of serpent is clearly shown in the collections of the museum. The pattern is changed from the shape of the coiling and intertwining serpent to the shape of an S or a C. The pattern is formed from solid broad lines to two lines. The bronze quality and the casting technique went from prosperity to decline. The decorative pattern formed by two lines were widely used in the bronze mirrors with gambing design and the bronze mirrors with interlaced hydras design in the early and middle Western Han Dynasty.

## Bronze Mirrors with inscription of "*shan*" (mountain) character

There are 14 bronze mirrors with inscription of "*shan*" (mountain) character, including the bronze mirror with inscription of four "*shan*" characters and design of eight leaves, the bronze mirror with inscription of four "*shan*" characters and design of eight leaves and four flowers, the bronze mirror with inscription of four "*shan*" characters and design of twelve leaves, the bronze mirror with inscription of four "*shan*" characters and design of sixteen leaves, the bronze mirror with inscription of four "*shan*" characters and design of four deer and the bronze mirror with inscription of five "*shan*" characters.

The bronze mirror with inscription of "*shan*" character is given widespread attention by the researchers of bronze mirrors. The researchers hold different views on the production place of the mirror because of diversified styles of the bronze mirrors with inscription of "*shan*" character. The eight mirror molds of the bronze mirrors with inscription of "*shan*" character were unearthed in Yi County, Hebei Province in the late 1930's; the mirror mold of the bronze mirrors with grass-leaf design was unearthed in Houma, Shanxi Province. But the mirror mold have not been found in Changsha, Hunan Province, Nanyang, Henan Province and Shou County, Anhui Province where the bronze mirrors of the Warring States Period were unearthed in great numbers. It can be concluded that the bronze mirrors with inscription of "*shan*" character were cast in Yi County where the mirror molds of the bronze mirrors with inscription of "*shan*" character were unearthed. Academia believes that the mirror with inscription of "*shan*" character was also cast in Changsha which was the casting center of the bronze mirrors of the Chu State. The shapes of the bronze mirrors with inscription of "*shan*" character unearthed show for us the evident regional characteristics. Some bronze mirrors with inscription of "*shan*" character, which were unearthed at the capital site of the Qi State in Linzi City, Shandong Province in recent years, distinguish clearly from the characteristics of the bronze mirrors of the Chu State. The two bronze mirrors unearthed in the tomb M198 and M429 of the Warring States Period in Yongliu Village[3], are decorated with inscription of "*shan*" character formed by four parallel lines and ground motif of coarse and big feather-like pattern cast shoddily. But a bronze mirror with inscription of four "*shan*" characters and design of eight leaves unearthed in the tomb M178 at the Fan Family Tomb[4], is similar to the bronze mirrors of the Chu State in decorative style but has a slight lack of refineness of the bronze mirrors of the Chu State for its shaggy ground motif and leaf design. With evident regional identity, the bronze mirrors with inscription of "*shan*" character unearthed in Linzi City should be cast in the capital city of the Qi State in the Warring States Period. The distinction is the difference between the Qi State and the Chu State in the Warring States Period. It is hard to distinguish among the different production places of the Chu State.

In the collections of the bronze mirrors with inscription of "*shan*" character, the three mirrors are worthy to be paid special attention. The first is the bronze mirror with inscription of four "*shan*" characters and design of four deer. The mirror was unearthed at the Hongwei Annular Kiln in Xiejiaji Distinct, adjacent to the site of Shouchun town, the capital of the Chu State in western Huainan City in December 1987. It is 15.7cm in diameter. It has a small knob with design of three bow strings and a two-layer square base. The inscription of four "*shan*" characters is inclined towards the left. The patterns of deer adorn among the four "*shan*" characters on the ground motif of feather-like pattern. The deer stand up on two feet and bend two feet. The bodies of the deer are covered with scale pattern. It is the most vivid picture of a vigorous and powerful deer with their heads holding high and looking back. The mirror is a rare treasure. According to the public articles in China, only the Shanghai Museum collects a bronze mirror with inscription of four "*shan*" characters and design of four deer. It has a two-layer round knob base. It is 17.03cm in diameter. The inscription of four "*shan*" characters is inclined towards the left. But its casting technique is not as good as the mirror in the museum, for the bad joint between the deer pattern and the ground motif of feather-like pattern and the unbalanced "*shan*" characters with the middle vertical stroke leaning to one side. The second is the bronze mirror with ground motif of feather-like pattern, inscription of four "*shan*" characters and design of four leaves. It is in a good appearance and is a rare exquisite treasure of bronze mirrors. It is also rare in the bronze mirrors of the Chu State that its knob and its knob base are in a shape of a two-layer knob base bigger in diameter than that of the knob under the knob. The ground motif with feather-like pattern is very elegant, showing in the pattern of the tail of fine feather rolling and raising. On this mirror, no mould mark can be found. It can be cast by the lost-wax method. Mr. Chen Peifen of the Shanghai Musuem observed some clear wax marks in the decorative patterns of the bronze mirrors of the Warring States Period and concluded that they could have been cast by the lost-wax method[5]. The lost-wax method was used in the early Spring and Autumn Period and the complex bronze wares were cast by the lost-wax method in the late Spring and Autumn Period. The bronze mirrors were therefore cast by the lost-wax method in reason. The third is the bronze mirror with inscription of four *"shan"* characters and design of twelve leaves. It is 15cm in diameter. It has a small knob with design of three bow strings and a two-layer knob base. It is decorated with the inscription of four *"shan"* characters inclining towards the left. It is special for its leaf design. Each decorative pattern in a shape of a standing man formed by branches, adorns the spaces among four *"shan"* characters. Each corner of the square knob base has a branch stretching out. Leaves at the top of the branch are in a shape of a human head. The leaves under the shoulders are in a shape of crossed arms and the leaves at the end are in a shape of human hands. The branches are overlaid in three layers, like a vivid dancer standing and crossing arms. The bronze mirror with inscription of four *"shan"* characters and design of twelve leaves is rare and it was cast by the lost-wax method is still a topic of research.

The three bronze mirrors above with inscription of *"shan"* character all have the features of the late period of the late Warring States Period, such as a slightly thick body, the flat rim changed from the sharp rim. It is deduced that all three mirrors were cast after the Chu State moved its capital to Shouchun town.

There are some other bronze mirrors with inscription of *"shan"* characters related to the collections of the museum. The brief introduction is as follows: The bronze mirror with inscription of three *"shan"* characters is collected at the Suzhou Museum, Anhui Province, which was unearthed in 2009 (Fig.1). The mirror is 9.7cm in diameter. It has a small knob with design of three bow strings and a two-layer round knob base. The inscription of three *"shan"* characters is inclined towards the right. In 2020, the bronze mirror with inscription of six *"shan"* characters was unearthed in the tomb M23 of the middle and late Warring States Period, at Wanda, Qiaocheng, Bozhou City. The entrance to the tomb is in a length of 6.1m and a width of 4.3m. The mirror is 17cm in diameter. It has a small knob with design of three bow strings and a two-layer round knob base. The inscription of *"shan"* characters is inclined towards the left. The ground motif with feather-like pattern is very elegant. In 2011, the bronze mirror with inscription of six *"shan"* characters in a diameter of 27cm was unearthed in the tomb M566 of the Warring States Period, Bailuzhou, Lu'an City[⑥]. The middle vertical strokes of *"shan"* characters are stretching out to the rim of the mirror. The inscription of four *"shan"* characters is inclined towards the right. The characters are interconnecting and the interiors of the joints are in a shape of hexagon. In the same tomb, there is the bronze mirror with inscription of four *"shan"* characters with a diameter of 17cm and the bronze mirror without design with a diameter of 8.1cm also found. The bronze mirrors with inscription of six *"shan"* characters remain in the world in relatively more numbers. According to incomplete statistics, the total may be over twelve mirrors, including two mirrors in the National Museum of China, the mirror in the Shanghai Museum, the mirror in the Museum of the Western Han Dynasty Mausoleum of the Nanyue King in Guangzhou, the mirror collected by private collector in Zhejiang Province, the mirror in the Tokyo National Museum in Japan, the mirror in the Arthur M. Sackler Gallery in America and the two mirrors unearthed in Anhui Province. Among these twelve bronze mirrors with inscription of six *"shan"* characters, the mirror unearthed in Lu'an City is decorated with the inscription inclining towards the right, and the others all are decorated with the inscription inclining towards the left. By contrast, the bronze mirrors with inscription of three *"shan"* characters are found few in number. Based on the statistics of the public information,

Fig.1 Bronze Mirror with inscription of three *"shan"* characters
(collected in Suzhou Museum)

there is the mirror in the Suzhou Museum, the two mirrors collected by private collector in Taiwan, China and the mirror with inscription of three "*shan*" characters and design of three deer in the Museum of East Asia in Sweden. The mirror with inscription of three "*shan*" characters and design of three deer is similar in ground motif and deer design to the bronze mirror with inscription of four "*shan*" characters and design of four deer in the museum, and it can be deduced that they were cast in the same place. It is said that a bronze mirror with inscription of four "*shan*" characters and animal design in a diameter of 14.6cm was unearthed in the tomb in Jin Village, Luoyang City[7]. Its decorative style of inscription and beast design is similar to the mirror with inscription of four "*shan*" characters and design of four deer in the museum. They are both the rare shapes of the bronze mirrors.

### Bronze Mirrors with motif of leaves

There are 15 bronze mirrors with motif of leaves in the book, including 9 mirrors with design of four leaves, 2 mirrors with design of eight leaves, 1 mirror with design of eight leaves and four flowers and 3 mirrors with design of twelve leaves. Of the 15 mirrors, five are decorated with the ground motif of design of cloud and thunder and ten are decorated with the ground motif of feather-like pattern. The mirrors with design of cloud and thunder as ground motif and design of leaves have a small and slim body with a diameter of less than 10cm. The mirrors with feather-like pattern as ground motif and design of leaves have a thick and solid body with a diameter of more than 10cm.

The mirror with design of cloud and thunder as ground motif and design of leaves is marked not only by the characteristic of a smaller diameter but also by the remarkable character of the elaborate decorative patterns. The mirror with design of twelve leaves has a small knob with design of three bow strings and a two-layer knob base. Each corner of the knob base has a branch stretching out. Each branch is adorned with two peach-shaped leaves. Each leaf is filled respectively in spaces among four leaves near the rim of the mirror. The mirror, with a diameter of 9cm, is decorated with finer ground motif. The granule-like patterns are less than 1mm in diameter. The pattern of cirrus cloud is formed with lines as thin as hair and is coiled clearly with more than five circles. The mirrors with design of cloud and thunder as ground motif and design of leaves are found in smaller numbers than the mirrors with feather-like pattern as ground motif and design of leaves. It was in wide use earlier than the mirror with feather-like pattern as ground motif. The collections at the museum are treasures in the mirrors with design of cloud and thunder as ground motif and design of leaves.

On the bronze mirrors with motif of leaves, we can observe the decorative method and the basic rule of the bronze mirrors of the Warring States Period. The ever-changing shapes of the pattern of a leaf, by using the method of adding lines and surfaces, such as the pattern of flat peach leaf, the pattern of long peach leaf and the pattern of salix leaf, can take on a different look of decorative patterns of the bronze mirrors. But the feather-like pattern and the inscription of "*shan*" character are the results of using and beautifying the part of the pattern. The changes are the embodiment of generations of craftsmen's pursuit and creation for beauty and the reflection of the aesthetic and thinking of ancient people.

### Bronze Mirrors with motif of beasts

There are four bronze mirrors with motif of beasts in the book, including the bronze mirror with design of *Tao Tie* (a monster with a head but no body). Fewer mirrors with design of *Tao Tie* were found, with only four to be found in the published articles. And only one of the mirrors has the exact location where it was unearthed. It is the mirror unearthed in the No.1 Tomb at the Mausoleum of the King of the Zhao State of the late Warring States Period at Zhouyao Village in Yi County, Handan City, Hebei Province[8]. There are evident differences in decorative style and casting technique between the bronze mirrors with design of *Tao Tie* and the bronze mirrors of the Chu State. Other bronze mirrors with design of stylized beasts are decorated with the ground motif of feather-like pattern and have a small knob with design of three bow strings and a round knob base. The decorative pattern of four stylized beasts is special due to its shape of square or round geometry changed from the beast pattern. The mirrors are more commonly found in the tombs of the Chu State in Hunan Province. The decorative pattern is changed from the shape of primate with head, eyes, a round and fat body and a long rolling tail into the shape of geometry with a C-shaped body and without head. The mirrors found in the tomb of the Chu State in Changsha City, Hunan Province, show various shapes of the beast pattern in the different periods. The mirrors are also found in Nanyang , Henan Province. It can be deduced that the mirrors were probably cast in Changsha.

## II. Understanding of Ground Motif of Bronze Mirrors in Museum

The Warring States Period is the first peak in the development of bronze mirrors in China. Most of the bronze mirrors of the Warring States Period are decorated with the ground motif. And the ground motif is the essential feature of the bronze mirrors of the Warring States Period. The ground motif provides the perfect foil for the main decorative patterns. The ground motifs of the bronze mirrors in the book can be classified into three shapes: plain pattern as ground motif, design of cloud and thunder as ground motif and feather-like pattern as ground motif.

The main decorative patterns of the bronze mirrors in the Warring States Period were various and complicated. The different main decorative patterns, changing from inscription motif of "*shan*" character to dragon design, phoenix design, serpent design and beast-shaped design, prevailed in the different periods and show different aesthetic trends of different periods. In particular, the decorative patterns of dragon are rich in shape. It takes more time to recognize some decorative patterns of dragon. It is one of the important features of the Warring States Period that the ground motif was stable compared to the main decorative patterns that were rich in shape, The ground motif was stable in shape and the shapes of the ground motif were all used for a long time. But the slight changes of the ground motif also show the features of the times and the regions.

The ground motif of design of cloud and thunder and the ground motif of feather-like pattern are the decorative mainstream of the ground motif of the bronze mirrors in the Warring States Period. Together with various main decorative patterns, they form the varied decorative patterns of bronze mirrors in the Warring States Period. For example, the mirrors with inscription motif of "*shan*" character are mostly decorated with the ground motif of feather-like pattern and the mirrors with motif of dragon and phoenix are mostly decorated with the ground motif of design of cloud and thunder. The relatively fixed collocation of the ground motif and the main decorative pattern was used not only in the Chu State but also in Northern regions. The style of fixed collocation had been continued for more than a hundred years. The fixed collocation embodies not only the passing on of technique by generations of craftsmen, but also the aesthetic focus and interest of the Chu State. In the meantime, some bronze mirrors of the Warring State Period are decorated with only ground motif and without main decorative patterns. For instance, the mirrors are only decorated with the cloud design, or the design of cloud and thunder, or the feather-like pattern. Some exceptional mirrors were found, whose main decorative patterns are the patterns used as ground motif. A bronze mirror with design of cloud and thunder as ground motif and design of feather-like pattern is recorded in the book (Fig.2). This mirror is very rare and is one of the most valuable materials for studying the changes of feather-like pattern.

Fig.2 Bronze Mirror with design of cloud and thunder as ground motif and design of feather-like pattern (collected in Huainan Museum)

## III. Understanding of Bronze Mirrors with Plain Pattern as Ground Motif in Museum

The bronze mirrors with plain pattern as ground motif include the bronze mirrors without design or the bronze mirrors with plain pattern as ground motif and design of bow string formed by single line, or design of broad band, or design of linked arcs formed by broad band. The book contains 23 bronze mirrors with plain pattern as ground motif, all of which are in the collections of the museum. Among these mirrors, eight bronze mirrors without design are between 8cm and 15cm in diameter; the bronze mirrors with plain pattern as ground motif and design of broad band and the bronze mirrors with plain pattern as ground motif and design of linked arcs formed by broad band are bigger, with a maximum diameter of 23cm; and the bronze mirrors with plain pattern as ground motif and design of bow string formed by single line are intermediate in size between the bronze mirrors without design and the bronze mirrors with plain pattern as ground motif and design of broad band, with a diameter of about 15cm. So there seems to be a suggestion of some regularity in the development of the bronze mirrors with plain pattern as ground motif. The bronze mirrors without design are small in size, have a flat surface and were cast crudely. Although the mirrors are unadorned, they can be distinguished for their different periods by their knobs. In the early stage, the bronze mirrors without design have a bow-shaped knob, such as the mirror with Collection No. 2418 and the mirror with Collection No. 2481 in the museum. The bronze mirror with Collection No. 2428 in the museum has a knob with exquisite design of three bow strings, and is distinguished from the two bronze mirrors above by features of a later period. Some mirrors can be found with rectangular mold marks under the knob. It is possible that they were cast by a second pour after the cast knob base was embedded in the mirror mold and that they were cast later.

The bronze mirrors without design appeared in the period from the late Spring and Autumn Period to the early Warring States Period and were popular in the middle Warring States Period. They are the earliest shape of the Chu-style mirrors. It has a bow-shaped knob in the early and middle periods and a knob with design of three bow strings in the late period. It remained in use for a long time. Based on the fifteen bronze mirrors without design unearthed in the tombs of the Western Han Dynasty in Nanyang, Henan Province[9], it can be deduced that these mirrors continued to be in use until the middle Western Han Dynasty. In the book *Tombs of the Chu State in Changsha City*[10], there are 34 bronze mirrors without design, all which were unearthed in the tombs of the Chu State in the Warring States Period. It follows from the above comparison that the bronze mirrors without design prevailed in the Central Plain for a longer time than in the central zone of the Chu State containing Changsha, Jingzhou and Shouchun. On the other hand, it is relatively easy to cast the bronze mirrors without design, considering the casting technique, and this is one of the reasons why they had long prevailed.

The bronze mirrors with plain pattern as ground motif and design of bow string, the bronze mirrors with plain pattern as ground motif and design of broad band and the bronze mirrors with plain pattern as ground motif and design of bow string and linked arcs were in use for a longer time than the bronze mirrors without design. The book contains fifteen bronze mirrors with plain pattern as ground motif and design of bow string. Their knobs come in four shapes, such as bow-shaped knob, knob with design of three bow strings, bridge-shaped knob and granule-shaped knob. The mirrors are adorned with the design of raised bow string formed by single line, or the design of raised bow string formed by two lines, or the design of two linked arcs formed by broad band, or the design of three linked arcs formed by broad band. The bronze mirrors with plain pattern as ground motif had been developed in a certain sequence, the small bronze mirrors without design appearing first, the bronze mirrors with design of linked arcs formed by single line the next, the big bronze mirrors with design of two broad bands, in a diameter of over 20cm, in the late period of the late Warring States Period. The collections of the bronze mirrors with design of broad band (Collection No.2541, Collection No.2425, Collection No.2426 and Collection No.2427), with a diameter of about 20cm, were cast in this period. The bronze mirror with plain pattern as ground motif and design of bow string, with a diameter of 17.8cm, was unearthed in the tomb of the Qin State in the period after when Bai Qi, a general of the Qin State, conquered Ying City, the capital city of the Chu State, in Changsha. The bronze mirror with design of broad band, with a diameter of 18.4cm, was unearthed in the tomb of the early Western Han Dynasty in Nanyang[11]. The big bronze mirrors with design of broad band are the product of the final stage in the development of the bronze mirrors with plain pattern as ground motif. Some are adorned with coloured patterns. In the two bronze mirrors of Collection No.2541 and Collection No.2405, we can find the remains of coloured patterns. It is deduced that the mirror of Collection No.2541 was coloured with zinnober and the mirror of Collection No.2405 was coloured with turquoise. This could be the beautifying and filling by craftsmen for the bronze mirrors with big size, simple design and blanks left.

In the collections of the bronze mirror with plain pattern as ground motif and design of bow string, there are seven mirrors which are the mirrors of the Qin State. It is generally believed that the mirrors with design of a bow string are the product of the Chu State and the mirrors with design of two raised bow strings formed by slender line and the mirrors with design of broad band with concave surface are the product of the Qin State. The conjecture is confirmed by the bronze mirrors unearthed in the tombs of the Qin State in Yunmeng County, Hubei Province, in Xianyang, Shaanxi Province and in Peiling, Sichuan Province. Among the mirrors, there are five mirrors with design of two raised bow strings formed by slender line, with a diameter of about 10cm in a small size. The bronze mirrors with design of two broad bands with concave surave, with a diameter of more than 20cm, are bigger in size than those unearthed in the tomb M7 of the Qin State at the Post Office of the Changsha Railway Station. (The groups and shapes of pottery unearthed in the tomb M7 show the typical features of the Qin State.)

## IV. Understanding of Bronze Mirrors with Motif of Dragons in Museum

The bronze mirrors with motif of dragons are one of the bronze mirrors that prevailed in the Warring States Period. Of the more than 120 bronze mirrors of the Warring States Period in the museum, there are 45 bronze mirrors with motif of dragons, with a higher percentage and including the decorative patterns of phoenix and serpent. There is no unified name for the bronze mirror with motif of dragons. The same decorative pattern can be called by different names. The objective cause is that the bronze mirrors with motif of dragons are adorned with varied and complicated patterns. The decorative patterns can be classified into two main shapes of dragon design and design of stylized dragon, which are further subdivided into design of interlaced hydras, design of coiled dragon, design of hornless dragon, serpent design and design of coiled serpent. There is the same understanding of the dragon design of the bronze mirrors of the Warring States Period that the patterns are in a shape of a complex whole of dragon and serpent, so it is also called the dragon with serpent body. In this book, the dragon patterns are referred to as dragon design or design of stylized dragon, and the patterns without features of dragon head are called serpent design.

In the museum, the bronze mirrors with motif of dragons have more than ten shapes, including the mirror with design of three dragons, the mirror with design of three dragons and three phoenixes, the mirror with design of three dragons and three leaves, the mirror with design of three dragons, three phoenixes and three leaves, the mirror with design of three dragons, three phoenixes and four leaves, the mirror with design of three dragons and three rhombuses, the mirror with design of four dragons, the mirror with design of four dragons and four leaves, the mirror with design of six dragons and six rhombuses, the mirror with design of three serpents, the mirror with design of three serpents and three rhombuses, the mirror with design of three stylized serpents and three rhombuses, the mirror with design of four serpents, the mirror with design of four serpents and four rhombuses, the mirror with design of four serpents and four leaves, the mirror with design of four serpents, four leaves and four rhombuses and the mirror with design of eight serpents. In these mirrors, the dragon pattern of the mirror with design of three dragons is in the concretest shape. In the museum, there are two bronze mirrors with design of cloud and thunder as ground motif and design of three dragons (Collection No.2411 and Collection No.2467). The decorative pattern of three dragons are arranged in a circle, with concrete shapes of head, wings and tail. The dragon pattern is similar in shape to that of the bronzes in the corresponding period and is in a shape commonly known. Few mirrors with dragon design in the same shape were unearthed in the tombs of the Chu State in Changsha and tombs in Yizheng, Jiangsu Province. The two other mirrors with design of three dragons (Collection No.2463 and Collection No.2450) in the museum are adorned with the pattern of dragon with a little changes in arrangement and the changed body in a shape of rhombus and the simplified wings. The mirrors with design of patterned dragon are rarely found and only one was unearthed in Nanyang, which is similar to the one in the museum. The dragon design was changed towards the patterned shape after the patterns of leaf or rhombus were filled among three dragons or four dragons. In the process of exaggerated change, the features of dragon head remained. For instance, the mirror with design of three dragons and three rhombuses (Collection No.2443) in the museum is adorned with the pattern of dragon head in front with two unusual round eyes, one big and the other small, and a tongue sticking out and rolling, and a patterned dragon body interlacing with rhombus as a whole. The design of patterned dragon changed more complicated and changed into a shape of intertwining branches which is hard to identify. The mirrors with design of realistic dragon are less than those with design of patterned dragon in number and use range. It is a reflection of the fact that the mirror with design of realistic dragon was only in use for a short time and the mirror with design of patterned dragon prevailed for a long time over a wide area. A swift transition of dragon design from the simple realistic shape to the patterned shape, was confirmed by the mirrors with dragon design unearthed. The evidences are all found in the mirrors of the Warring States Period unearthed in Hunan Province, Hubei Province, Anhui Province, Henan Province, Jiangsu Province, Shaanxi Province and Shandong Province. And there are about 60 bronze mirrors with dragon motif from the late Warring States Period to the early Western Han Dynasty unearthed in Nanyan, Henan Province. All mirrors have only three mirrors with design of realistic dragon.

The decorative patterns of the bronze mirrors with motif of dragons are the best indication of aesthetic ideas and cultural trait of the Chu State. People of the Chu State were fond of red, and the evidence of this can be found in color of lacquer wares and textiles unearthed in the tombs of the Chu State. But in the monochrome bronze mirrors, the changes of the design reflect the inner world of the people of the Chu State. The book *The Songs of Chu* records the inner world of people of the Chu State, a world full of illusions, mythologies and witchcrafts with heaven, earth, man and god as a whole. It was expressed most fully in the bronze mirrors with design of dragon and phoenix of the late Warring States Period that the dragon and phoenix were revered in the Chu State. In the realm of fantastical and variable dragon patterns, the overelaborate and exquisite patterns of interlacing and flying dragons reflect the inner world of people of the Chu State and show a mysterious scene. The bronze mirror with design of simplified dragon was the main shape of the bronze mirrors in the late period of the late Warring States Period. The design of simplified dragon contains phoenix pattern and serpent pattern. The changes from the design of realistic and simple dragon to design of mysterious and complicated dragon to design of simplified dragon, reflect the process from prosperity to decline of the bronze mirrors in the late Chu State and is a miniature of the bronze mirrors of the Chu State from glory to decay. By observing the bronze mirrors with design of simplified dragon, it can be seen that the material quality of the bronze mirrors was changed and its molding technique got worse. One of the important reasons is that the times was changed. There were more people in the late Warring States Period. And in the early Han Dynasty, however, a sharp increase in population was made possible by provision to recover from the effects of war. As a result, the bronze mirrors became more widely available. As a result of the increased demand, the bronze mirrors were cast in great numbers with low quality. The style of the bronze mirrors of the Han Dynasty laid the foundation.

The two bronze mirrors with dragon design in the museum, in a big size with a diameter of about 20cm, are the representative of this type of the bronze mirrors. The two bronze mirrors with dragon design have a similar decorative style and are adorned with the design of cloud and thunder as ground motif. With a diameter of 24cm, the bronze mirror with dragon design has a knob base with rare design of small linked arcs. The mirror shows the features of a later period. The other bronze mirror with design of four dragons and four leaves (Collection No.2479), with a diameter of 19.8cm, is rare in shape. The decorative patterns of four leaves divide the dragon patterns into four sections and are used mainly in partitions and not in decoration. The decorative style not only reflects the process of changing the dragon pattern but also shows craftsmen of the Warring States Period thinking and overcoming the arrangement in a circle. So the decorative patterns of the bronze mirrors, simple or complicated, all give us an aesthetic rule with careful observation.

There are four rare bronze mirrors with design of six dragons and six rhombuses in the museum. The four bronze mirrors (Collection No.2486, Collection No.2543, Collection No.1927 and Collection No.2478) are similar in size with a diameter of about 16cm. The four bronze mirrors are adorned with the fine design of cloud and thunder as ground motif and the design of stylized dragon as major motif. The rhombus design is peculiar to its arrangement. The outside of the knob base is adorned with three small patterns of rhombuses and above these patterns of rhombuses are three small patterns of rhombuses near the rim of the mirror. The arrangement of six patterns of rhombuses staggered up and down is used mainly in partitions and not in decoration and serves as a decorative effect in highlighting the dragon pattern. Each pattern of rhombus is interlaced with the horn on the head of the dragon pattern as a whole. The four mirrors are similar in size, decorative patterns and casting technique, so they should be cast in the same place. But the mirrors with similar design have not been found in the tombs of the Chu State in Hunan Province, Hubei Province and Henan Province. So the mirrors were probably cast after the Chu State moved its capital to Shouchun town.

There are some bronze mirrors with phoenix design in the museum that are similar in decorative style to the bronze mirrors with dragon design. The bronze mirrors with phoenix design prevailed at the same time as the bronze mirrors with dragon design and was used until the late period of the late Warring States Period. Like the bronze mirrors with dragon design, the bronze mirrors with phoenix design had been changed into the mirror shape of the early Western Han Dynasty.

There are six bronze mirrors with phoenix design in the museum. They can be classified into two main shapes. The first is the decorative pattern of phoenix standing alone in a circle around the knob base on the ground motif. The patterns of phoenix are not connected to one another. The shape of phoenix is relatively realistic. The patterns of leaf or rhombus fill up the blanks between phoenixes. Not many mirrors were unearthed in Sichuan Province, Hunan Province and Henan Province. The second is the decorative pattern of patterned phoenix. Fewer mirrors were found. Most were found in the Huainan region and a few were found in Hunan Province.

## V. Discussion on Bronze Mirrors Casted in Ying Capital renamed from Shouchun

After the capital city of the Chu State was moved to Shouchun town in the Warring States Period, was the bronze mirror cast in Shouchun City? One view is that it's most likely the bronze mirror with inscription of four "*shan*" characters and design of four deer unearthed in Huainan City was cast in Huainan, for the reason that the bronze mirrors with inscription of "*shan*" character mostly found in Hunan Province are not adorned with deer pattern[12]. The deer pattern of the bronze mirror unearthed in Huainan is the same as the deer pattern of the bronze mirror with inscription of four "*shan*" characters and design of four deer collected in the Shanghai Museum. Statistically, there are more bronze mirrors with special design than this. Since the foundation of the People's Republic of China, the bronze mirrors of the Warring States Period have been found in great numbers in Huainan. Some mirrors have unique shapes not seen in other areas, such as the four mirrors with design of six dragons and six rhombuses, the mirror with design of three dragons, three phoenixes and four leaves, the mirror with design of three dragons and three phoenixes, the mirror with inscription of four "*shan*" characters and design of twelve leaves and the mirror with design of twelve leaves, all which are collected in the museum. These decorative patterns of the bronze mirrors are rarely found in the published articles on the bronze mirror. From this it can be deduced that the mirrors were most likely cast in Shouchun town. We believe that the handicraft industry of casting bronze mirror was essential for Shouchun town, the capital city. When the Chu State moved its capital to Shouchun town, the craftsmen of casting bronze mirror were supposed to come here. The bronze mirrors, as a daily necessity, should be cast here. Even before the relocation of the capital, the industry of casting bronze mirror appeared on a small scale in Shouchun town, as the important city of the North of the Chu State.

In 241 BC (the 22nd year of the King Kaolie of the Chu), the Chu State moved its capital to Shouchun town and Shouchun was renamed Ying. In the 1980s, Mr. Ding Bangjun in the Institute of Cultural Relics and Historical Relics and Archaeology, Anhui Province, took care of routine matters in Shou County. And the location and area of Shouchun town were determined approximately, through ways of field research, archaeological prospecting and telemetry[13]. Mr. Ding concluded that Shouchun city lies to the southeast of the county town of Shou County and covers a total area of 26.35 square kilometers, from Dongjindu in the east to the west bank of Slender West Lake in the west and from Shilitou in the south to the Feihe River in the north. The large remains of buildings found at Baijiatai at the west bank of the Feihe River, have an area of 3,000 square meters, with 11 *kaijian* (the standard width of a room in an old-style house, about the length of a purlin) and a depth of 42 meters. The Shouchun town is larger in area than Jinan town, Linzi town, town of the Jin Sate in Houma, town of the Lu State in Qufu, town of the Zhao State in Handan and town in Zhengzhou. Shouchun town has a perfect layout including palace area, high-platform building for ritual regulations, waterway and city gates. The industry of casting bronze mirrors, as one of the essential handicraft industry, was an important component of the capital city. The potter-making site was found in the north of the town in 1987. The pottery workshop site was found at Niuweigang in the southeast of the town in recent years, where the building materials were baked for the construction of the capital.

For over 70 years since the foundation of the People's Republic of China, after the long-term and unremitting efforts of cultural workers, the distribution of the tombs of the Warring States Period in Huainan City and Shou County has been discovered. The tombs of the Chu State with high mound are densely scattered at Sanhe Town, Yanggong Town, Wangfenggang Town and Liyingzi Town in Huainan City seated at the southern foot of Shungeng Mountain, the northern bank of Wabu Lake and the eastern bank of East Feihe River. These areas are the areas of high-level tombs of the Chu State. The Tomb of the King You of the Chu at Lisangudui, the Tomb of the Marquis Sheng of the Cai and other tombs were found successively in these regions. Since 2019, the salvage excavation of the Wuwangdun Tomb at Xuwa Village, Sanhe Town, Huainan City has been underdone. The mound of the tomb was uncovered and the coffin chamber is being excavated. The archaeological reconnaissance shows that the tomb is in a large shape of "*jia*" character (the first of the ten Heavenly Stems) with an open of 50m in length and 50m in width, and has a tomb passage with a length of 42m. There is a chariot pit with a length of 147m about 60 meters away from the west side of the tomb. The archaeological reconnaissance also reveals it is a mausoleum with the Wuwangdun Tomb as the center and the surrounding park. It is in a squarish shape protected by the ditch and covers an area of 2.04km². It is rare for its large scale and perfect structure in the king mausoleums in the pre-Qin Period. At Zhujiaji, Yanggong Town about 14.6 kilometers away from the south of the Wuwangdun Tomb, there is a Lisangudui Tomb found in the 1930s. The tomb was excavated by the Institute of Cultural Relics and Historical Relics and Archaeology, Anhui Province in 1983. The excavation result shows the opening of the tomb is 41m in length and 41m in width and the tomb passage is 22.4m in length. In 1958 and 1959, two tombs of the late Spring and Autumn Period were excavated at Zhaojiagudui, Caijiagang, Huainan City. It is generally believed that they are the tombs of the marquises of the Cai State. Between 1977 and 1982, there were eleven middle-scale tombs of the Chu State of the Warring States Period excavated at Yanggong Town, Huainan City. In recent years, some tombs of the Chu State of the Warring States Period were excavated in Lu'an City and the tombs of the Chu State were excavated in Qianshan and Zongyang, Anqing City. Some bronze mirrors of the Warring States Period are collected in the museums in the above cities and counties and Fuyang City and Bozhou City, most of which are unearthed by archaeological excavation.

The bronze mirrors were unearthed in the neighbouring area of the capital of the Chu Sate, now known as Huainan City, Lu'an City and Fuyang City around Shouchun town. It reflects that there was a great demand for bronze mirrors here in the late Warring States Period. In 1957, the bronze mirror with inscription of four "*shan*" characters, four flowers and four leaves was unearthed in the tomb of the Warrring States at Qiujiagang, Tangshan Commune, Xiejiaji District, Huainan City. In 1958, the two bronze mirrors with feather-like pattern as ground motif and design of leaves were unearthed in two tombs of the Warring States Period at Jiuli Brigade, Tangshan Commune. One has a square knob base and is adorned with rough decorative patterns of four small leaves; and the other has a square knob base and is adorned with exquisite decorative patterns of twelve leaves. In 1972, the bronze mirror with feather-like pattern as ground motif and four-leaf design was unearthed in the tomb of the Warring States Period at Hongwei Annular Kiln Works in Xiejiaji District not far from the Qiu's Family Garden in Shou County. It is later than the bronze mirror with design of four leaves unearthed at Jiuli Brigade. It has a fine round knob base and is adorned with fine ground motif of feather-like pattern and exquisite design of four small leaves, all which show the changes of the bronze mirror with design of four leaves in the Huainan region. In August, 1982, the bronze mirror with dragon design was unearthed in the tomb of the Warring States Period at Lianhua Brigade, Laishan Commune, Xiejiaji District. Its decorative pattern of dragon with simplified shape and style had changed from the complicated and fine pattern. In 1986, the bronze mirror with feather-like pattern as ground motif and four-leaf design unearthed in the tomb of the Warring States Period was collected from Mr. Jiang Chengmi in Shijiahu Town, Xiejiaji District. It is adorned with design of four bud-shaped leaves encircling the knob base. The decorative style of four small leaves encircling the knob base is the final shape of the bronze mirror with design of four leaves and was evolved into the pattern of branches or the pattern of stylized leaf shortly afterwards. In 1987, the bronze mirror with feather-like pattern as ground motif, inscription of four "*shan*" characters and design of four deer was unearthed in the tomb of the Warring States Period at Hongwei Annular Kiln Works in Xiejiaji District. The mirror was found in the officially recorded site and is an important and rare bronze mirror. In 2010, the bronze mirror with feather-like pattern as ground motif and four-leaf design was unearthed in the tomb of the Warring States Period at Liyingzi Town, Xiejiaji District. It is cast exquisitely and is adorned with well-arranged and clear decorative patterns. Based on a preliminary judgment, the mirror may be cast by the lost-wax method. The mirror has the distinguishing features of the late period of the late Warring States Period due to its thicker and wider rim. In 2020, the bronze mirror with design of four dragons, four phoenixes and linked arcs formed by broad band was unearthed in the tomb of the Warring States Period in the High-tech Zone, Huainan City. In recent years, some tombs of the late Warring States Period were excavated in Huainan City and Shou County by the Shou County Workstation of the Institute of Cultural Relics and Historical Relics and Archaeology, Anhui Province, and more than 10 bronze mirrors were unearthed. There are twenty bronze mirrors of the Warring States Period collected in the *Bronze Mirrors Unearthed in Lu'an*. There are twelve bronze mirrors of the Warring States Period collected in the *Treasures of Bronze Mirrors Collected in Shou County Museum*. There are five bronze mirrors of the Warring

States Period collected in the *Treasures of Cultural Relics Collected in Wanxi Museum*.

The *Huai Nan Zi*, a book compiled by the Emperor Wu of the Han Dynasty, records the history of casting bronze mirrors from another side. In the *Xiu Wu Xun* of *Huai Nan Zi*, there is a detailed account of how bronze mirrors were used. It is likely that people who took part in casting bronze mirrors wrote down the process. In 1974, The bronze mirror with inscription of "*Long Di Zhang He Shi Huai Nan*" and design of dragon and tiger was unearthed in Banqiao Town, Shou County. It is rare in reflecting the production level of local handicraft in the Eastern Han Dynasty. The inscription of the mirror tells the time and producing place of casting this mirror. The mirror was cast in Shouchun town in the first year of Zhanghe of the Emperor Zhang of the Eastern Han Dynasty. In the book of *Later Han Dynasty*, there is a historical record of the Emperor Zhang, Liu Da, who came to Shouchun town in the first year of Zhanghe, 87AD, on an inspection in the south. The Long's Family in Shouchun town, a family of casting bronze mirrors, cast this meaningful mirror with a chronological record to mark the event. This mirror evidences that casting bronze mirrors did not decline and continued to be inherited and developed in the Han Dynasty after the Chu State was conquered.

Director of Huainan Museum
Mr. Wang Maodong

❶ Henan Province Institute of Cultural Relics and Historical Relics and Archaeology, Archaeological Team of Danjiangkou Reservoir of Henan Province, Xichuan County Museum, *Tombs of the Spring and Autumn Period at Xiasi Town, Xichuan County*. Cultural Relics Press, 1991.

❷ Gao Zhixi, "On the Bronze Mirror of the Chu". *Cultural Relics*, 1991. 5.

❸ Linzi District Administration of Cultural Heritage, Zibo City (ed.), *Study on Bronze Mirrors Unearthed at the Tombs from the Warring States Period to the Han Dynasty at Linzi, Shandong Province*. Cultural Relics Press, 2017.

❹ Linzi District Administration of Cultural Heritage, "Tombs of the Warring States Period at the Cemetery of the Fan Family in Linzi District, Zibo City, Shandong Province". *Cultural Relics,* 2016.2.

❺ Shanghai Museum, *Ancient Bronze Mirrors from the Shanghai Museum*. Shanghai Calligraphy and Painting Publishing House, 2005.

❻ Anhui Province Institute of Cultural Relics and Historical Relics and Archaeology, Lu'an City Administration of Cultural Heritage, "Excavation of M566 of the Tombs of the Warring States Period at Bailuzhou, Lu'an City, Anhui Province". *Cultural Relics,* 2012.5.

❼ Huo Hongwei, Shi Jiazhen (eds.), *Discovery and Research of Bronze Mirrors at Luoyang City*. Science Press, 2013.

❽ Hebei Province Administration of Cultural Heritage, "Mausoleum of the King of the Zhao State in Handan City, Hebei Province". *Cultural Relics,* 1982.6.

❾ Nanyang City Institute of Cultural Relics and Historical Relics and Archaeology, *Bronze Mirrors Unearthed at Nanyang City*. Cultural Relics Press, 2010.

❿ Hunan Museum et al. *Tombs of the Chu State in Changsha City*. Cultural Relics Press, 2010.

⓫ Nanyang City Institute of Cultural Relics and Historical Relics and Archaeology, *Bronze Mirrors Unearthed at Nanyang City*. Cultural Relics Press, 2010.

⓬ He Gang, "On the Bronze Mirrors with Inscription Motif of 'Shan' Character". *Analects of Research of the Chu Culture (6),* Hubei Education Press, 2005.

⓭ Ding Bangjun, "Li Dewen, New Investigation of Remote Sensing of the Site of Shouchun Town". *Analects of Research of the Chu Culture (2),* Hubei People's Press, 1991.

图版 Plates

## 1. 十二叶镜

战国晚期
直径 9.0 厘米，厚 0.1 厘米，重 37 克
2019 年 11 月征集入藏

　　圆形。小三弦钮，方形钮座，呈双层叠压凹弧面方框状。地纹由细密的卷云纹和细小圆粒点组成的勾连三角形纹饰组成。从接范的痕迹判断是由三块范上下拼接而成。每区有六个卷云纹组成，卷云纹线条细如发丝。地纹上下排列形成二方连续图案。方形钮座的四角伸出四个花叶枝（每个花枝有两片扁桃形叶片片），八片扁桃叶形叶片片呈十字交叉分布。近镜缘处对应方钮座四边布置四片扁桃叶，近缘处饰一周细线弦纹，镜缘微弧，上卷。

　　此镜尺寸虽不大，但镜面的装饰纹样极其细密，粒状小点直径不足 1 毫米，如此精细的纹样用陶范制作需要十分高超的技艺。十二片扁桃形花叶叶面成凹弧面状，模铸得十分清晰，反映出当时工匠艺人的高超水平。在荆州、益阳、长沙、南阳楚墓中出土有羽状地叶纹镜，很少见到云雷地的花叶镜。但在淮南寿县地区发现不少此类铜镜，这可能是楚国晚期晚段在郢都寿春一带铸造的产品。

# 1. Mirror with design of twelve leaves

Late Warring States Period
Diameter: 9.0cm, Thickness: 0.1cm, Weight: 37g
Collected in November, 2019

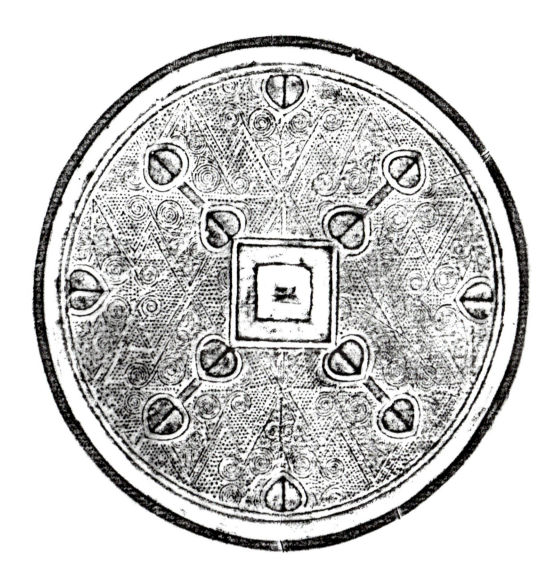

The mirror is round in shape. It has a small knob with design of three bow strings on a square two-layer base with concave surface. The ground motif is the design of interlaced triangle consisting of fine design of cirrus cloud and design of tiny spots. To judge from mold marks, the ground motif was cast in three molds placed together up and down. Each section is composed of six designs of cirrus cloud that is formed by lines as thin as hair. The ground motifs are consecutively and repeatedly arranged up and down. Four branches extend from each corner of the knob base in each direction of cross. Each branch has two peach-shaped leaves. There are four peach-shaped leaves near the rim of the mirror, corresponding to four sides of the knob base. A band of string design is close to the rim of the mirror. The rim, in a shape of slight arc, rolls up.

The mirror is small in size, but is adorned with exquisite decorative patterns. The design of tiny spots is less than 1mm in diameter. The delicate decorative patterns were cast in pottery mold with wonderful skill. The twelve leaves, in a shape of arc with concave surface, with clear molding, show the excellent skill of the craftsmen of that period. In the tomb of the Chu State at Jingzhou, Yiyang, Changsha and Nanyang, the bronze mirrors with feather-like pattern as ground motif and design of leaves were unearthed and few bronze mirrors with cloud and thunder pattern as ground motif and design of leaves were found. But in Shou County, Huainan City, some bronze mirrors with pattern of cloud and thunder as ground motif and design of leaves were found in large numbers. Thus, it is inferred that the bronze mirror was cast in the area of Shouchun town, Ying Capital of the Chu State, in the late period of the late Chu State.

## 2. 羽状纹镜

战国晚期

直径 11.2 厘米，厚 0.3 厘米，重 71 克

2018 年 5 月征集入藏

圆形。小桥钮，圆钮座。钮座外饰凹弧面宽带纹。镜面平直，满铺羽状纹，羽状纹精细规范，每组四个卷羽斜向对称，呈方形布局。宽平缘。

此镜的每单个羽翅的形态特征与早期羽翅相比有了明显变化。早期羽翅更接近写实风格，羽翅的轮廓由多道细长弧线组成；此镜羽翅已演化成羽翅边缘线高高突起、轮廓细长、弧线弱化、拐弯处平直，更具装饰意味，这可能是羽状纹演化到战国晚期晚段时的特征。此镜还有一个重要特点，即在羽状纹的卷羽之间有细小的三角雷纹，是以雷纹为地，主纹是羽状纹，不易发现，所以这面铜镜应称之为雷纹地羽状纹镜。这面铜镜的装饰方法十分少见。以雷纹为地，将通常用作地纹的羽状纹作为主体纹饰。

## 2. Mirror with feather-like design

Late Warring States Period
Diameter: 11.2cm, Thickness: 0.3cm, Weight: 71g
Collected in May, 2018

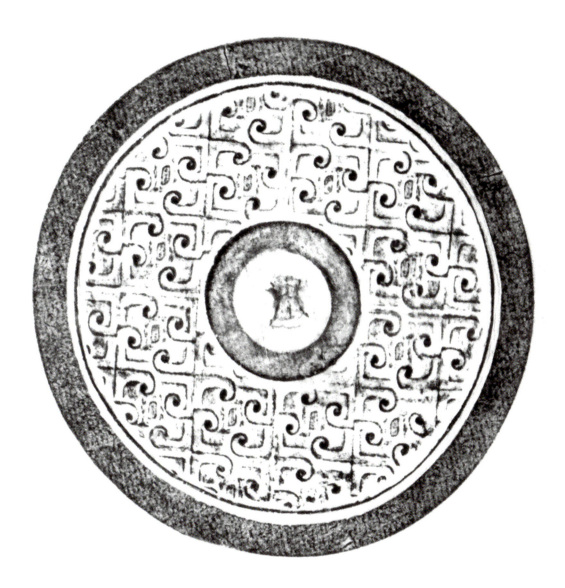

The mirror is round in shape. It has a small bridge-shaped knob on a round base. The outside of the knob base is adorned with a broad band with concave surface. The surface of the mirror is flat and straight and fills with feather-like patterns. The feather-like patterns are exquisite and well-regulated. Each group has four feather-like patterns. Four feather-like patterns are slantly symmetrical and are arranged in a square. The rim of the mirror is broad and flat.

Each feather pattern on this mirror differs in the shape from that of the earlier period. The feather pattern in the early period has a realistic style and is formed by several long and slender arcs. The feather patterns on this mirror are in the shape of raised edge lines, long

and slender outline formed by attenuated arcs and flat turns and have a decorative feel, indicating the features of the feather pattern in the late period of the late Warring States Period. This mirror is distinguished by another important feature of tiny design of triangle-shaped thunder among feather-like patterns. It is not easy to find for its ground motif of thunder design and its major motif of feather-like patterns. So this mirror is also seen as the bronze mirror with thunder design as ground motif and design of feather-like patterns. The decorative style on this mirror is rarely seen, with the thunder design as ground motif and the feather-like patterns as major motif. The feather-like patterns were often used as the ground motif.

## 3. 云雷纹镜

战国晚期
直径9厘米，厚0.2厘米，重38克
2018年5月征集入藏

　　圆形。小三弦钮。钮形制不规范，穿孔处疑为整体浇铸后打破而成，故留下不规则的碴口；三弦钮一侧伸出三道细范线，似为工匠有意为之，但其功能不明。圆钮座，外饰二周细线弦纹。镜面平直，镜体轻薄。中区满饰云雷纹。近缘处的云雷纹被一圈凸起的细线弦纹打破。缘弧凹，卷沿。

　　此镜钮座较小，单组云雷纹的形制较大，较本馆另一件同类镜时代稍早一些。国内出土的纯云雷纹镜不多，湖南长沙楚墓出土两件此类铜镜，其中编号 M1458：4[1] 的云雷纹镜与此件相似，应是同一时期楚墓出土。

[1] 湖南省博物馆、湖南省文物考古研究所、长沙市博物馆、长沙市文物考古研究所：《长沙楚墓》，文物出版社，2000年。

## 3. Mirror with design of cloud and thunder

Late Warring States Period
Diameter: 9cm, Thickness: 0.2cm, Weight: 38
Collected in May, 2018

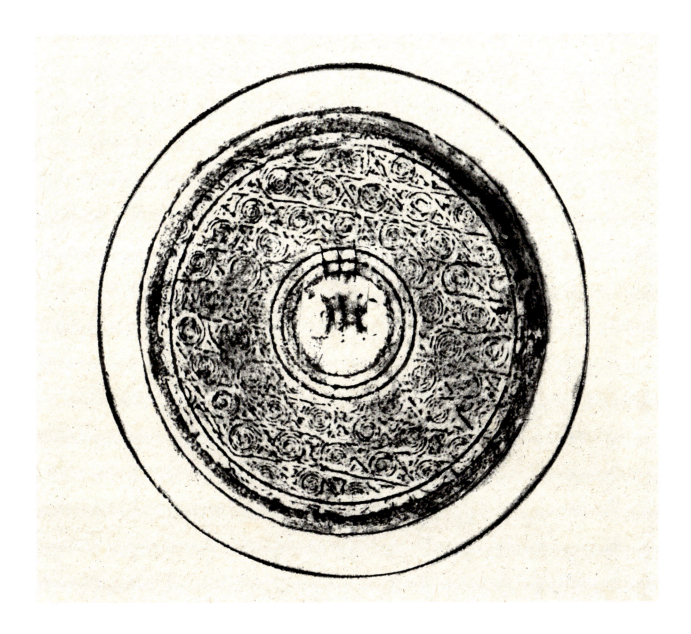

The mirror is round in shape. It has a small knob with design of three bow strings on a round base. The knob has an irregular shape. The irregular hole of the knob may be made by breaking the cast knob. There are three slender molded lines extending from one side of the knob, which are inferred to be made intentionally by the craftsmen but it is not possible to deduce how they were used. The outside of the knob base is adorned with two bands of bow string design formed by thin lines. The surface of the mirror is flat and straight and the body of the mirror is thin. The middle of the mirror is adorned with design of cloud and thunder. The design of cloud and thunder, close to the rim, is broken by a raised band of bow string design. The rim of the mirror rolls and the edge of the rim has a concave surface.

This mirror has a smaller knob base and the design of cloud and thunder is in a big shape. This mirror predates the other one of its kind in the museum. The mirrors with only design of cloud and thunder as ground motif were unearthed in small numbers. There are two mirrors of this kind unearthed in the tombs of the Chu State in Changsha, Hunan Province. One, with its number M1458:4[1], is similar to this mirror, and both mirrors were unearthed in the tombs of the Chu State in the same period.

❶ Hunan Museum, Hunan Province Institute of Cultural Relics and Historical Relics and Archaeology, Changsha Museum (eds.), *Tombs of the Chu State in Changsha City*. Cultural Relics Press, 2000.

## 4. 四山十二叶镜

战国晚期

直径 15 厘米，厚 0.55 厘米，重 330 克

2018 年 5 月征集入藏

　　圆形。小三弦钮，双层小方钮座。镜面满铺羽状纹，精细有致，找不到模印拼接痕，与本馆的四山四鹿镜铸造工艺相同，是否为失蜡法铸造，还有待研究。方钮座四角各伸出一立杆，杆顶端饰一桃形叶片，叶片下二枝绚带弯曲交叉后各生出一叶片，一枝向前叠压在直立的立杆上，一枝向后叠压在立杆之下；在羽状纹之上，大致成一个舞动的人形，四角对称，很是生动。其间四山字左旋，山字外廓为双层叠压，四个山字纹的底边，与方形钮座平行。宽平缘，近缘处饰一周单线弦纹。

　　整个镜面的纹饰，布置疏朗有致，尽管纹饰内容丰富，但是没有臃塞感。此类镜从四叶演化到十二叶这种特有的布局，十分少见，这种装饰风格从时代上看，应该是战国晚期晚段作品，有可能是楚国迁都寿春后所铸。

## 4. Mirror with inscription of four *"shan"* characters and design of twelve leaves

Late Warring States Period
Diameter: 15cm, Thickness: 0.55cm, Weight: 330g
Collected in May, 2018

The mirror is round in shape. It has a small knob with design of three bow strings on an overlaid square base. The surface of the mirror is full of the feather-like patterns which were exquisitely cast so that the joint marks of molding are barely visible. The mirror is similar in casting technique to the mirror with inscription of four *"shan"* characters and design of four deer collected in the museum. But it requires further research to confirm if the mirror was cast by the lost-wax method. Each corner of the square knob base has a pole that extends out. At the tip of the pole is a peach-shaped leaf. Under each leaf are the two designs of rope interlaced with each other. At the end of each rope design has a leaf. One leaf is overlaid forward on the pole, and the other is overlaid backward under the pole. On the feather-like patterns is the vivid design of a dancer. The inscription of *"shan"* characters is inclined towards the left. The vertical strokes of the character on both sides are formed by double lines. The bottom sides of the characters are parallel to the bottom sides of the square knob base. The rim is broad and flat. A band of bow string formed by single line approaches the rim.

The decorative patterns of the mirror are well arranged. It has an orderly layout with rich decorative patterns. Its arrangement is rarely seen in the changes of the decorative pattern from four leaves to twelve leaves. The decorative style suggests that it can date from the late period of the late Warring States Period after the Chu State moved its capital to Shouchun town.

## 5. 四花八叶镜

战国晚期

直径 10.5 厘米，厚 0.1 厘米，重 85 克

2018 年 11 月征集入藏

　　圆形。三弦钮，方钮座。钮座外饰以凹弧面的双层方框。纹饰由地纹和主纹构成。地纹是单线的涡纹和三角形纹构成的云雷纹。在钮座四角处和镜缘处各饰一片双层叠压的桃形花叶，中间以花枝相联；枝叶纹间饰四个四花瓣纹，圆形花蕊为双层叠压，花蕊中间凹陷较深，疑曾有镶嵌物。近缘处饰二周细弦纹。卷素缘。

　　此镜镜面纹饰布局均匀和谐，疏朗有致，十分美观。从工艺上看，先是在模制好的云雷纹地纹上装饰主纹；方形钮座内部纹饰与钮座外的地纹相联，能区别出钮座的叠压模制痕。四片桃形花叶正好与方形钮座的四角相接，给人以自然和谐之美。

## 5. Mirror with design of four flowers and eight leaves

Late Warring States Period
Diameter: 10.5cm, Thickness: 0.1cm, Weight: 85g
Collected in November, 2018

The mirror is round in shape. It has a knob with design of three bow strings on a square base. The outside of the knob base is adorned with two-layer squares with concave surface. The decorative pattern consists of the ground motif and the major motif. The ground motif is the whorl design formed by single line and the triangle-shaped design of cloud and thunder. Each corner of the square base and its opposite rim of the mirror is adorned with an overlaid peach-shaped leaf, the two leaves being joined by a branch. Four flowers with four petals are spaced between the branches. The flower has a round overlaid pistil. The middle of the pistil is sunken deeply and above it is suspected to be an inset. Two bands of string design are close to the rim of the mirror. The rim is unadorned and rolls.

This mirror is perfect, with its well-arranged and harmonious layout. The major motif was cast over the ground motif first molded. The decorative patterns on the inside of the square base and the ground motif on the outside of the knob base are connected and the mold marks of overlaid base are clearly visible. There is a natural combination of each peach-shaped leaf and each corner of the square base.

## 6. 云雷纹镜

战国晚期

直径 9.5 厘米，厚 0.3 厘米，重 60 克

1987 年 10 月淮南市谢家集区唐山乡双古堆东侧砂场工地出土

　　圆形。三弦钮，圆钮座。钮座外和镜缘边各饰二周弦纹，弦纹之间满铺云雷纹。云雷纹为圆涡纹及两个底边相对的双线三角纹相间排列，呈四方连续式排列。在斜穿镜钮方向，有模制范线。卷缘。

　　战国时期云雷纹多作地纹，常出现于龙纹镜中，纯地纹镜比较少见。楚镜中的地纹除云雷纹外，还有羽状纹，是由同一印模连续压印而成。该镜镜体轻薄，较《中国铜镜图典》收录的直径 15.5 厘米云雷地纹镜和湖南长沙年嘉湖出土的直径 11 厘米的同类镜直径都要小，钮座所占镜面比例也小，其时代要稍早一些，时间应在楚国迁都寿春之前。

## 6. Mirror with design of cloud and thunder

Late Warring States Period
Diameter: 9.5cm, Thickness: 0.3cm, Weight: 60g
Unearthed at a Sand Workshop, east of Shuanggudui in Xiejiaji District, Huainan City in October, 1987

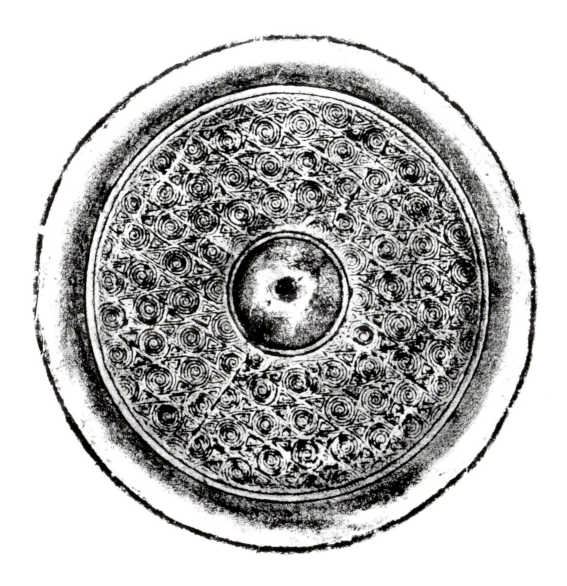

The mirror is round in shape. It has a knob with design of three bow strings on a round base. The outside of the knob base and the inside of the rim are adorned with two bands of bow string design, respectively. The design of cloud and thunder is filled in between the two bands. The design of cloud and thunder is in the shape of an alternating arrangement of the whorl pattern and two triangles that are formed by double lines and are opposite to each other with their base lines, and is arranged repeatedly toward four directions. A molding line is placed in the direction of slanting the knob. The rim of the mirror rolls.

In the Warring States Period (475 BC – 221 BC), the design of cloud and thunder was used as the ground motif and mostly adorned on the mirrors with dragon design. The mirrors with only design of cloud and thunder as ground motif are rarely seen. The design of cloud and thunder and feather-like pattern were often used as the ground motif of the bronze mirrors of the Chu State and were pressed continuously by the same mold. The mirror has a thin body. It is shorter in diameter than the two mirrors with the same design, one of which is recorded in the *A Catalogue of Chinese Bronze Mirror* with a diameter of 15.5cm and the other is unearthed at Nianjia Lake, Changsha City, Hunan Province with a diameter of 11cm. The knob base has a small share of the surface of the mirror. It can date from an earlier period before the Chu State moved its capital to Shouchun town.

## 7. 四叶镜

战国中晚期
直径 11.6 厘米，厚 0.4 厘米，重 72 克
2018 年 2 月征集入藏

　　圆形。三弦钮，圆钮座。镜面满铺羽状地纹，分七层，每层有四个方块组成，单个方块呈长方形状。钮座外呈"十"字形伸出四花叶，叶片呈花蕾状，由中间大叶片和两侧小叶片组成，叶柄与钮座相连。宽素缘，卷边。

　　此镜与本馆收藏的 1986 年谢家集区出土的四叶镜十分相似。湖南资兴出土的战国中期四叶镜与此镜造型基本相同，湖北、安徽都有此类镜出土。说明这种形制的铜镜出现时间较早，流行区域广泛。

# 7. Mirror with design of four leaves

Middle and Late Warring States Period
Diameter: 11.6cm, Thickness: 0.4cm, Weight: 72g
Collected in February, 2018

The mirror is round in shape. It has a knob with design of three bow strings on a round base. The back of the mirror is adorned with the seven-layer ground motif of feather-like pattern. Each layer is formed by four rectangles. The four branches extend from the knob base in each direction of cross. The branch, in the shape of bud, consists of a big leaf in the middle and two small leaves on either side. The petioles approach the knob base. The mirror has a broad rim that rolls up and is decorated without design.

The mirror is similar to the mirror with design of four leaves in the museum, which was unearthed in Xiejiaji District in 1986. The mirror is basically the same as the mirror with design of four leaves of the middle Warring States Period unearthed in Zixing, Hunan Province. The mirrors with design of four leaves were also unearthed in Hubei Province and Anhui Province. All the evidence tells the mirrors with design of four leaves appeared much earlier and were used over a wide area.

　　圆形。小三弦钮，双层宽带凹弧面方钮座。纹饰由三层组合而成，最下层的是模印清晰的羽状地纹，在羽状地纹上装饰十二叶纹，最上层是叠压在地纹和草叶纹上的四左旋山字纹。地纹是由排列五层的羽状纹组合而成，模印结合处很细腻，不易察觉，卷羽的涡纹和弯曲羽状纹很有立体感。方形钮座四角伸出的八叶片，与山字中间一竖右上的叶片以细绹带叠压成枝相连，非常生动。具体的制模方法是，在钮座方角处的叶片以条带交叉叠出，与上方叶片、左右两侧山字上的叶片连接，山字纹上的叶片又与相邻的钮座角的叶片相连。在本馆所藏另一件直径 9.7 厘米的镜面上，只能观察到用枝干相连，但看不到其细部构成。由于此镜模制精美，可以窥其细微之处。近缘处饰一周凸弦纹，沿口弧起，窄平。

## 8. Mirror with inscription of four "*shan*" characters and design of twelve leaves

Late Warring States Period
Diameter: 14.8cm, Thickness: 0.5cm, Weight: 292g
Transferred by Xiejiaji District Public Security Bureau in Huainan City in 2018

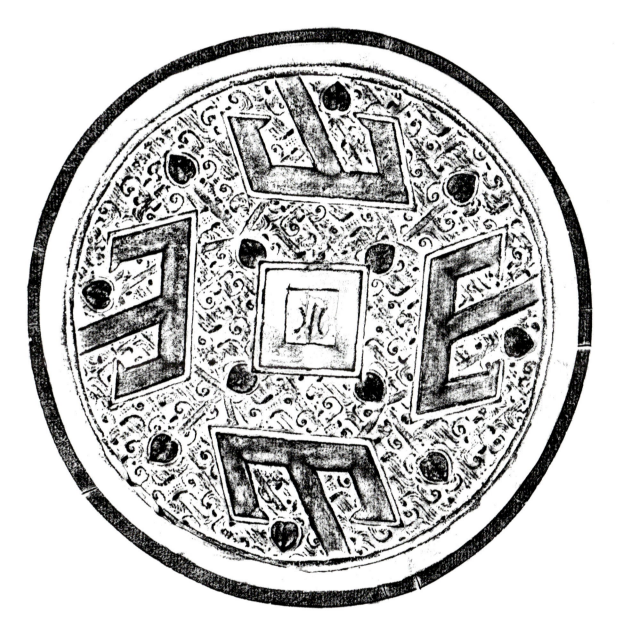

The mirror is round in shape. It has a small knob with design of three bow strings on an overlaid square base formed by broad band with concave surface. The decorative patterns are a combination of three layers. The lowest layer is adorned with the ground motif of feather-like patterns with clear molding marks. The design of twelve leaves adorns on the ground motif of feather-like patterns. The upper layer is adorned with the inscription of four "*shan*" characters that is inclined towards the left and is overlaid on the ground motif and the leaf design. The ground motif is the feather-like patterns in five layers, with barely visible molding marks. The patterns of the whorl design with rolling feather and the crooked feather-like pattern give a stereoscopic effect. Eight leaves extend out from each corner of the square knob base. The leaves are joined by the rope design with the

leaves on the top right-hand corner of the middle vertical strokes of the characters, and the rope designs are overlaid to be the shape of branches. It is a vivid picture. The details of the picture are as follows: the leaves on each corner that interlace to each other and extend out are connected with the leaves on the upper corners of both sides of the middle vertical strokes of the characters; the leaves on the characters are connected with the leaves on the adjacent corner of the knob base. On the surface of another mirror with a diameter of 9.7cm, which is in the museum, we can observe only the leaves are connected by the branches, but no other details of the mirror. This mirror was delicately cast so that its details could be observed. A band of raised bow string approaches the rim of the mirror. The rim is in the shape of arc and is narrow and flat.

## 9. 四叶镜

战国晚期

直径 13 厘米，厚 0.6 厘米，重 278 克

2010 年 8 月淮南市谢家集区李郢孜镇塌陷区

改造工程谢家集小区 21 号楼工地出土

　　圆形。三弦钮，小圆钮座。双层钮座仅比镜钮稍大，此种钮座十分少见。座外等距伸出四桃形叶，叶形饱满，中间隆脊，短粗无柄，长度不及钮座直径。镜面满铺羽状地纹，羽状地纹较大，但十分清晰、规整，每一羽尾卷而凸起，极细密，是羽状地纹中比较少见的精细作品。羽状地纹边缘以弦纹为栏。镜缘弧形，宽缘。

　　羽状地纹早期采用模印制范，一面直径不足 10 厘米的镜上，有时有多达 30 个羽状纹模印痕迹，模印之间的连接处多见不规则接缝。脱范时，为保护镜体，多将泥范揭破，故很少有完全相同的铜镜，是一镜一范所致。而此镜羽状地纹和四叶纹观察不到任何模印的接范痕。陈佩芬先生在观察有些铜镜花纹上具有明显的缩蜡痕迹后认为，"山字纹镜从羽翅纹的地纹看，它是用失蜡法铸造的。"此镜纹饰清晰，铸造精良，镜体厚重，已无楚镜之轻薄特征，是楚国晚期晚段用失蜡法铸造，弥足珍贵。

## 9. Mirror with design of four leaves

Late Warring States Period

Diameter: 13cm, Thickness: 0.6cm, Weight: 278g

Unearthed at a construction site of No.21 Building site, Xiejiaji housing estate under a project of rebuilding subsidence area, in Liyingzi Town, Xiejiaji District, in Huainan City, in August, 2010

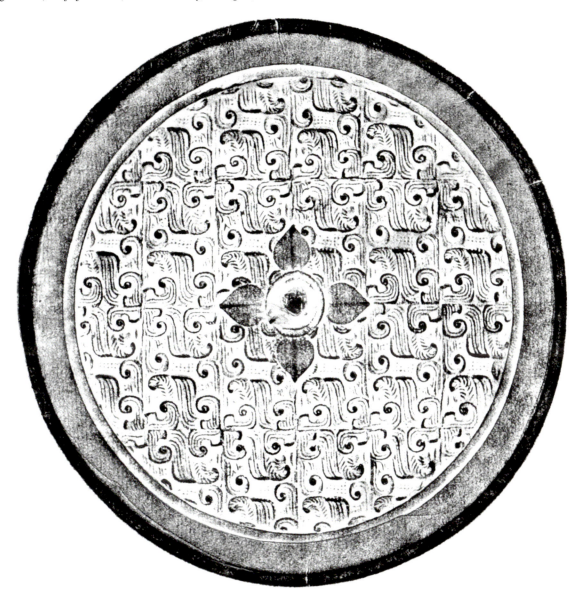

The mirror is round in shape. It has a knob with design of three bow strings on a small round base. The two-layer knob base, slightly bigger than the knob, is rarely seen. Four peach-shaped leaves extend out at equally spaced intervals around the knob base. Each leaf is of a plump shape and has a raised vein in the middle. Each leaf is short and stubby and is decorated without a petiole. The length of each leaf is less than the diameter of the knob base. The back of the mirror is adorned with feather-like pattern as ground motif. The ground motif of feather-like pattern is big in size and is clearly arranged in order. The end of each feather is rolled up and raised. The ground motif of the mirror is an elaborate treasure of the ground motifs of feather-like pattern. The edge of the ground motif is adorned with a band of string design that serves as a fence. The mirror has a broad rim raised in arc shape.

The technique of molding was used in the early period to cast the mirror with feather-like pattern as motif ground. More than 30 mold marks with irregular joints can be found in a mirror with a diameter of less than 10cm. To protect the mirror, the clay model was often broken while being demolded. So each mirror has its unique mold and it is rare to find the same mirror. But in this mirror, no trace of mold is to be found on the ground motif of feather-like pattern and design of four leaves. Mr. Chen Peifen observed that some clear wax marks are on the decorative patterns of bronze mirrors and inferred that the mirror with inscription of "*shan*" character was cast by lost-wax method from its ground motif with feather-like pattern. The mirror, with its clear design, fine cast and thick body, was cast by the lost-wax method in the late period of the late Chu State, which does not possess the light and slender features of bronze mirrors of the Chu State. The mirror is of high value.

## 10. 六龙六菱镜

战国晚期

直径 16.1 厘米，厚 0.4 厘米，重 245 克

2018 年 1 月征集入藏

　　圆形。三弦钮，圆钮座。钮座外饰一圈凹弧面宽圈带纹，宽圈带纹内外饰单弦纹。镜面平直，满铺细密的云雷纹。主纹由龙纹和小菱形纹组成。每个菱形纹都与龙首的角相连接。龙纹结构复杂，尤其是在龙首部分，上、下小菱形近似"回"形纹，菱形纹的收口线即是龙的角，近镜缘处的龙首向镜钮方向张口吐舌，口中有二牙，钮座处小菱形纹伸出的龙首，张口，无牙，圆目，二龙首相互贴于对方弯曲腹部上。龙的身体向两侧展开，盘曲交错呈蔓枝状。由于此镜保存完整，通过放大可以见到龙首处制模的过程的痕迹。近缘处的龙颈部在下方先行制作，龙角在中间，上层叠压着相连接的小菱形纹伸出的边线。近钮座处龙的颈部叠压下方的龙腹部，并贴服其上，其是生动，仔细观察，是二龙相交的写实画面。宽素缘，平沿。

　　本馆收藏的有 4 面六龙六菱镜，此镜是模印最清晰的，前三面曾被误读为三龙，依据此镜清晰的纹饰才辨识出是六龙。六龙六菱镜的布局独特，尤其是上、下各三个小菱纹布置很特别，在长沙楚墓和荆州楚墓中没有看到这类材料，而本馆的 4 面铜镜，尺寸、纹饰布局、铸造工艺都十分相似，由此推测，存在着此类铜镜是楚国迁都寿春后在淮南地区铸造的可能。

## 10. Mirror with design of six dragons and six rhombuses

Late Warring States Period
Diameter: 16.1cm, Thickness: 0.4cm, Weight: 245g
Collected in January, 2018

The mirror is round in shape. It has a knob with design of three bow strings on a round base. The outside of the knob base is adorned with a broad band with concave surface. Both sides of the broad band are adorned with the design of bow string formed by single line. The surface of the mirror is flat and straight and is full of the fine design of cloud and thunder. The major motif is the decorative patterns of the dragon design and the small design of rhombus. Each rhombus is connected with the horn on the head of the dragon. Each dragon is in the complex shape, especially its head with horns formed by seam lines of rhombus. The head of each dragon, which is close to the rim, has an open mouth with a tongue protruding towards the knob and two teeth. The head of each dragon, which extends from the small design of rhombus out of the knob base, has round eyes and an open toothless mouth. The heads of both dragons were close to each other's crooked belly. The body of each dragon is spread towards both sides and is curled and interlaced like a branch. This mirror is kept in good condition, so that it can provide a zoom-in observation of the molding process. The neck of the dragon, close to the rim, was cast first. The

horns of the dragon are located in the middle and are overlaid with side lines of small design of rhombus joined. The neck of the dragon, close to the knob base, is vividly overlaid on the belly of the other dragon. On closer observation, it is a picture of two intersecting dragons. The broad rim is unadorned and has a flat edge.

There are four bronze mirrors with design of six dragons and six rhombuses in the museum. Of these, this mirror has the clearest molding marks. The three mirrors above were erroneously believed to be the mirror with design of three dragons. Based on the clear decorative patterns of this mirror, their decoration is recognized as the design of six dragons. The mirrors with design of six dragons and six rhombuses are peculiar in their arrangement, especially in their three small design of rhombuses above and below, respectively. The mirrors were not found in the published articles on the tombs of the Chu State in Changsha and Jingzhou. All four mirrors are similar in size, decorative layout and casting technique. Thus, it is deduced that the mirrors of this kind could be cast in the Huainan region after the Chu State moved its capital to Shouchun town.

## 11. 三龙镜

战国中晚期

直径 15.6 厘米，厚 0.3 厘米，重 209 克

2018 年 5 月征集入藏

　　圆形。三弦钮，圆钮座，钮座外饰凹弧面宽圈带纹，钮座内饰蒲谷纹。纹饰由地纹和主纹组合而成。地纹十分细密，以双线勾连雷纹填以细密的谷纹。双勾线内谷纹略高，线外谷纹稀松。地纹之上环绕镜钮饰三条右向奔走姿态的侧影龙纹。龙小首，腹部硕大呈菱形，龙口向下张开，长唇外卷，曲颈，单足，爪部蹬于钮座外缘，长尾向内卷起，一龙尾中部饰玉兰花苞状纹飘起，二龙尾中部有燕尾式小翼。近缘处饰一圈细线凸弦纹。宽素缘，缘微卷，平沿。

　　此类铜镜在江苏仪征、湖南长沙、河南南阳的西汉早期墓葬都有出土。勾连雷纹出现的较早，商代中期用于青铜器上，西周时流行，用于铜镜上的时代在战国中晚期。南阳汉代中期墓葬出土的一批同类铜镜的镜缘增加了连弧纹，说明这类铜镜在中原地区流行时间更长。

## 11. Mirror with design of three dragons

Middle and Late Warring States Period
Diameter: 15.6cm, Thickness: 0.3cm, Weight: 209g
Collected in May, 2018

The mirror is round in shape. It has a knob with design of three bow strings on a round base. The outside of the knob base is adorned with a broad band with concave surface and the inside of the base is adorned with design of unhusked rice. The decorative patterns consist of the ground motif and the major motif. The fine ground motif is the thunder design that is formed by two interlaced lines and the design of unhusked rice spaced among the thunder design. The design of unhusked rice is raised on the inside of the two interlaced lines and is loose on the outside of the two interlaced lines. There are silhouette of three dragons flying towards the right around the knob on the ground motif. The dragons have small heads, big rhombus-like bellies, downward-opening mouths, long rolling lips, crooked necks, single feet that step on the rim of the knob base and long tails that roll inwards. The design of magnolia bud adorns on the middle of the tail of the one dragon and the swallow-tail-shaped wings adorns on the middle

of the tails of the two dragons. A band of design of raised bow string is decorated near the rim. The broad flat rim is unadorned and slightly rolls.

The bronze mirror with the same shape were often unearthed in the tombs of the early Western Han Dynasty in Yizheng, Jiangsu Province, in Changsha, Hunan Province, and in Nanyang, Henan Province. The design of thunder scrolls, which appeared earlier, was used as decorative patterns on the bronzes in the middle Shang Dynasty and prevailed in the Western Zhou Dynasty. In the middle and late Warring States Period, the bronze mirrors were adorned with the design of thunder scrolls. The design of linked arcs was found on the bronze mirrors with the same shape unearthed in the tombs of the middle Han Dynasty in Nanyang, which is evidence that the mirrors were in use in the Central Plain for a much longer time.

## 12. 饕餮纹镜

战国晚期
直径 8.2 厘米，厚 0.1 厘米，重 38 克
2018 年 11 月征集入藏

　　圆形。小三弦钮，圆钮座。钮座外饰凹弧面宽带纹。纹饰由地纹和主纹组成。地纹以细密的卷云纹和网格纹组成，局部较清晰。主纹为两组上下对称的饕餮纹，饕餮鼻目夸张，目上有弯曲的眉，眉上有弯曲的角，鼻下有隆起的口，两侧为盘曲的身躯。整个主纹的卷曲端都饰明显的涡状乳钉纹，身体部分填以网格地纹。宽素平缘。

　　饕餮纹镜发现的较少，见于已公开的材料有 5 面。美国收藏家罗伊德·扣岑捐赠给上海博物馆铜镜中有 1 面❶，直径 12.1 厘米，主纹特征与此镜相似，模印清晰，能看到饕餮纹身体上的鳞纹，眼部、鼻部的凸起更清晰，尤其眼珠更逼真。《中原藏镜聚英》❷收录的出土于河南洛阳金村的 1 面，也与此镜纹饰风格、布局相似。浙江私人收藏家收藏 1 面，与此镜在尺寸、纹饰特征上十分相似❸，应属同一产地、同一工匠制模浇铸。此类镜考古发掘品出土于河北、河南一带。1978 年河北邯郸赵王陵周窑一号墓出土了 1 面❹，直径 14 厘米，纹饰与此镜相似。发掘者推测该墓是赵国迁都邯郸后五代国君王陵之一，时间在

战国晚期。但该墓出土的饕餮纹镜在铸造工艺上要远逊于楚镜。《欧洲所藏中国青铜器遗珠》❺收录的巴黎赛努奇博物馆的蟠龙纹镜，与上述 4 面饕餮纹镜在纹饰的风格尤其是镜缘上很相似。

　　此外，20 世纪 80 年代，在江陵九店楚墓中发现的饕餮纹镜，出土时放置于竹笥内，保存完好，光可鉴人，品相非常好。其直径 12.2 厘米，纹饰布局大致相同，模铸精细，纹样直接取材于青铜器，具有显著的黄河流域铜镜特征，与楚镜面貌不同。

　　河北邯郸和湖北江陵九店 2 面有确切出土地点的饕餮纹镜，反映出战国晚期饕餮纹镜的流通是相当广泛的。

❶ 上海博物馆：《镜映乾坤——罗伊德·扣岑先生捐赠铜镜精粹》，上海书画出版社，2012年。
❷ 王趁意：《中原藏镜聚英》，中州古籍出版社，2011年，第107页。
❸ 浙江省博物馆：《古镜今照——中国铜镜研究会成员藏镜精粹》，文物出版社，2012年。
❹ 河北省文管处等：《河北邯郸赵王陵》，《考古》1982年第6期。
❺ 李学勤、艾兰：《欧洲所藏中国青铜器遗珠》，文物出版社，1995年，第151页。

## 12. Mirror with design of *Tao Tie* (a monster with a head but no body)

Late Warring States Period

Diameter: 8.2cm, Thickness: 0.1cm, Weight: 38g

Collected in November, 2018

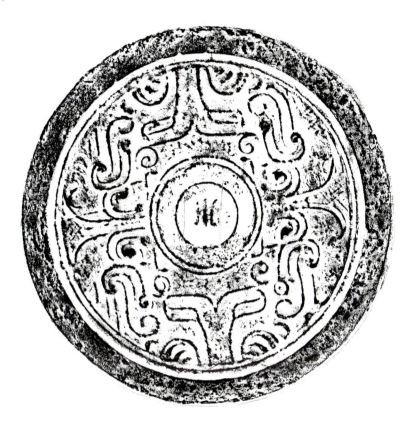

The mirror is round in shape. It has a small knob with design of three bow strings on a round base. The outside of the knob base is adorned with a broad band with concave surface. The decorative patterns consist of the ground motif and the major motif. The ground motif is formed with fine design of cirrus cloud and the grid design, the part of which is more defined. The major motif is a symmetrical design of two groups of *Tao Tie* up and down. *Tao Tie* has an exaggerated nose, exaggerated eyes, eyebrows with curved arches, a raised mouth and coiled bodies on either side of its head. The curling ends of decorative patterns of the major motif are adorned with the whorl-shaped design of nipple. The bodies of *Tao Tie* are filled with the ground motif of the grid design. The broad and flat rim is unadorned.

The mirrors with design of *Tao Tie* have been found in small numbers. In all, there are five bronze mirrors recorded in the published articles. Of these, the one donated by American collector Lioyd Cotsen is collected in the Shanghai Museum.[1] That mirror, with a diameter of 12.1cm, is similar in major motif to this mirror. The major motif of that mirror shows clear molding marks and is the design of *Tao Tie* with scales, eyes with realistic eyeballs and a clearly raised nose. Another one, unearthed in Jin Village, Luoyang, Henan Province, is recorded in the book *Treasures of Bronze Mirrors in Central Plains*.[2] That mirror is similar in its decorative style and arrangement to this mirror. Another is in the possession of a private collector in Zhejiang Province.[3] That mirror, similar in size and decorative style, should be cast by the same craftsmen at the same place. The mirrors of this kind were often unearthed in the area of Hebei Province and Henan Province. In 1978, a mirror, with a diameter of 14cm and decorative patterns similar to this mirror, was unearthed at the No.1 tomb of the King Mausoleum of the Zhao State at Zhouyao, Handan, Hebei Province.[4] It is inferred

that the mausoleum is one of the mausoleums of five kings after the Zhao State moved its capital to Handan and dates from the late Warring States Period. But the mirror unearthed in the tomb was cast with worse technique than those of the Chu State. There is a bronze mirror with design of coiled dragon recorded in the book *Chinese Bronzes: A Selection from European Collections*, which is collected in the Cernuschi Museum in Paris.[5] The one is similar in decorative style and the rim of the mirror to the above four mirrors with design of *Tao Tie*.

In addition, in the 1980s, a mirror with design of *Tao Tie* was unearthed in the tomb of the Chu State at Jiudian, Jiangling. It was preserved in a bamboo-plaited basket and in excellent condition. Its surface is brilliant enough to reflect the image. It is 12.2cm in diameter and of good quality. Its decorative arrangement is approximately the same as that of this mirror. It was exquisitely cast. Its decorative patterns were drawn from those of the bronzes and show the typical features of the Huanghe Valley, unlike the bronze mirrors of the Chu State.

The two mirrors unearthed in Handan, Hebei Province and Jiudian, Handan, Hubei Province indicate that the mirrors with design of *Tao Tie* prevailed widely in the late Warring States Period.

[1] Shanghai Museum, *Treasures of Bronze Mirrors Donated by Lioyd Cotsen.* Shanghai Calligraphy and Painting Publishing House, 2012.

[2] Wang Chenyi, *Treasures of Bronze Mirrors in Central Plains.* Zhongzhou Ancient Books Publishing House, 2011.

[3] Zhejiang Musuem, *Light Today on Ancient Mirrors.* Cultural Relics Press, 2012.

[4] Hebei Province Administration of Cultural Heritage et al. "Mausoleum of the King of the Zhao State in Handan City, Hebei Province". Cultural Relics, 1982.6.

[5] Li Xueqin, Ai Lan, *Chinese Bronzes: A Selection from European Collections.* Cultural Relics Press, 1995.

## 13. 十二花叶镜

战国晚期

直径 6.8 厘米，厚 0.1 厘米，重 29 克

2018 年 11 月征集入藏

　　圆形。小三弦钮，双层凹弧面宽圈带纹圆钮座。镜体小巧平直。地纹为三角形雷纹和卷云纹、碎粒点组成的云雷纹。主纹呈米字形布局，二片扁桃叶串联以十字形沿钮座伸出，间以长形双层叶片。近缘处饰一周细弦纹。镜缘稍宽，缘内凹弧。

　　镜面布置舒展匀称，十分美观，与本馆收藏的另一件扁桃叶和长花叶组成的八花叶纹镜，尺寸相近，地纹和主纹的模印方法以及镜表面的氧化程度都十分相似。这两面铜镜应是同一时期、同一地区的产品，也有可能是同一制镜作坊的产品。

## 13. Mirror with design of twelve leaves

Late Warring States Period
Diameter: 6.8cm, Thickness: 0.1cm, Weight: 29g
Collected in November, 2018

The mirror is round in shape. It has a small knob with design of three bow strings on a two-layer round base with broad concave surface. The body of the mirror is delicate and flat. The ground motif is the design of cloud and thunder consisting of triangle-shaped design of thunder, cirrus cloud design and design of tiny spots. The major design is arranged in Chinese character "*mi* (rice)" and is the design of branches with two peach-shaped leaves which extend from the knob base in each direction of cross and the design of long two-layer leaves among branches. A band of string design is close to the rim of the mirror. The rim is slightly broad and has an arc-like shape with concave surface.

The mirror, well-arranged, is very beautiful. The mirror is similar in size to another bronze mirror with design of twelve leaves that is formed by peach-shaped leaves and long leaves. And both mirrors are similar in mold casting of the ground motif and the major motif and oxidation of the mirror surface. Both the mirrors may be cast in the same area at the same time, or may be cast by the same workshop.

## 14. 羽状纹镜

战国晚期
直径 9.1 厘米，厚 0.3 厘米，重 94 克
2018 年 5 月征集入藏

　　圆形。小四弦钮，圆钮座。钮座外饰一周凹弧面宽圈带纹。镜面平直。满铺羽状纹，羽状纹分层模印而成。近缘处饰双层圈带纹。镜缘上卷，平沿。

　　羽状纹，又称羽翅纹，是变形兽纹的局部放大，一般认为是龙蛇身体上的小羽翅，截取后以二方连续、四方连续组合而形成，一般用作地纹，用作主纹的比较少见，最先在春秋晚期到战国早期的青铜器上流行使用。

　　此镜虽然镜钮很小，但镜缘已变得宽厚，时代在战国晚期。

## 14. Mirror with feather-like design

Late Warring States Period
Diameter: 9.1cm, Thickness: 0.3cm, Weight: 94g
Collected in May, 2018

The mirror is round in shape. It has a small knob with design of four bow strings on a round base. The outside of the knob base is adorned with a broad band with concave surface. The surface of the mirror is flat and straight and full of feather-like patterns. The feather-like patterns were molded in layers. The two bands are close to the rim of the mirror. The rim of the mirror rolls up and has a flat edge.

The feather-like pattern, also known as feather-wing pattern, is the enlarged part of the pattern of stylized beast. It is generally supposed that the pattern of small feather wings, taken from the bodies of dragon and serpent, is consecutively and repeatedly arranged up and down or toward four directions. The feather-like pattern was often used as the ground motif and rarely as the major motif. It first prevailed on the bronzes from the late Spring and Autumn Period to the early Warring States Period.

This mirror, with a small knob and a broad and thick rim, dates from the late Warring States Period.

## 15. 四山四鹿镜

战国晚期

直径 15.7 厘米，厚 0.5 厘米，重 230 克

1987 年 12 月淮南市谢家集区红卫轮窑厂出土

　　圆形。三弦钮，双层方形宽带钮座。镜背通体以精美的羽状纹为地，成四方连续排列，四山纹粗壮有力，以鹿形瑞兽间隔。鹿做回首态，小短尾，三足落地，右前腿抬起弯曲，身饰鳞状纹，造型生动。山字左旋，中间一笔向左伸向镜缘，两侧的竖划上端向内折成尖角。宽缘，边缘上卷。

　　该镜制作十分规整，模范精细，为战国晚期楚国铜镜。此镜 1987 年在淮南市谢家集区红卫轮窑厂发现时已残破，后经修复完整。山字纹镜中饰瑞兽类纹饰的比较罕见，尤显此镜珍贵。

## 15. Mirror with inscription of four *"shan"* characters and design of four deer

Late Warring States Period
Diameter: 15.7cm, Thickness: 0.5cm, Weight: 230g
Unearthed at Hongwei Annular Kiln Works, Xiejiaji District, Huainan City in December, 1987

The mirror is round in shape. It has a knob with design of three bow strings on an overlaid square base formed by broad band. The back of the mirror is filled up with the feather-like patterns as the ground motif which is arranged consecutively and repeatedly towards the four directions. The inscription of four *"shan"* characters is powerful and strong and is spaced in the design of deer-like beast. Each deer turns its head vividly. Its three legs are landed and its right foreleg is bent and raised. Each deer has a short tail and a body with design of scale. The inscription of *"shan"* characters is inclined towards the left. The middle vertical stroke of each character projects to the rim and the vertical strokes on both sides of each character turn inwards and take in the shape of closed angle. The broad rim has a rolling edge.

This mirror, with its well arrangement and delicate molding marks, can date from the Chu State in the late Warring States Period. This mirror was broken when it was found at the Hongwei Annular Kiln Works, Xiejiaji District, Huainan City in 1987. But it was beautifully restored. The design of lucky beast on the mirrors with inscription of *"shan"* characters is rarely seen. So this mirror is very valuable.

## 16. 龙纹镜

战国晚期

直径 23.8 厘米，厚 0.5 厘米，重 818 克

2010 年 9 月淮南市谢家集公安分局移交

圆形。宽弦钮，圆钮座。七个浅凹弧面连弧纹绕钮座一周，镜面以细密的云雷纹铺地，外饰一圈凹弧面宽带纹。主区在云雷纹地上饰八龙纹。龙大口，小圆目，长舌卷起，角部后翻，身躯平起，足踏镜缘，身形变化复杂，缠绕交错，勾连奇曲。外以一周细弦纹和栉齿纹为栏。宽素缘，缘边卷起，窄平。此镜形制硕大，纹饰繁缛华丽，是战国晚期楚镜的代表作品。

## 16. Mirror with design of dragon

Late Warring States Period
Diameter: 23.8cm, Thickness: 0.5cm, Weight: 818g
Transferred by Xiejiaji District Public Security Bureau in Huainan City in September, 2010

The mirror is round in shape. It has a knob with broad string design on a round base. The outside of the knob base is adorned with a band of seven linked arcs with concave surface. The mirror surface is decorated with fine design of cloud and thunder as ground motif. There is a broad band with concave surface on the exterior of the ground motif. The major motif is the design of eight dragons on the ground motif with design of cloud and thunder. The dragons are interlaced with each other and are in the complex shape of a big mouth, small round eyes, a rolling tongue, horns turning backwards, a flat body and feet that step on the rim of the mirror. A band of bow string design and fine-toothed pattern serves as a fence around the exterior of the major motif. A broad rim rolls up and is unadorned. The rim is narrow and flat. The mirror, with its large size and exquisite decoration, is the typical of the mirrors of the Chu State in the late Warring Stats Period.

## 17. 六龙六菱镜

战国晚期
直径 16.1 厘米，厚 0.4 厘米，重 232 克
2018 年 11 月淮南市谢家集公安分局移交

　　圆形。小三弦钮，圆钮座。钮座外饰一圈凹面宽圈带纹，宽圈带纹内外饰一周细线凸弦纹。镜面平直，满铺云雷纹至钮座外，可以判断出凸弦纹、宽带纹和主纹都是在铺好后的地纹上装饰的。六龙纹自近缘处的小菱纹开始，菱形纹下端伸出龙的角，龙首向下张口，吐舌，口中有二獠牙，龙腹如"S"状卷曲，羽翼呈蔓枝状盘曲。镜面的主纹在很小的空间中交错、穿插，使龙的身影上下、左右舞动，而镜面的布置仍然疏朗有致。宽素缘，平沿。

　　战国晚期龙纹镜的形态多样，而此六龙六菱镜在淮南地区以外并不多见。

## 17. Mirror with design of six dragons and six rhombuses

Late Warring States Period
Diameter: 16.1cm, Thickness: 0.4cm, Weight: 232g
Transferred by Xiejiaji District Public Security Bureau in Huainan City in November, 2018

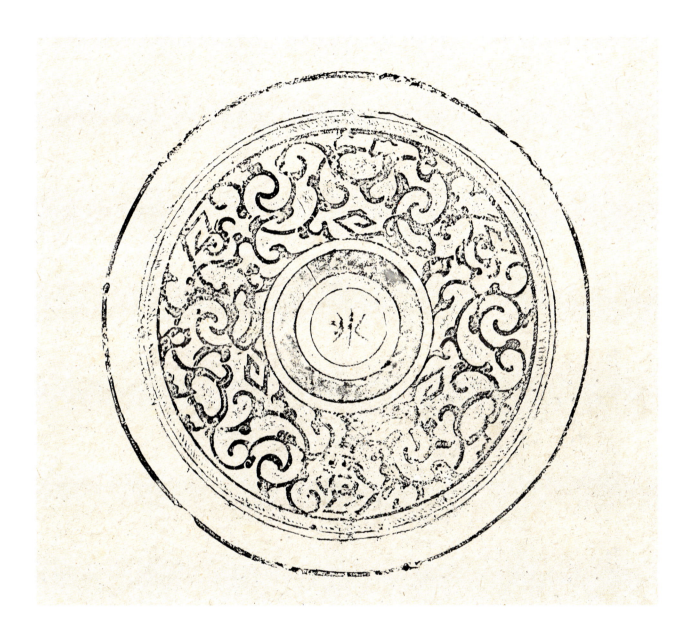

The mirror is round in shape. It has a small knob with design of three bow strings on a round base. The outside of the knob base is adorned with a broad band with concave surface. Both sides of the broad band are adorned with a band of raised bow string formed by slender line. The surface of the mirror is flat and straight and is full of the design of cloud and thunder that extend to the outside of the knob base. It can be deduced that the design of raised bow string, the broad band and the major motif are arranged on the cast ground motif. The design of six dragons begins with the small design of rhombuses near the rim of the mirror. The horns of each dragon extend under the design of rhombus. Each dragon has a head with a downward-opening mouth with a protruding tongue and two buckteeth, a belly curled in the shape of an S and wings coiled like branches. The major motif is interlaced and intersected in small spaces, showing images of dragons flying up and down, right and left and a well-arrangement of the surface of the mirror. The broad rim is unadorned and has a flat edge.

The mirrors with dragon design come in a variety of shapes in the late Warring States Period. But the mirrors with design of six dragons and six rhombuses are rarely seen outside the Huainan region.

## 18. 三龙镜

战国晚期
直径 12.1 厘米、厚 0.25 厘米、重 84 克
2018 年 11 月征集入藏

　　圆形。小三弦钮，圆钮座。钮座外饰凹弧面双层宽圈带纹。纹饰由地纹和主纹构成。地纹是由菱形方块为单元的卷云纹、三角雷纹和略呈方形的涡纹相间组成，成四方连续的云雷地纹；钮座内纹饰与圈带外纹饰本来是相连接的，被其上的宽圈带打破。主纹三龙绕钮环列布置，龙曲颈向后伸展，短角，张口，露牙，圆目。胸、腹部饱满，一足上翘，一足蹬踏镜钮座，尾部高高拱起后向内收卷，尾中部有小燕尾翼。宽素缘。

　　此镜龙纹造型十分生动，龙的形态没有图案化，而是将龙的各个部分以写实方法表现出来，是同类镜中的上乘之作。中国国家博物馆收藏的一面三龙镜与之相近，只是龙首及身体运动方向相反。这类铜镜发展到战国晚期晚段时，龙的身躯是方形图案状。此镜与本馆所藏另一件三龙镜不同，其三龙中，二龙尾有小燕翼，一龙尾有玉兰花苞式纹饰，这种区别的原因尚不清楚。

## 18. Mirror with design of three dragons

Late Warring States Period
Diameter: 12.1cm, Thickness: 0.25cm, Weight: 84g
Collected in November, 2018

The mirror is round in shape. It has a small knob with design of three bow strings on a round base. The outside of the knob base is adorned with two broad bands with concave surface. The decorative patterns consist of the ground motif and the major motif. The ground motif is the alternate decorative patterns of the design of cirrus cloud, or triangle-shaped thunder in a rhombus and design of square-shaped whorl, and is arranged consecutively and repeatedly toward four directions. The decorative patterns on either side of the broad band are separated by the broad band. The major motif is the design of three dragons surrounding the knob. The dragons have crooked necks towards the back, short horns, open mouths, teeth and round eyes. The shape of the dragon is that of a full belly, a full chest, an arching tail with swallow-tail-shaped wings on the middle and the end of the tail

rolled inwards, one foot stepping on the knob base and the other turned up. The broad rim is unadorned.

The dragon design on the mirror is vivid. The dragon design is of remarkable quality, for realistic dragons rather than patterned ones. There is a similar bronze mirror collected in the National Museum of China, but on this one the heads and the bodies of the dragons are turned in the opposite direction. In the late period of the late Warring States Period, the bronze mirror with design of three dragons is adorned with the design of dragon with square body. The mirror differs from another bronze mirror with design of three dragons in the museum. On the decorative patterns of three dragons on that mirror, two of them have small swallow-tail-shaped wings on their tails, and one of them has a magnolia bud. The reason for the difference is unclear.

## 19. 素面镜

战国晚期

直径 13.6 厘米，厚 0.15 厘米，重 168 克

2018 年 5 月征集入藏

圆形。小十字钮。素面。无缘。镜体平直，呈黑漆古状。保存完好。

## 19. Mirror with plain ground

Late Warring States Period
Diameter: 13.6cm, Thickness: 0.15cm, Weight: 168g
Collected in May, 2018

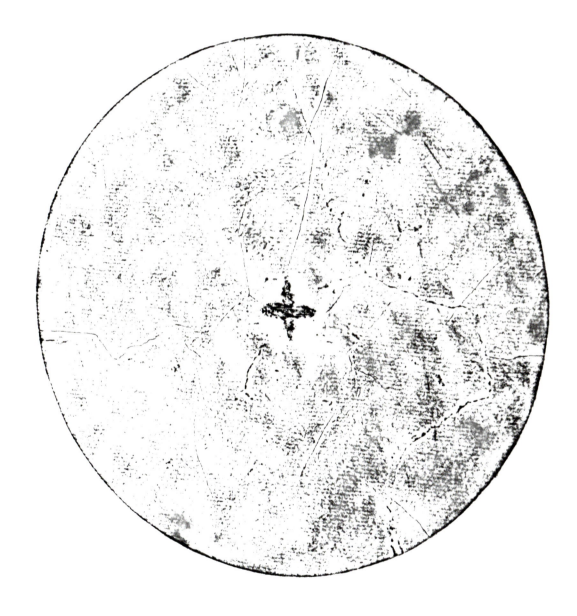

The mirror is round in shape. It has a small knob in a shape of small cross. The mirror is adorned without design. It has no rim. The body of the mirror is flat and straight, with an old-fashioned black lacquer. It is kept in good condition.

## 20. 八叶镜

战国晚期
直径9.1厘米，厚0.2厘米，重72克
2018年11月征集入藏

## 20. Mirror with design of eight leaves

Late Warring States Period
Diameter: 9.1cm, Thickness: 0.2cm, Weight: 72g
Collected in November, 2018

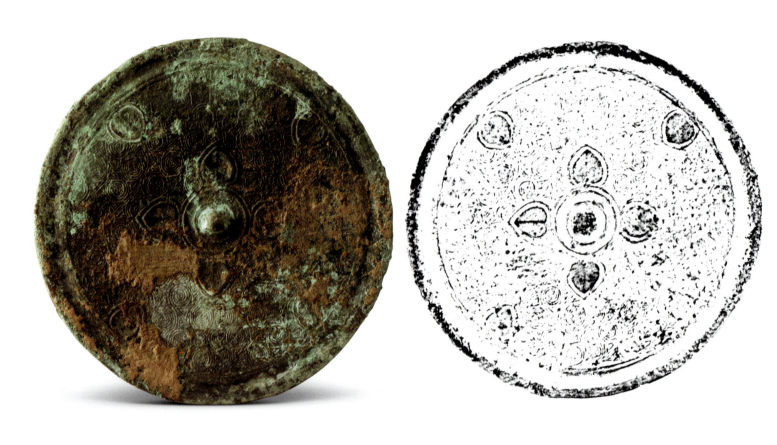

圆形。小桥钮，圆钮座。钮座外饰双层凹弧面圈带纹。云雷地纹，主纹为钮座外饰四片桃形花叶，呈十字形分布，与镜钮组合成花瓣状。近缘处均匀分布四片桃形花叶，叶片为双层叠压。近缘处饰二周细弦纹。卷缘。

此镜虽地纹较模糊，但主纹分布匀称疏朗，十分美观。

The mirror is round in shape. It has a small bridge-shaped knob on a round base. The outside of the knob base is adorned with two bands with concave surface. The ground motif is the design of cloud and thunder. The major motif is a petal-like combination of the knob and four peach-shaped leaves around the knob base in each direction of cross. There are four peach-shaped leaves evenly spaced near the rim. Each leaf is covered in two layers. Two bands of string design are close to the rim. The rim rolls up.

The ground motif in the mirror is not clear, but the major motif, with its well-proportioned arrangement, is very beautiful.

## 21. 素面镜

战国早期

直径 8.8 厘米，厚 0.1 厘米，重 31 克

2018 年 11 月征集入藏

## 21. Mirror with plain ground

Early Warring States Period

Diameter: 8.8cm, Thickness: 0.1cm, Weight: 31g

Collected in November, 2018

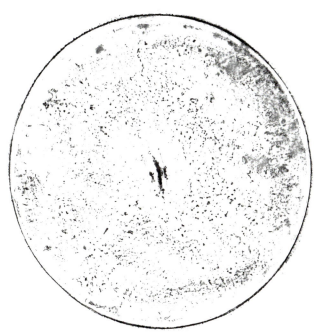

　　圆形。扁弓形钮，方钮座。弓孔两侧饰很小的兽纹，一侧模糊不清。兽纹的形态似饕餮纹，扁弓形钮一侧纹饰可见饕餮纹上部和鼻部特征，另一侧可见眼部特征。镜面平直，镜体保存完好。方钮座及钮座外的纹饰模印很浅，呈素面状。平沿。此镜具有战国早期铜镜特征。

　　The mirror is round in shape. It has a flat-bow-shaped knob on a square base. Both sides of the hole on the bow-shaped knob are adorned with tiny design of beast and the beast design on the one side is not clear. The decorative pattern of beast is in a shape of *Tao Tie*. The decorative pattern on the one left side of the knob can show the features of the upper part, the nose, the other side can show the eye of *Tao Tie*. The surface of the mirror is flat and straight. It is kept in good condition. The square knob base and the outside of the knob base are adorned with decorative patterns in light molding and appear to be unadorned. The rim of the mirror is flat. This mirror holds the features of the bronze mirrors of the early Warring States Period.

## 22. 八花叶镜

战国晚期
直径 7.1 厘米，厚 0.1 厘米，重 32 克
2018 年 2 月征集入藏

## 22. Mirror with design of eight leaves

Late Warring States Period
Diameter: 7.1cm, Thickness: 0.1cm, Weight: 32g
Collected in February, 2018

　　圆形。小三弦钮，圆钮座。钮座外饰叠压的双层宽圈带纹。纹饰由主纹和地纹构成。地纹为双线菱形格内饰涡纹，菱形边线中填圆点纹、卷云纹，其形制、布局与通常的云雷纹形态和布局不同。主纹是从钮座伸出四片双层长形桃叶间以四片双层短叶，与钮座搭配形似一花朵。宽缘，缘边微卷。

　　此镜小巧玲珑，镜面纹饰布置精美，地纹与主纹层次分明，十分可爱。

The mirror is round in shape. It has a small knob with design of three bow strings on a round base. The outside of the knob base is adorned with two overlaid broad bands. The decorative pattern consists of the major motif and the ground motif. The ground motif is the design of whorl in rhombus formed by two lines. There are spot design and cirrus cloud design in the middle of sidelines of the rhombus, which differ in shape and arrangement from the usual design of cloud and thunder. The major motif is a flower-like combination of the knob and four two-layer short leaves among four two-layer peach-shaped leaves extending from the knob base. The broad rim slightly rolls up.

The mirror is small and exquisite, with its elaborate decorative patterns. Its ground motif and major motif are well arranged.

## 23. 素面镜

战国晚期
直径 10.2 厘米，厚 0.1 厘米，重 37 克
2019 年 11 月征集入藏

## 23. Mirror with plain ground

Late Warring States Period
Diameter: 10.2cm, Thickness: 0.1cm, Weight: 37g
Collected in November, 2019

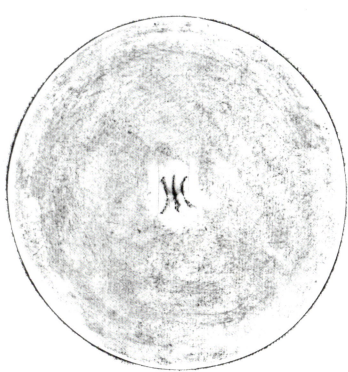

圆形。小三弦钮，无钮座。素面无纹，镜面平直。

The mirror is round in shape. It has a small knob with design of three bow strings and has no knob base. The mirror is unadorned. The surface of the mirror is flat and straight.

## 24. 四山十六叶镜

战国晚期
直径 13.6 厘米，厚 0.35 厘米，重 176 克
2019 年 11 月征集入藏

　　圆形。小三弦钮，钮座是以双层凹弧面宽圈带围成的方框。纹饰由三层组合而成。地纹满铺羽状纹，中层是十六叶纹，最上层是左旋的四山字纹。钮座四角角尖上各伸出一叶片，叶尖引出三条窄绹带与另一叶片相连，并在叶尖甩出左向长叶片，左右两条斜向与相邻绹带连接成四角形图案。左旋四山字纹底部与方形钮座平行，山字的底边与两侧竖笔为双层叠压。近缘处饰二周细凸弦纹。缘呈弧面卷起。

　　此镜是十六叶纹镜中制作最规整的一类。这一类铜镜大多称之为"四山十二叶"，忽略了四长形叶的存在，应当以"四山十六叶"称之。

## 24. Mirror with inscription of four "*shan*" characters and design of sixteen leaves

Late Warring States Period
Diameter: 13.6cm, Thickness: 0.35cm, Weight: 176g
Collected in November, 2019

The mirror is round in shape. It has a small knob with design of three bow strings on an overlaid square base formed by broad band with concave surface. The decorative patterns are in three layers. The ground motif is full of feather-like patterns. The middle layer is the design of sixteen leaves. The upper layer is the inscription of four "*shan*" characters that are inclined towards the left. The leaves extend out from each corner of the square knob base. At the top of the leaf are three rope designs and the three rope designs are joined with another leaf. At the top of the leaf is also a long leaf that extends towards the left. The leaves extending towards the right and the left and the adjacent design of rope are in the shape of quadrangle. The bottom sides of the characters are parallel to the bottom sides of the knob base. The bottom sides and the vertical strokes on both sides of the characters are formed by double lines. Two bands of raised bow string formed by slender line approach the rim. The rim is in the shape of arc and rolls up.

This mirror belongs to the well-arranged type of the mirrors with design of sixteen leaves. The mirrors of this kind are known as the mirrors with inscription of four "*shan*" characters and design of twelve leaves. But the name does not include the decorative patterns of the design of four long leaves, so it is reasonable that the mirrors of this kind are called the mirrors with inscription of four "*shan*" characters and design of sixteen leaves.

## 25. 三虺三菱镜

战国晚期
直径 10 厘米，厚 0.2 厘米，重 44 克
2018 年 2 月征集入藏

圆形。小三弦钮，圆钮座。钮座外饰凹面宽圈带纹、单线凸弦纹各一周。以疏朗的卷云纹为地，主纹由变形虺纹和连体的菱形纹相间组成。虺首居中，向下弯曲，两侧为盘曲的身体，与相邻的菱形纹勾连。连体菱形纹形状不对称，折口不相连。虺纹、菱形纹已简化为由粗细相同的线条组成，虺的形态已简化得没有细部特征，虺首只是稍稍大一些的圆点。宽素缘，微弧上卷。此镜简化的虺纹装饰风格主要流行于战国晚期到西汉早期。

# 25. Mirror with design of three serpents and three rhombuses

Late Warring States Period
Diameter: 10cm, Thickness: 0.2cm, Weight: 44g
Collected in February, 2018

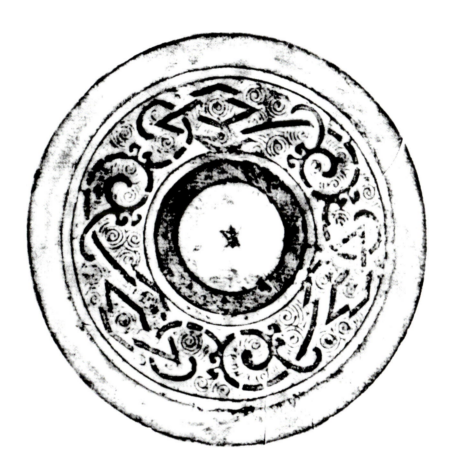

The mirror is round in shape. It has a small knob with design of three bow strings on a round base. The outside of the knob base is adorned with a broad band with concave surface and a band of raised bow string formed by single line. The ground motif is the design of cirrus cloud. The major motif is an alternating arrangement of the design of stylized serpent and the joined designs of rhombuses. Each serpent has a head in the middle that bends downward and the coiled bodies on either side of the head that are interlaced with the adjacent

designs of rhombus. The joined design of rhombus is asymmetric in shape and the joints of the patterns are not connected. The serpent design and the rhombus design are simplified to the shapes that are formed by uniform lines. The serpents are in a simplified shape without detailed features and with a slightly big circle dot. The broad rim is unadorned and rolls up in the shape of arc. The simplified design of serpent prevailed from the late Warring States Period to the early Western Han Dynasty.

　　圆形。小双弦钮，圆钮座。钮座外饰凹面宽圈带纹、短斜线纹、单线凸弦纹各一周。地纹为疏朗的卷云纹，不甚清晰。主纹为菱形纹与虺纹相间，分成四区。虺的身躯纤细，虺首居中，立于宽带纹上，身体翻转，对称卷曲，与菱形纹相接。宽素缘。

　　本馆收藏有此类铜镜 2 面，另 1 面的菱形纹是双层变形。此镜的菱形纹更趋简单，是战国铜镜走向衰微的表现。

## 27. Mirror with design of four serpents and four rhombuses

Late Warring States Period
Diameter: 13.1cm, Thickness: 0.15cm, Weight: 89g
Collected in May, 2018

The mirror is round in shape. It has a small knob with design of two bow strings on a round base. The outside of the knob base is adorned with a broad band with concave surface, a band of short slanted lines and a band of raised bow string formed by single line. The ground motif is the dim design of cirrus cloud. The major motif is an alternating arrangement of the rhombus design and the serpent design and is divided into four sections. Each serpent has the slender bodies that turn and coil symmetrically and a head in the middle that is connected with the rhombus design. The broad rim is unadorned.

Two such mirrors are in the museum. The other is adorned with the design of overlaid and stylized rhombus. This mirror is adorned with the design of simple rhombus, indicating the decline of bronze mirrors in the Warring States Period.

## 28. 弦纹镜

战国

直径 9.9 厘米，厚 0.1 厘米，重 79 克

2018 年 11 月征集入藏

圆形。弓形钮，无钮座。钮外饰两周细弦纹。镜身平直，镜面锈蚀较重。仅饰弦纹的素面铜镜，使用时间跨度较长，自战国中期至西汉早期的墓葬中都有发现，这类铜镜一般尺寸较小，这种长时间延续使用可能是与制范相对简单、易于铸造相关。

## 28. Mirror with design of bow string

Warring States Period
Diameter: 9.9cm, Thickness: 0.1cm, Weight: 79g
Collected in November, 2018

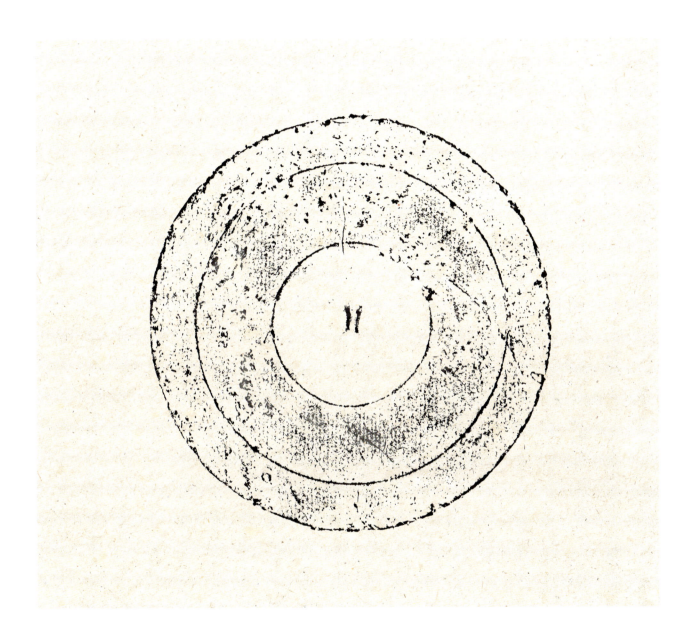

The mirror is round in shape. It has a bow-shaped knob and has no knob base. The outside of the knob is adorned with two bands of slender bow string. The body of the mirror is flat and straight and is heavily rusted. The bronze mirrors, adorned only with design of bow string, were in use for a long period, and were unearthed in the tombs from the middle Warring States Period to the early Western Han Dynasty. The mirrors of this kind are often small in size. The mirrors remained in use for a long time because of their simple molds and easy casting.

## 29. 四山八叶镜

战国晚期
直径 12 厘米，厚 0.4 厘米，重 119 克
2018 年 11 月征集入藏

　　圆形。小三弦钮，双层方形钮座。地纹满铺羽状纹，清晰、规整，由六层排列模印而成，每组由卷羽涡纹和羽翅纹、谷纹组成。方形钮座四角伸出两片间以绚带纹枝杆相连接的叶片，叶片是叠置在绚带纹枝杆相扣的环套上。四个右旋的山字纹底部与钮座边平行。沿口弧起，窄平。

　　山字纹中加叶纹，是一个逐渐增多以至变形的过程。从早期的四叶发展到后期十二叶、十六叶，直至增加花朵、花苞，这种过程是当时的工匠根据铜镜尺寸的大小、纹饰间空隙，通过审美判断而不断变化的。可能每一种叶纹山字镜，都有其流行的区域和时间。

# 29. Mirror with inscription of four "*shan*" characters and design of eight leaves

Late Warring States Period
Diameter: 12cm, Thickness: 0.4cm, Weight: 119g
Collected in November, 2018

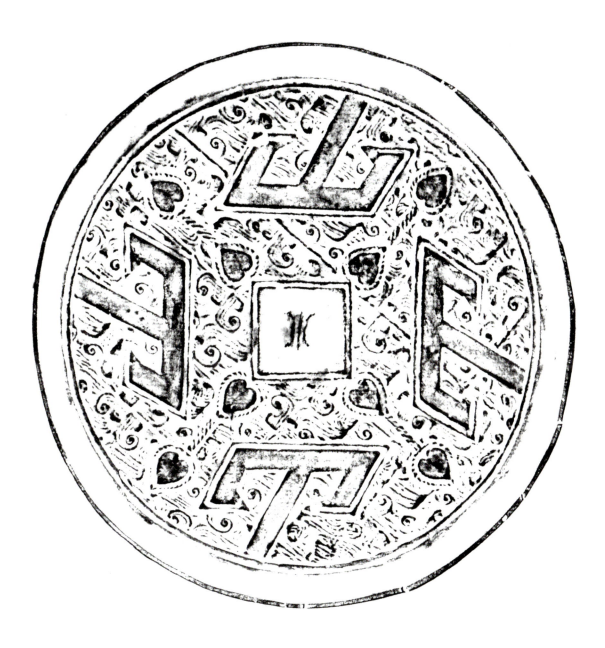

The mirror is round in shape. It has a small knob with design of three bow strings on an overlaid square base. The ground motif is full of the clear and symmetrical feather-like pattern and was cast in six layers with molding. Each group of the ground motif consists of the design of whorl in a shape of rolling feather, feather-wing design and design of unhusked rice. Two leaves, that are connected with the branches with rope design between the leaves, extend from each corner of the square knob base and are overlaid with the rings that are interlocked with the branches. The inscription of four "*shan*" characters is inclined towards the right. The bottom sides of "*shan*" characters are parallel to the base line of the knob base. The rim of the mirror, narrow and flat, is in a shape of arc.

The leaf design on the mirror with the inscription of "*shan*" character, is a change process of gradually increasing and stylizing from the design of four leaves in the early period to the design of twelve leaves or sixteen leaves in the late period up to the leaf design with flower pattern or bud pattern. The changing process was prompted by the aesthetic of the ancient craftsmen to the size of the mirror and the gap between decorative patterns. It is deduced that each mirror with inscription of "*shan*" character and leaf design had its prevailing area and period.

## 30. 七宽带连弧纹镜

战国晚期

直径 14.5 厘米，厚 0.1 厘米，重 151 克

2018 年 2 月征集入藏

圆形，三弦钮。钮外和镜缘饰凹面宽圈带纹。镜面中区饰内向凹面七宽带连弧纹。凹面宽带连弧纹镜在长沙、益阳、南阳等地楚墓中都有出土，直径大多在 15 厘米左右，时代在战国晚期晚段到西汉中期。

## 30. Mirror with design of seven linked arcs formed by broad band

Late Warring States Period
Diameter: 14.5cm, Thickness: 0.1cm, Weight: 151g
Collected in February, 2018

The mirror is round in shape. It has a knob with design of three bow strings. The outside of the knob and the rim of the mirror are adorned with the broad bands with concave surface. The major motif is the design of seven linked arcs formed by broad band with concave surface and oriented inwards. The bronze mirrors with design of linked arcs formed by broad band with concave surface, with a diameter of about 15cm, were unearthed in the tombs of the Chu State in Changsha, Yiyang and Nanyang, which are deduced to be in the period from the late period of the late Warring States Period to the middle Western Han Dynasty.

## 31. 四叶镜

战国晚期
直径 9.2 厘米，厚 0.5 厘米，重 134 克
2019 年 11 月征集入藏

　　圆形。小三弦钮，双层叠压圆钮座。镜面平直，满铺精美的羽状纹，从模印痕迹看，是由上下六层组合而成。镜钮周边方形整块模印上下排列，形成二方连续图案。圆钮座外呈十字方向向外伸出四片小花叶，无柄，叶片中间有筋脉纹、微凹。宽素缘，平沿。

　　羽状地纹镜，早期镜钮一般很小，无钮座，后期钮逐渐变大，有圆形、方形钮座。羽状纹也从早期的线条粗犷简单，逐渐演变得细密，发展到战国晚期时，羽状纹一般用作山字纹、龙凤纹为主纹的地纹。早期纯羽状纹镜发现不多，这可能与之流行时间较短有关，但是战国晚期晚段时，也有以羽状纹用作主纹装饰的铜镜。

## 31. Mirror with design of four leaves

Late Warring States Period
Diameter: 9.2cm, Thickness: 0.5cm, Weight: 134g
Collected in November, 2019

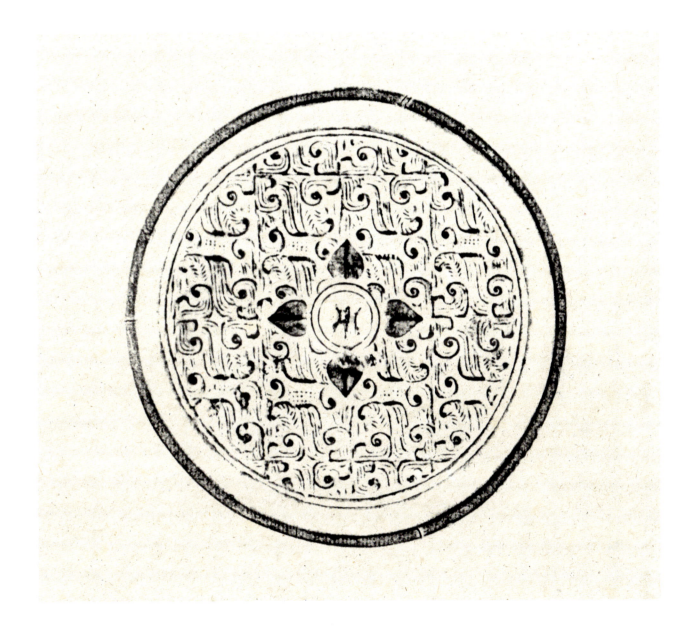

The mirror is round in shape. It has a small knob with design of three bow strings on a round two-layer base. The surface of the mirror is flat and is decorated with the elaborate ground motif of feather-like pattern. The mold marks show that the ground motif is a six-layer combination. The decorative patterns around the knob are consecutively and repeatedly arranged in rectangular shape up and down. Four small leaves extend from the round knob base in each direction of cross. Each leaf has no petiole. In the middle of the leaf there is a slightly concave vein. The broad rim has a flat edge and is unadorned.

In the early period, the bronze mirror with ground motif of feather-like pattern has a small knob and has no knob base; in the late period, the mirror has a big knob on a round or rectangular base. The feather-like pattern was changed from the straightforward lines in the early period to the elaborate lines. In the late Warring States Period, the feather-like pattern was served as the ground motif to the major motif of inscription of "*shan*" character or pattern of dragon and phoenix. The bronze mirrors with ground motif of feather-like pattern in the early period have been found in small numbers, presumably because they were in widespread use for a short time. But in the late period of the late Warring States Period, some bronze mirrors were adorned with feather-like pattern as major motif.

## 32. 三凤三菱镜

战国晚期

直径 11.7 厘米，厚 0.55 厘米，重 118 克

2018 年 5 月征集入藏

　　圆形。小三弦钮，绳纹框圆钮座。钮座外饰云雷地纹一周，外饰以凹弧面宽圈带纹，宽圈带纹外有短斜线纹和单线凸弦纹。镜面中区由地纹和主纹构成，地纹为满铺的云雷纹，主纹是以三个连体菱形纹将镜面分成三区，每区饰一凤纹。凤居二菱形中间，回首衔尾羽，双足立于钮座之上，二翼向两侧卷起，穿过两侧相邻的卷羽。三立凤之间的卷羽与凤身并不连接，很像龙纹形态，但不见龙

首，比较罕见。宽素缘。

　　本书收录的有同样特点的 4 面三凤镜。其中另 1 面直径 14.2 厘米铜镜，风格相同，直立的凤身与两侧卷羽虽不相连，但在凤与凤之间饰有龙首。这 4 面铜镜尺寸、纹饰风格相同。将凤纹之间的装饰简化，是工匠有意为之，还是粗心少饰龙首就不得而知了。但此镜装饰纹样匀称细腻，以双勾线条方法装饰，也是这类铜镜的尾声了。

## 32. Mirror with design of three phoenixes and three rhombuses

Late Warring States Period
Diameter: 11.7cm, Thickness: 0.55cm, Weight: 118g
Collected in May, 2018

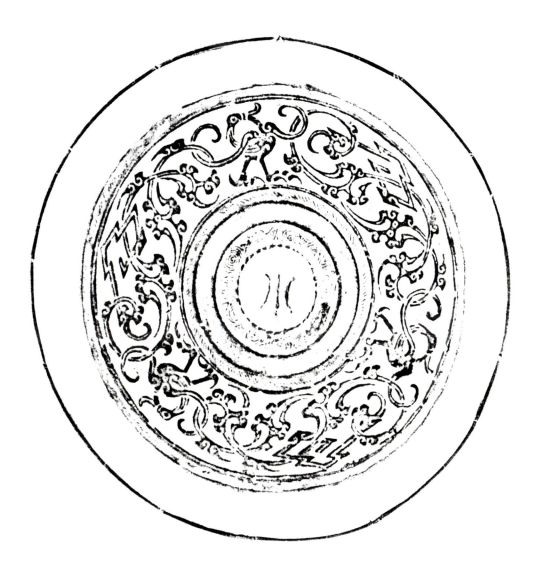

The mirror is round in shape. It has a small knob with design of three bow strings on a round base with the rope design as the fence. The outside of the knob base is adorned sequentially with a band of the design of cloud and thunder, a broad band with concave surface and a band of short slanted lines and a band of raised bow string formed by single line. The middle surface of the mirror consists of the ground motif and the major motif. The ground motif is the design of cloud and thunder that fill the surface of the mirror. The major motif is divided into three sections by three designs of joined rhombuses. Each section is adorned with the design of phoenix. Each phoenix, situated between two rhombuses, turns its back, holds its tail in its mouth, steps on the knob base with both legs, spreads its two rolling wings towards the sides which cross through the neighbouring rolling feathers of the two

side. The rolling feathers, located among three standing phoenixes, are not connected with the body of the phoenix and resemble a dragon without its head, which is rarely seen. The broad rim is unadorned.

Four such mirrors are recorded in the book. Another one, with a diameter of 14.2cm, is similar in style. Its decorative pattern of a standing phoenix is not connected with the rolling feather on both sides, but a dragon's head adorns between the phoenixes. The four mirrors are the same in size and decorative style. It is hard to know whether this happened by accident or by intention to simplify the pattern without the head between phoenixes. The well-arranged and elaborate decoration, which is formed by double lines, is the last glory of the mirrors of this kind.

## 33. 羽状纹镜

战国晚期

直径 11.2 厘米，厚 0.3 厘米，重 65 克

2018 年 5 月征集入藏

　　圆形。小三弦钮，无钮座。镜面平直，满铺羽状纹，每块羽状纹有四个羽翅，逆时针方向上卷，空隙处铺以方形碎粒状纹饰。宽素缘，内凹。镜面锈蚀较重。

## 33. Mirror with feather-like design

Late Warring States Period
Diameter: 11.2cm, Thickness: 0.3cm, Weight: 65g
Collected in May, 2018

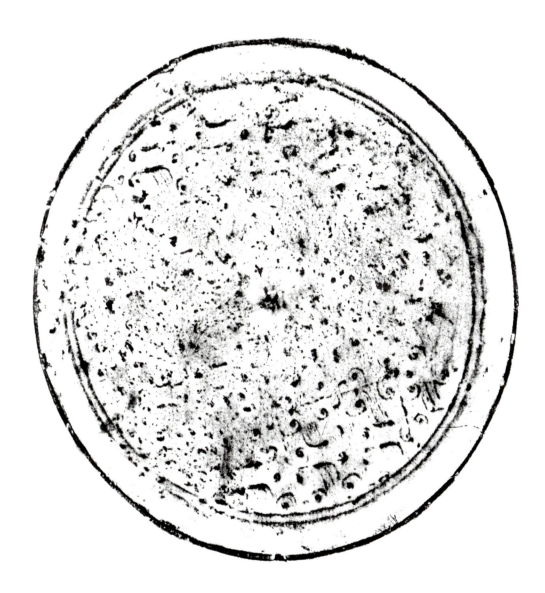

The mirror is round in shape. It has a small knob with design of three bow strings and has no knob base. The surface of the mirror is flat and straight and full of feather-like patterns. Each feather-like pattern has four feathery wings that roll up in an anticlockwise direction. The designs of tiny square spots adorn the space. The broad rim of the mirror is unadorned and has a concave surface. The mirror was heavily rusted.

## 34. 素面镜

战国晚期

直径 14.1 厘米，厚 0.15 厘米，重 117 克

2018 年 2 月征集入藏

圆形。小三弦钮，无钮座。素面无纹，镜面平直。

## 34. Mirror with plain ground

Late Warring States Period
Diameter: 14.1cm, Thickness: 0.15cm, Weight: 117g
Collected in February, 2018

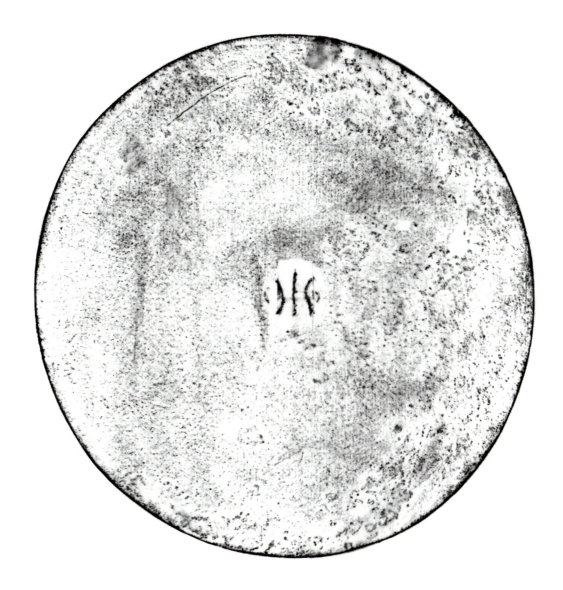

The mirror is round in shape. It has a small knob with design of three bow strings and has no knob base. The mirror is unadorned. The surface of the mirror is flat and straight.

## 35. 变形四龙镜

战国晚期
直径 14.9 厘米，厚 0.5 厘米，重 222 克
2018 年 5 月征集入藏

　　圆形。三弦钮，圆钮座。钮座外围饰一周凹面宽圈带纹，宽圈带纹外饰一周细线凸弦纹，弦纹与宽圈带纹间饰一周短斜线纹。地纹由细密的云雷纹和粒状碎点纹组成。从模印痕迹看，地纹由上下八层模制而成，贯通包括钮座在内的整个镜面。

　　四条龙的布局很有特点，没有采取对称布置，而是右顺向一致排列。龙首居近钮座的宽圈带纹处，大张口，有上下两只大獠牙，大圆目，脑后起尖角，身体呈蔓枝状卷曲，与相邻的龙身勾连。龙的造型遒劲有力，整个镜面以卷曲的"S"状体态均匀分布。宽素缘，缘边卷起，窄平。

　　此镜是龙纹镜中装饰纹样的上乘之作。

## 35. Mirror with design of four stylized dragons

Late Warring States Period
Diameter: 14.9cm, Thickness: 0.5cm, Weight: 222g
Collected in May, 2018

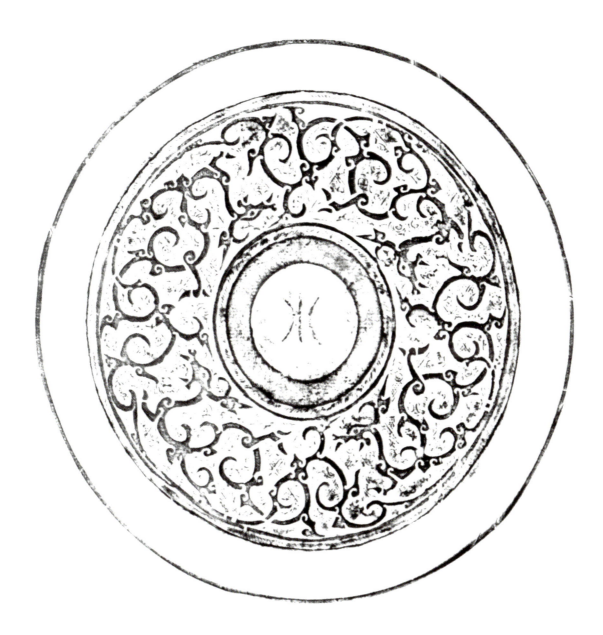

The mirror is round in shape. It has a knob with design of three bow strings on a round base. The outside of the knob base is adorned with a broad band with concave surface. A band of raised bow string design adorns the outside of the broad band. A band of short slanted lines is spaced between the broad band and the band of string design. The ground motif is composed of the fine design of cloud and thunder and the design of tiny spots. Mold marks indicate that the ground motif was cast in eight layers of molding above and below and is filled in on the whole surface of the mirror including the knob base.

The arrangement of four dragons is distinguished by the layout

rightwards in order, rather than by the symmetrical layout. Each dragon has a head close to the broad band on the outside of the knob base, an open mouth, two buckteeth up and down, big round eyes, sharp horn on the back of the head, a body in the shape of a curled branch. Each dragon is interlaced with another. Each dragon is in the vigorous and vivid shape of an S. The broad rim is unadorned and the narrow and flat edge of the rim rolls.

This mirror is of remarkable quality among the bronze mirrors with dragon design.

## 36. 素面镜

战国晚期

直径 10.1 厘米，厚 0.1 厘米，重 50 克

2019 年 11 月征集入藏

圆形。小三弦钮，无钮座。素面无纹，镜面平直。

## 36. Mirror with plain ground

Late Warring States Period
Diameter: 10.1cm, Thickness: 0.1cm, Weight: 50g
Collected in November, 2019

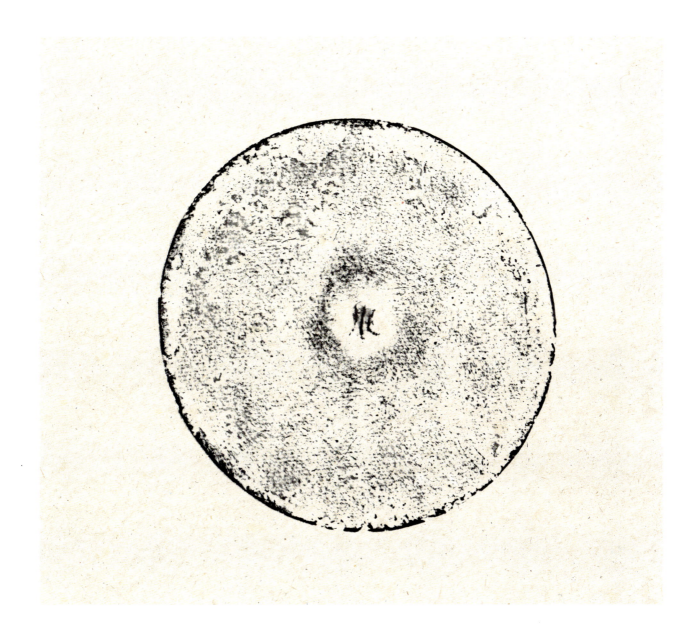

The mirror is round in shape. It has a small knob with design of three bow strings and has no knob base. The mirror is unadorned. The surface of the mirror is flat and straight.

## 37. 四山十六叶镜

战国晚期

直径 13.8 厘米，厚 0.3 厘米，重 175 克

2018 年淮南市谢家集公安分局移交入藏

　　圆形。小三弦钮，小方形钮座。钮座以双层凹弧面宽带围成方框。纹饰由地纹和主纹组成。羽状地纹细密，有锈蚀，局部不清晰。主纹由十二叶片和四长叶片及左旋的四个山字纹构成。钮座四角向外各伸出一叶片，以绚带纹与一叶片相连，叶尖甩出一长叶片，与左旋山字中间一竖右侧的叶片连接后，形成四角形花。四个长形叶片在一些铜镜中很长，甚至有弯曲的弧度，此镜的长叶片较短，无弧度，应该是同类镜中较早流行的品种。缘内饰一周细线弦纹。缘呈弧面卷起。

## 37. Mirror with inscription of four "*shan*" characters and design of sixteen leaves

Late Warring States Period
Diameter: 13.8cm, Thickness: 0.3cm, Weight: 175g
Transferred by Xiejiaji District Public Security Bureau in Huainan City in 2018

The mirror is round in shape. It has a small knob with design of three bow strings on an overlaid square base formed by broad band with concave surface. The decorative patterns consist of the ground motif and the major motif. The fine ground motif of feather-like patterns was slightly rusted and the part of the ground motif is not clearly defined. The major motif is the design of twelve leaves, the design of four long leaves and the inscription of four "*shan*" characters inclined towards the left. Each corner of the knob base has an extending leaf. Each leaf is joined by the rope design to the other. At the top of each leaf is a long projecting leaf. The long projecting leaf is connected with the leaf on the right side of the middle vertical stroke of the characters and they are in the shape of quadrangle flower. The design of four long leaves is longer on some mirrors and some of the leaves even have crooked arcs. In contrast to the others, the long leaves on this mirror are shorter and do not have a crooked arc. So this mirror may be an early product of the mirrors of this kind. A band of bow string formed by slender line adorns the inside of the rim. The rim of the mirror has an arc and rolls up.

## 38. 三凤三菱镜

战国晚期

直径 11.7 厘米，厚 0.4 厘米，重 116 克

2017 年 12 月征集入藏

　　圆形。小三弦钮，圆钮座。钮座外饰一周单线弦纹，弦纹内饰短斜线纹，外饰云雷纹。钮座外围以凹弧面宽圈带纹。云雷纹地纹不甚清楚。主纹由三凤与三菱相间环列布置，凤立于菱纹之间，凤首回勾向下，小圆目，尖喙，凤冠向后飘起，两翼勾卷，与缠枝状菱形纹交错叠压。宽卷素缘。

　　本馆收藏有多面三凤三菱纹镜，此镜的线条已开始向双线分离，与河北省博物馆收藏的三凤三菱纹镜在装饰手法上很相近，应是同时代的产品 ❶。

❶ 河北省文物考古研究所：《历代铜镜纹饰》，河北美术出版社，1996年。

## 38. Mirror with design of three phoenixes and three rhombuses

Late Warring States Period
Diameter: 11.7cm, Thickness: 0.4cm, Weight: 116g
Collected in December, 2017

The mirror is round in shape. It has a small knob with design of three bow strings on a round base. The outside of the knob base is adorned with a band of bow string formed by single line. The inside of the design of bow string is adorned with the design of short slanted lines, and the outside of the design of bow string is adorned with the design of cloud and thunder. A broad band with concave surface adorns on the outside of the knob base. The ground motif is the dim design of cloud and thunder. The major motif is an alternating arrangement of three phoenixes and three rhombuses. Each phoenix stands between rhombuses. Each phoenix has its back turned, small round eyes, a sharp beak, a phoenix coronet flying backwards and two wings that roll and

are interlaced and overlaid with branch-shaped rhombus. The broad rim is unadorned and rolls.

Several such mirrors are in the museum. The decorative lines on this mirror appear in the shape of two separated lines. This mirror is similar in decorative style to the mirror with design of three phoenixes and three rhombuses in the Hebei Museum, both of which can date from the same time[1].

❶ Hebei Province Institute of Cultural Relics and Historical Relics and Archaeology. *Bronze Mirrors through the Ages,* Hebei Fine Arts Publishing House, 1996.

## 39. 素面镜

战国晚期

直径 10.3 厘米，厚 0.1 厘米，重 40 克

2018 年 2 月征集入藏

圆形。小三弦钮，无钮座。素面无纹，镜面平直。

## 39. Mirror with plain ground

Late Warring States Period
Diameter: 10.3cm, Thickness: 0.1cm, Weight: 40g
Collected in February, 2018

The mirror is round in shape. It has a small knob with design of three bow strings and has no knob base. The mirror is unadorned. The surface of the mirror is flat and straight.

## 40. 三龙镜

战国晚期

直径 8.6 厘米，厚 0.2 厘米，重 41 克

2018 年 2 月征集入藏

圆形。小桥钮。钮外环绕双层凹弧面宽圈带纹。地纹由涡状卷云纹和谷纹组成，满铺镜面，钮座外的圈带纹是在地纹上装饰的，圈带内的纹饰与中区纹饰相通。主纹由三条粗壮的龙环绕钮座布置，龙小首圆目，张口卷舌，长曲颈拱起，腹部呈菱形，足部硕壮，蹬踏钮座，尾向后抛起内卷，二条龙尾中段有小燕尾翼，一条龙尾

饰玉兰花苞纹。宽素缘。

三角雷纹和云纹组成的地纹，比较常见，此镜的特点在于地纹用谷粒纹与涡状卷云纹组成，比较少见。每个单元的地纹由四个卷云纹组成，周边满布细小谷粒纹，从制模工艺上判断，是在模印好的地纹上装饰主纹。整个镜面装饰纹样均匀饱满，是以小见大的精美铜镜。

# 40. Mirror with design of three dragons

Late Warring States Period
Diameter: 8.6cm, Thickness: 0.2cm, Weight: 41g
Collected in February, 2018

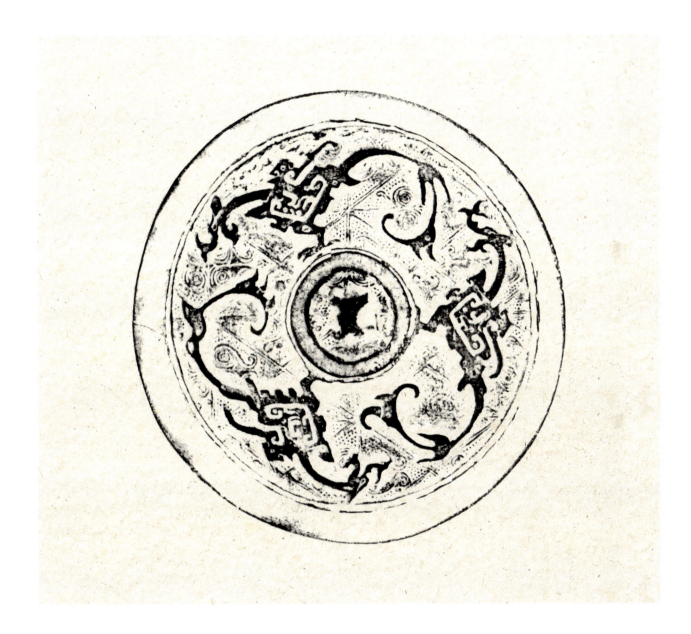

The mirror is round in shape. It has a small bridge-shaped knob. The outside of the knob is adorned with two broad bands with concave surface on the ground motif. The back of the mirror is decorated with the ground motif consisting of the whorl-shaped design of cirrus cloud and the design of unhusked rice. The decorative patterns on the inside of the band are connected to the patterns on the middle part of the mirror. The major motif is the design of three powerful dragons surrounding the knob base. The dragons have small heads, round eyes, open mouths, curled tongues, long crooked necks, rhombus-shaped bellies, strong feet stepping on the knob base, tails rolled inwards with swallow-tail-shaped wings in the middle on two of the dragons and magnolia bud on one of them. The broad rim is unadorned.

The ground motif with design of triangle-shaped thunder and cloud is more common. In this mirror, the ground motif with design of whorl-shaped design of cirrus cloud and design of unhusked rice is rare. In each section, the ground motif consists of four designs of cirrus cloud and the surrounding design of tiny unhusked rice. It is deduced that the major motif was cast on molded ground motif according to the mold masks. The mirror, with its well-arranged decorative patterns, is typical of fine bronze mirrors.

## 41. 四山十六叶镜

战国晚期

直径 13.4 厘米，厚 0.4 厘米，重 136 克

2018 年淮南市谢家集公安分局移交

　　圆形。小四弦钮，双层方形钮座。纹饰由地纹、中层的有柄草叶纹和叠压在上层的山字纹组成。羽状地纹模印十分清晰，底层羽状纹的细部线条以及谷粒纹非常精细。尽管铜镜破碎后经修复完整，由于不缺肉，所以得以完美复原。叠压在地纹上的十二叶片，以绚带纹相连，叶片凹弧面中间出筋；两山字纹之间的叶片，向镜缘处各甩出一个长叶片，生动自然。四个右旋山字纹的底边与方钮座平行，并且叠压斜向叶柄之上，构成了三层纹饰的立体效果。一般将此类镜纹饰分为地纹和主纹，但此镜为三层装饰，层次分明，总体来说，还是以山字纹为主，十六叶片纹也是环绕山字布局，突出了主题，其他两层是起烘托作用。近缘处饰二周细线弦纹。缘呈弧面卷起。

## 41. Mirror with inscription of four "*shan*" characters and design of sixteen leaves

Late Warring States Period
Diameter: 13.4cm, Thickness: 0.4cm, Weight: 136g
Transferred by Xiejiaji District Public Security Bureau in Huainan City in 2018

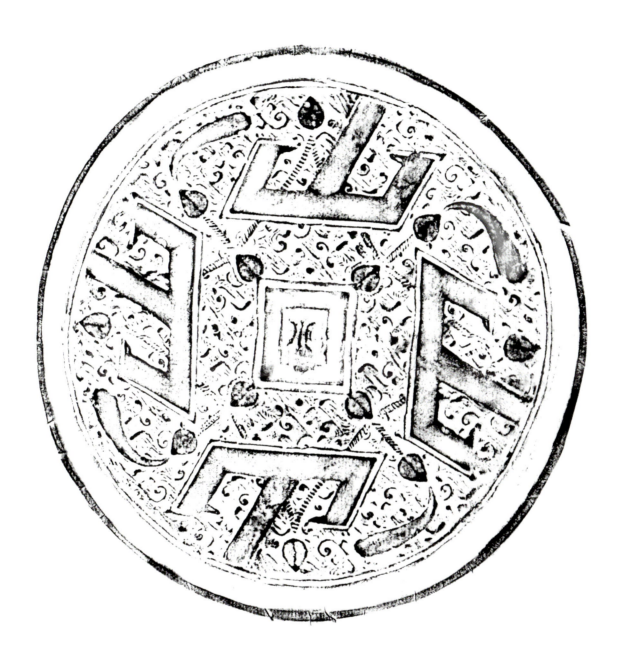

The mirror is round in shape. It has a small knob with design of four bow strings on an overlaid square knob base. The decorative patterns consist of the ground motif and the design of leaf with a petiole on the middle layer and the overlaid inscription of "*shan*" characters on the upper layer. The ground motif of feather-like patterns has clear molding marks and the lines of feather-like patterns and the design of unhusked rice are exquisitely cast. The mirror was in excellent repair. The twelve leaves overlaid on the ground motif are connected by the rope design. In the middle of the concave surface of the leaf is the raised vein. A long leaf naturally and vividly projects from the leaf between the characters to the rim of the mirrors. The inscription of four "*shan*" characters is inclined towards the right. Their bottom sides are parallel to the bottom sides of the square knob base and are overlaid on the slant petioles, giving a stereoscopic effect in three layers. The mirrors of this kind are often adorned with the ground motif and the major motif. But this mirror is adorned with the decorative patterns in three layers. Generally speaking, the design of sixteen leaves encircles the inscription of "*shan*" characters to make the inscription stand out. Two bands of bow string formed by slender line approach the rim. The rim of the mirror rolls up in an arc shape.

## 42. 十一连弧纹镜

战国晚期
直径 16 厘米，厚 0.3 厘米，重 227 克
2018 年 2 月征集入藏

　　圆形。三弦钮，方形钮座与三弦钮成一体状，疑为预先制好嵌入镜模内整体浇铸而成。钮外饰凹面宽带纹。中区饰十一单线连弧纹，弧度平缓。宽缘，卷沿。本馆收藏有同类尺寸的单线连弧纹镜 3 面，其中 1 面出土于战国寿春城遗址东侧的谢家集区红卫轮窑厂，当地分布着众多的战国楚国晚期小型土坑墓。这 3 面连弧纹镜直径在 14～16 厘米之间，装饰风格相近，有着共同的时代特征。

## 42. Mirror with design of eleven linked arcs

Late Warring States Period
Diameter: 16cm, Thickness: 0.3cm, Weight: 227g
Collected in February, 2018

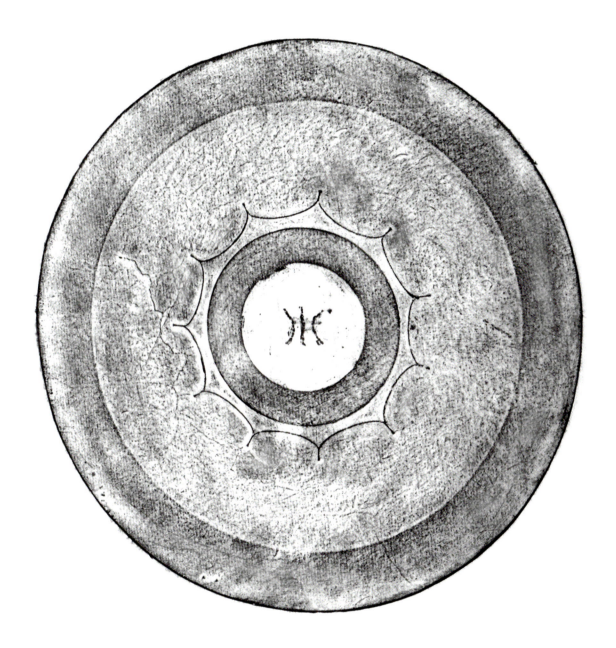

The mirror is round in shape. It has a knob with design of three bow strings. The square knob base and the knob with design of three bow strings are taken as a whole, and it is suspected that the mirror was cast after the cast knob and base were inserted into the mirror mold. The outside of the knob is adorned with a broad band with concave surface. The major motif is the design of eleven gently linked arcs formed by single line. The broad rim rolls. There are three mirrors with design of linked arcs formed by single line in the same size collected in the museum. One of them was unearthed at the Hongwei Annular Kiln Works, in Xiejiaji District, east of the site of Shouchun town of the Warring States Period where a number of small shaft tombs of the late Chu State of the Warring States Period are distributed. All three mirrors, ranging in diameter from 14cm to 16cm, have similar decorative style and marks of the period.

## 43. 六龙六菱镜

战国晚期

直径 16.1 厘米，厚 0.4 厘米，重 287 克

本馆旧藏

　　圆形。三弦钮，圆钮座。钮座外饰凹面宽圈带纹和细线凸弦纹。在钮座外和镜缘内侧交错饰三个小菱形纹，将镜面分为三区。二龙首为左右相对，身体向前后展开。龙首在菱形纹的下方伸出，大张口，身体自镜缘处向内卷起，呈蔓枝状勾连，足部蹬踏钮座。近缘处饰两周弦纹，间饰短斜线纹。宽缘边卷起。

　　战国晚期的龙纹镜，龙纹造形风格和铸造工艺水平各有不同，铸造地分布较广，是广泛流行的镜种，也是战国晚期楚镜中的主要产品。而此六龙六菱纹镜却十分少见。

## 43. Mirror with design of six dragons and six rhombuses

Late Warring States Period
Diameter: 16.1cm, Thickness: 0.4cm, Weight: 287g
Collection of Huainan Musuem

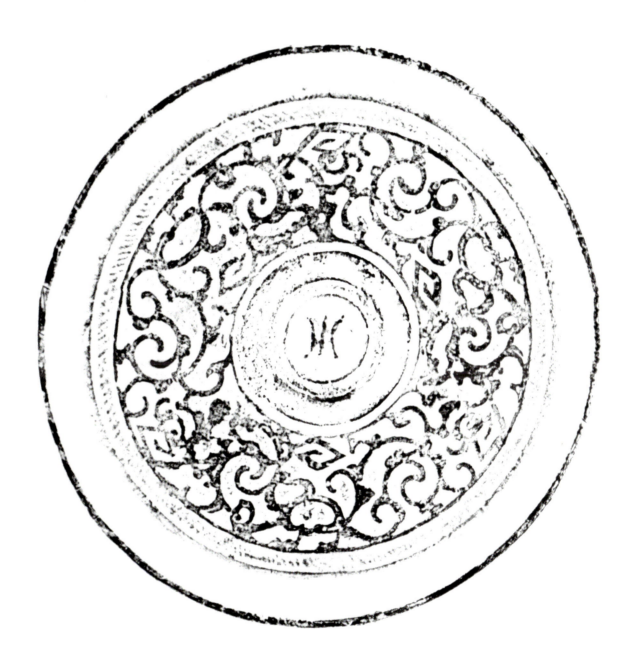

The mirror is round in shape. It has a knob with design of three bow strings on a round base. The outside of the knob base is adorned a broad band with concave surface and a band of raised bow string formed by slender line. Between the outside of the knob base and the inside of the rim is an alternate arrangement of three small rhombus designs that divide the surface of the mirror into three sections. The heads of the two dragons are opposite to each other and both bodies of the two dragons are spread out forward and backward. Each dragon has a head with a downward-opening mouth under the rhombus design, a body that rolls inward from the rim and is interlaced like branches

and feet that tread on the knob base. Two bands of bow string adorn near the rim and two bands are filled in with the design of short slanted lines. The broad rim rolls up.

In the late Warring States Period, the mirrors with dragon design differed in their dragon shapes and casting technique. The mirrors were cast over a wide area. The mirrors with dragon design prevailed widely and these were the dominant shape of bronze mirrors of the Chu State in the late Warring States Period. This mirror with design of six dragons and six rhombuses is rarely seen.

## 44. 八宽带连弧纹镜

战国晚期
直径 17.8 厘米，厚 0.15 厘米，重 278 克
2018 年 2 月征集入藏

　　圆形。三弦钮。钮外饰凹面宽圈带纹，镜中区饰云雷地纹，地纹上叠压八凹面宽带连弧纹。从残留的色彩判断，云雷地纹上覆盖的是孔雀蓝颜料，弦纹和连弧纹的凹面上填的是石青类颜料。两种颜料在凹面宽带纹和连弧纹的边缘处十分明显。云雷纹地纹上的孔雀蓝颜料比较薄，局部脱落处能看到镜体本身的氧化层。战国彩绘镜发现较少，山东临淄出土的 2 面彩绘镜，是以三种不同颜色颜料绘出龙凤的形态。此镜是以两种不同颜色的颜料填在模铸好的镜面上，颜料层很薄，能够透出镜体的花纹。所以，从残留的色彩看，此镜不能算作彩绘，仅仅是填彩，以达到美化的作用。

## 44. Mirror with design of eight linked arcs formed by broad band

Late Warring States Period
Diameter: 17.8cm, Thickness: 0.15cm, Weight: 278g
Collected in February, 2018

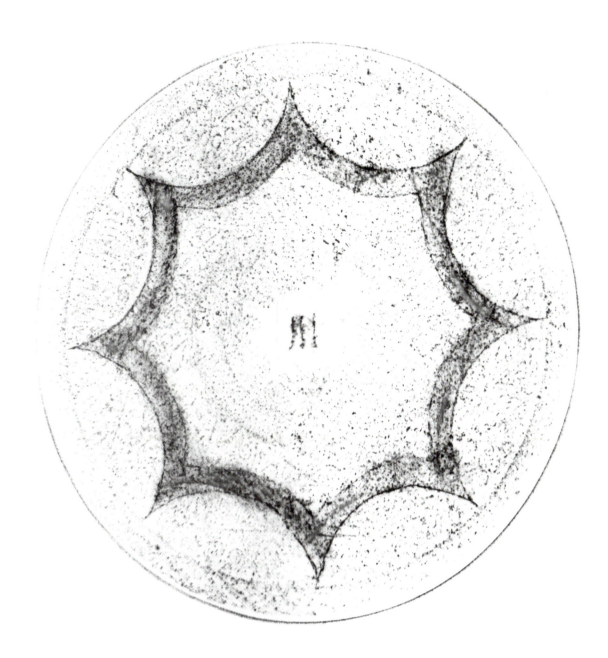

The mirror is round in shape. It has a knob with design of three bow strings. The outside of the knob is adorned with a broad band with concave surface. The middle of the mirror is adorned with the ground motif of patterns of cloud and thunder and the design of eight linked arcs formed by broad band with concave surface that is overlaid on the ground motif. According to the remaining pigments, the ground motif of patterns of cloud and thunder is painted with peacock blue pigment and the concave surfaces of the string design and the design of linked arcs are painted with azurite pigment. The two pigments are strikingly visible on the edges of the broad band with concave surface and the design

of linked arcs. The peacock blue pigment is comparatively thin on the ground motif of patterns of cloud and thunder. The layer of oxidation can be seen on the chipped paint of the mirror part. The painted mirrors of the Warring States Period were found in small numbers. There are two painted mirrors unearthed in Linzi, Shandong Province, with the shapes of dragon and phoenix painted in three pigments. But this mirror is filled with two pigments on the molded mirror and the layers of pigments are thin enough to see the decorative patterns of the mirror. So this mirror, based on the remaining pigments, is not regarded as the painted mirror, and is only filled with pigments for the purpose of beautifying the effect.

## 45. 四龙四叶镜

战国晚期
直径 19.8 厘米，厚 0.7 厘米，重 505 克
2018 年 5 月征集入藏

圆形。三弦钮，圆钮座。环钮饰一周凹弧面宽圈带纹，宽圈带纹内外各饰一周细线凸弦纹。纹饰由地纹和主纹组成。地纹为满铺十分细密的云雷纹和小粒点纹，主纹以四小叶纹分隔成四部分，饰四条舞动的龙，龙首左向回勾，头上部有小角，长直颈，身、腹部呈"S"状弯曲，前后饰卷曲羽翅拱护小花叶。宽素缘，缘边卷起，窄平。

此镜是淮南市博物馆收藏的三十余面龙纹镜中的佳品。镜面的纹饰层次分明，地纹细腻精致，主纹舒展自如、布局均匀，尤其是龙的形态如四个舞者，形态矫健有力，充满张力。

## 45. Mirror with design of four dragons and four leaves

Late Warring States Period
Diameter: 19.8cm, Thickness: 0.7cm, Weight: 505g
Collected in May, 2018

The mirror is round in shape. It has a knob with design of three bow strings on a round base. The knob base is adorned with a broad band with concave surface, and on each side of the broad band is a band of raised bow string. The decorative patterns consist of the ground motif and the major motif. The ground motif is composed of the fine design of cloud and thunder and the design of tiny spots. The major motif is divided into four sections by four small leaves. Each section is adorned with the design of a flying dragon, with its head tuning the left, small horns on the upper part of the head, a long and straight neck, an

S-shaped body and the curled wings on the front and back to protect the leaves. The broad rim is unadorned and the narrow and flat edge rolls.

Among the about thirty bronze mirrors with dragon design collected in the Huainan Museum, this mirror stands for the remarkable quality, with its well-arranged arrangement of decorative patterns. Its ground motif is exquisite and delicate and the major motif, with vigorous and powerful dancer-like dragons, is arranged skilfully and symmetrically.

## 46. 四山镜

战国晚期
直径 13.7 厘米，厚 0.4 厘米，重 165 克
1957 年淮南市唐山公社邱家岗出土

　　圆形。三弦钮，双层方形钮座。钮座四角饰四片花瓣，主纹为四山字纹，山字底边与方钮座四边平行排列，间饰四花，以羽状纹为地，构成三层重叠式图案，布局细致，主次分明。窄斜素缘。

　　山字纹镜在战国时十分流行，多以羽状纹作地纹。上饰三山、四山、五山或六山纹，尤以四山纹为多。镜中的山字，其寓意有不同解释，一般认为是从青铜器上的勾连云雷纹演化而来。在圆形镜面上以三个或数个山字纹作纹饰，是比较难以排列布局的，但是我们现在见到的每一面山字纹镜均十分匀称美观，古代工匠技艺之精巧可见一斑。此镜四个山字左旋，避免了构图的呆板，产生了律动。虽然单个山字缺少平衡，但整体有一种旋转的韵律。方形钮座四角伸出四叶纹，四山之间饰四瓣花纹，下层再以细密的羽状纹铺地，使观者感受到镜面纹饰繁缛精细，有生动的美感。该镜胎体轻薄，能够保存如此完好十分难得。

# 46. Mirror with inscription of four "*shan*" characters

Late Warring States Period
Diameter: 13.7cm, Thickness: 0.4cm, Weight: 165g
Unearthed at Qiujiagang, Tangshan Commune, Huainan City in 1957

The mirror is round in shape. It has a knob with design of three bow strings on a two-layer square base. A petal casts outside each corner of the square. The mirror is decorated with a three-layer overlapping pattern consisting of the inscription of four "*shan*" characters symmetrically arranged, four flowers with which four "*shan*" are spaced and feather-like pattern as ground motif. The bottom strokes of the characters are in parallel with the four sides of the square. The decoration of the mirror has an exquisite layout and shows a distinction between the primary design and the lesser one. It has an inclined narrow rim without design.

During the Warring States Period, the mirrors with inscription of "*shan*" character were prevailed , most of which are adorned with feather-like pattern as the ground motif. The mirrors were usually decorated with inscription of three, four, five or six "*shan*" characters, especially four "*shan*" characters design more. The "*shan*" character is given different meaning. It is generally thought that "*shan*" is derived from cloud and thunder pattern on the bronzes. It is hard to arrange three or several "*shan*" characters on a round surface. The ancient craftsmen were great talents with considerable creative spirit, so every mirror with inscription of "*shan*" characters found shows us aesthetic and symmetrical design. The four "*shan*" characters inclining to left form circulating composition as a whole. The mirror with intricate and elegant decorations brings a strong aesthetic feeling. It is rare that the mirror with thin body is kept in good condition.

**47. 四山八叶镜**

战国

直径 11.3 厘米，厚 0.25 厘米，重 77 克

2018 年 11 月征集入藏

　　圆形。小三弦钮，方形钮座。镜面铺满羽状地纹，羽状纹和卷羽纹、谷粒纹线条粗犷。方形钮座四角各伸出以绹带纹相接的二叶片，八叶片与地纹融为一体。右旋的四个山字纹的底边与方钮座平行，山字纹中间一竖顶至镜缘内侧。镜面平直，缘边呈弧面卷起。

　　此镜的制模略显粗糙，但从其小方钮座看，是此类镜的早期作品。

## 47. Mirror with inscription of four "*shan*" characters and design of eight leaves

Warring States Period
Diameter: 11.3cm, Thickness: 0.25cm, Weight: 77g
Collected in November, 2018

The mirror is round in shape. It has a small knob with design of three bow strings on a square knob base. The surface of the mirror is full of the ground motif of the feather-like patterns. The feather-like pattern, the pattern of rolling feather and the design of unhusked rice are formed with rough lines. Each corner of the square knob base has the design of two leaves joined with the rope design. All eight leaves are combined with the ground motif as a whole. The inscription of "*shan*" characters is inclined towards the right. The bottom sides of "*shan*" characters are parallel to the square knob base. The middle vertical strokes of "*shan*" characters extend to the rim of the mirror. The surface of the mirror is flat and straight. The rim of the mirror is in a shape of arc and rolls.

The mirror was roughly molded. Based on its small square knob base, it is inferred to be an early product of the mirrors of this kind.

## 48. 弦纹镜

战国晚期
直径 9.9 厘米，厚 0.1 厘米，重 60 克
2018 年 5 月征集入藏

　　圆形。宽弓形钮，无钮座。钮外饰二周细弦纹，镜体平直。单弦纹镜、双弦纹镜一般尺寸较小，直径大都是 5 ～ 10 厘米。此类铜镜中镜缘未凸起的时代要早一些，此镜属于这一类。

## 48. Mirror with design of bow string

Late Warring States Period
Diameter: 9.9cm, Thickness: 0.1cm, Weight: 60g
Collected in May, 2018

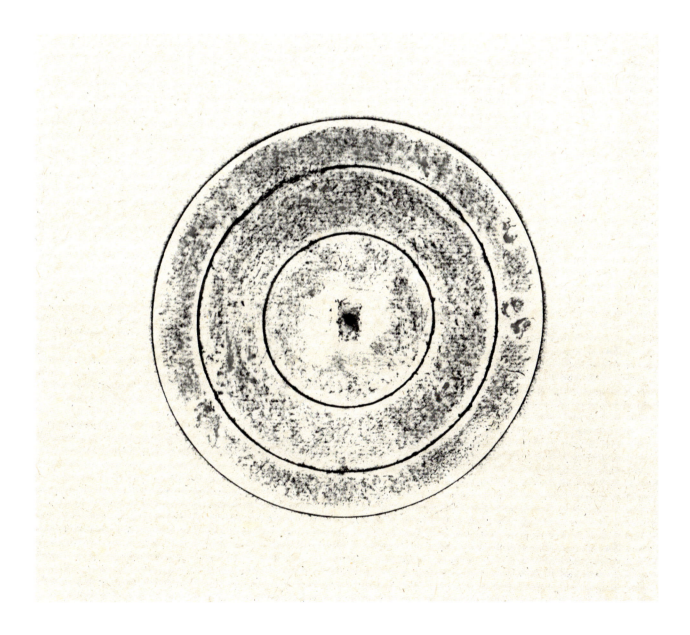

The mirror is round in shape. It has a broad-bow-shaped knob and has no knob base. The outside of the knob is adorned with two bands of slender bow string. The body of the mirror is flat and straight. The mirrors with design of single bow string and the mirrors with design of two bow strings are often small in size, ranging from 5cm to 10cm in diameter. The mirrors, with its rim that is not raised, appeared earlier. This mirror belongs to the mirrors of this kind.

Bronze Mirrors of the Warring States Period
Collected in Huainan Museum

## 49. 三凤三菱镜

战国晚期

直径 11 厘米，厚 0.5 厘米，重 138 克

2018 年 5 月征集入藏

圆形。三弦钮，圆钮座。贴钮座饰一周短斜线纹，绕钮座饰一圈凹弧面宽圈带纹，宽圈带纹外饰有单线凸弦纹，凸弦纹与宽圈带纹之间各饰反向的短斜线纹一周。镜面满铺云雷地纹，不甚清晰。三个双线菱形纹将镜面分为三区，每区各饰一凤。凤首居中，小圆目，张口衔羽翅，凤冠向后飘起，凤身向后拱起，斜穿菱形纹后与相邻的凤羽勾连。凤的羽翼与身体交叉呈穿花状。宽素缘。

此镜小巧精致，尤其是双线菱形纹的装饰方法说明已经到了战国晚期晚段，这种风格到汉代早期被广泛应用。

## 49. Mirror with design of three phoenixes and three rhombuses

Late Warring States Period
Diameter: 11cm, Thickness: 0.5cm, Weight: 138g
Collected in May, 2018

The mirror is round in shape. It has a knob with design of three bow strings on a round base. The outside of the knob base is adorned sequentially with a band of short slanted lines, a broad band with concave surface and a band of raised bow string formed by single line. Between the band of bow string and the broad band is a band of short lines slanting in the opposite direction to the lines above. The surface of the mirror is full of the ground motif of the dim design of cloud and thunder. The surface of the mirror is divided into three sections by three rhombuses formed by double lines. Each section is adorned with a phoenix. Each phoenix has a head in the middle, small round eyes, an opening mouth to hold its feather wing, a phoenix coronet flying backwards and a body that arches backwards and interlaces with the neighbouring feathers after crossing slantwise through the rhombus. The wings and the body of each phoenix are in the interlaced shape. The broad rim is unadorned.

This mirror is small in size and was exquisitely cast. The decorative patterns of rhombus that are formed by double lines appeared in the late period of the late Warring States Period and prevailed in the early Han Dynasty.

## 50. 三虺三菱三叶镜

战国晚期
直径 13.1 厘米，厚 0.55 厘米，重 158 克
2018 年 5 月征集入藏

　　圆形。小三弦钮，圆钮座。钮座外饰二周单线凸弦纹。纹饰由地纹和主纹构成。地纹是细密的云雷纹，满铺镜面至钮座。主纹由虺纹、连体菱形纹和小草叶纹组成，以三扁平圆钉和矮小草叶纹上下布置，将镜面分成三区。每区左大右小的连体菱形纹与翻卷的虺纹纠缠在一起，菱形纹在上，虺纹在下；虺纹的形态十分活泼，虺首呈小圆形状，无目，身体穿过钮座外弦纹后向上卷起穿过菱形纹。宽素缘。

　　本馆藏有此类造型的铜镜 2 面，此镜更显精细。这类铜镜在战国晚期流行的时间不长，发现的也很少。

## 50. Mirror with design of three serpents, three rhombuses and three leaves

Late Warring States Period
Diameter: 13.1cm, Thickness: 0.55cm, Weight: 158g
Collected in May, 2018

The mirror is round in shape. It has a small knob with design of three bow strings. The outside of the knob base is adorned with two bands of raised bow string formed by single line. The decorative patterns consist of the ground motif and the major motif. The ground motif is the fine design of cloud and thunder and is filled in on the surface of the mirror to the knob base. The major motif is composed of the serpent design, the joined design of rhombuses and the leaf design and is divided into three sections by three flat nails and design of short leaf all of which are arranged up and down. Each section is adorned with the joined design of rhombuses, big on the left and small on the right, and the design of coiling serpent that are interlaced with the rhombus, with the rhombus design above and the serpent design below. Each serpent has a vivid shape, with a small round head without eyes, a body that rolls up and passes through the rhombus after crossing the design of bow string on the outside of the knob base. The broad rim is unadorned.

Two such mirrors are in the museum. This mirror is more delicate. The mirrors of this kind prevailed for a short time in the late Warring States Period and were found in small numbers.

## 51. 三凤三龙镜

战国晚期

直径 14.2 厘米，厚 0.6 厘米，重 243 克

2018 年 10 月征集入藏

　　圆形。三弦钮，制作精致。围钮座饰一圈清晰的云雷纹，云雷纹外围饰一周凹弧面宽圈带纹，宽圈带纹外饰短斜线纹和扁平的凸弦纹。地纹为云雷纹。主纹是以三凤三龙相间环列，凤纹占据主要部分。这种装饰方法与三龙三菱纹镜相似，以三凤替代了三菱，纹饰的风格仍然未变。凤单足立于钮座之上，勾回首，小目，短喙，凤口衔尾羽，两翼勾连两侧的龙羽。龙的布局与凤相反，以头部顶托钮座。龙首硕大，回首，双目，大张口，口中露六獠牙，足踏镜缘，前后翼与相邻的凤羽穿花勾连，凤、龙的身躯呈蔓枝状缠绕。镜面的空间布局十分匀称有致。宽素缘。

　　凤的形态在三凤三菱镜中多有见到，龙的形态十分生动有趣，龙虽张口獠牙，但又有笑面之容。从平面布置上看，凤立于上，正下方是龙首，龙的姿态又有呼唤凤的感觉，这既有传统的楚人尚凤，将凤置于龙之上的习惯，又有将狰狞的龙演化成世俗的审美，反映了时代变化的特征。

　　此镜是龙凤纹镜中的精品。其装饰纹样在战国晚期中十分少见，从纹样的布置到模铸工艺均非常精美，是楚镜发展到最后的精品之作。

# 51. Mirror with design of three phoenixes and three dragons

Late Warring States Period
Diameter: 14.2cm, Thickness: 0.6cm, Weight: 243g
Collected in October, 2018

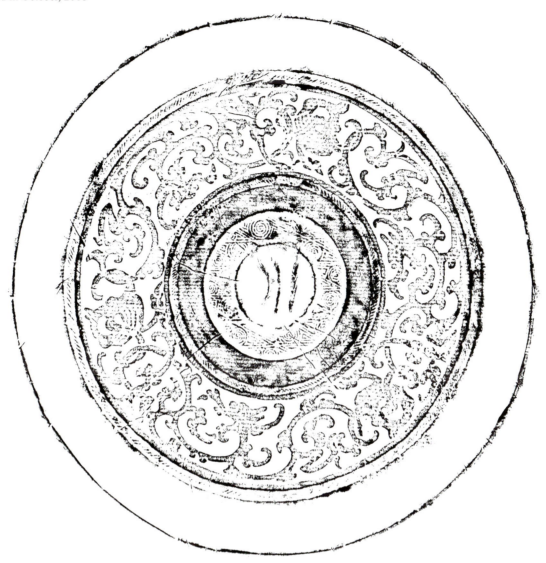

The mirror is round in shape. It has an exquisite knob with design of three bow strings. The outside of the knob base is adorned with a clear band of cloud and thunder pattern, a broad band with concave surface, a band of short slanted lines and a flat band of raised bow string. The ground motif is the design of cloud and thunder. The major motif is an alternating arrangement of three phoenixes and three dragons. The phoenix designs take up most of the mirror. The decoration of the mirror is similar to that of the mirrors with design of three dragons and three rhombuses, except that the design of three phoenixes is used instead of the design of three rhombuses. Each phoenix steps on the knob base with its one leg, turns its back and holds its tail in its mouth. Each phoenix has small eyes, a short beak and two wings that are interlaced with the feathers of the dragons on both sides. Each dragon is opposite to the phoenix, with its head supporting the knob base. Each dragon has a big head turned back, two eyes, an opening mouth with six buckteeth, feet stepping on the rim of the mirror and front and back wings that are interlaced with the feathers

of the neighbouring phoenix. The bodies of the dragon and the phoenix are interwoven like branches. The surface of the mirror is arranged symmetrically. The broad rim is unadorned.

The shapes of the phoenixes are commonly seen on the bronze mirrors with design of three phoenixes and three rhombuses. The dragon is in the lively and interesting shape, showing an opening mouth with buckteeth but a smiling face. The decorative arrangement of the phoenix above and the dragon below, as a picture that the dragon is calling the phoenix, indicates the tradition of the Chu State that the phoenix was revered and was superior to the dragon and the changing features of the times that the ferocious dragon was changed to the shape of popular aesthetic.

This mirror is a treasure of the mirrors with design of dragon and phoenix. Its decoration was rarely seen in the late Warring States Period. The mirror, with its delicate decorative layout and elaborate mold casting, is a product of the high quality of the bronze mirrors in the last period of the bronze mirrors of the Chu State.

## 52. 四龙镜

战国晚期

直径 14.3 厘米，厚 0.4 厘米，重 162 克

2017 年 12 月征集入藏

　　圆形。三弦钮，圆钮座。钮座外饰一周细线凸弦纹，弦纹内外铺细密的云雷纹，凹弧面宽圈带纹围绕一周。地纹为模印清晰的云雷纹，环钮座饰四只对称的龙纹，每两只龙首相向，龙尾处有分隔线。龙首居于中部近镜缘处，形象写实，大张口，曲颈呈"S"状，腹部卷曲，一足向前蹬踏在钮座上，尾部向后上部翻卷。龙的形态很有张力，生动活泼。宽素缘，缘边卷起，窄平。

　　龙纹镜上的龙纹，有称蟠螭纹、蟠龙纹、螭龙纹、变形龙纹等，其中的区别比较细微，认识上有差别。对有龙首这一典型特征的，一般可称之为龙纹。

## 52. Mirror with design of four dragons

Late Warring States Period
Diameter: 14.3cm, Thickness: 0.4cm, Weight: 162g
Collected in December, 2017

The mirror is round in shape. It has a knob with design of three bow strings on a round base. The outside of the knob base is adorned with a band of raised bow string design. The design of cloud and thunder adorns either side of the bow string design and the broad band with concave surface surrounds the design of cloud and thunder. The ground motif is the design of cloud and thunder with clear mold marks. Four dragons surround well-arrangedly the knob base. The dragons look at each other in pairs. On the tail of the dragon is a dividing line. The dragons are in the realistic and vivid shape of heads in the middle close to the rim of the mirror, big open mouths, crooked necks in the shape of an S, curled bellies, one foot stepping on the knob base and tails rolling backwards and upwards. The broad rim is unadorned and the narrow and flat edge of the rim rolls.

The dragon design is also known as the design of interlaced hydras, the design of coiled dragon, the design of hornless dragon and the design of stylized dragon. The distinction of all is subtle. But the decorative patterns with characteristic features of the dragon's head are generally considered to be the dragon design.

## 53. 四山八叶镜

战国晚期
直径 8.7 厘米，厚 0.4 厘米，重 64 克
2018 年 5 月征集入藏

　　圆形。小三弦钮，双层圆钮座。纹饰由地纹和主纹组成。地纹是较为粗犷的羽状纹。以钮座为中心，向十字方向伸出四花叶，花叶尖部的花枝连接镜缘处的花叶。右旋四个山字纹分置在十字形花叶间，山字粗壮。素卷缘，微弧，短平沿。

　　圆形钮座上饰四山八花叶纹，比较少见。常见的在方形钮座外装饰花叶和山字纹。叶片之间相连接的细条纹不是以绹带纹构成，而是扁平的长杆相接，很少见。山字纹镜中的圆钮座，一般在五山镜、六山镜上使用，所以，此镜算是四山八叶镜中的罕见之作，甚是珍贵。从其小巧的三弦钮和很小的圆钮座上看，此镜是同类镜中较早时期的产品。

## 53. Mirror with inscription of four "*shan*" characters and design of eight leaves

Late Warring States Period
Diameter: 8.7cm, Thickness: 0.4cm, Weight: 64g
Collected in May, 2018

The mirror is round in shape. It has a small knob with design of three bow strings on an overlaid round base. The decorative patterns consist of the ground motif and the major motif. The ground motif is the rough feather-like pattern. Four leaves extend from the knob base in each direction of cross. The branches at the tip of each leaf are joined with the leaves that are close to the rim of the mirror. The inscription of four "*shan*" characters is inclined towards the right and is arranged among leaves in each direction of cross. The characters are in the strong shape. The unadorned rim of the mirror rolls and has a slight arc. The edge of the rim is short and flat.

It is rarely seen that the decorative patterns of the inscription of four "*shan*" characters and the design of eight leaves adorn on the round knob base. It is commonly seen that the outside of the square knob base is adorned with the decorative patterns of the leaf design and the inscription of "*shan*" characters. It is also rarely seen that the joints between the leaves are formed by the flat long poles rather than by the rope design. The inscription of "*shan*" characters on the round knob base was often used on the mirrors with inscription of five or six "*shan*" characters. So this mirror is a rare treasure of the mirrors with inscription of four "*shan*" characters and design of eight leaves. From its small knob with design of three bow strings and round base, it is inferred to be an early product of the mirrors of this kind.

## 54. 三虺三菱镜

战国晚期

直径 12 厘米，厚 0.5 厘米，重 145 克

2018 年 5 月征集入藏

　　圆形。小三弦钮，圆钮座。钮座外饰单线凸弦纹两周。镜面平直。纹饰由地纹和主纹构成。镜面满铺云雷地纹，细密清晰。主纹模印精致，很有特点。三菱纹将镜面分为三区，菱纹左右连体，一大一小；虺纹与菱纹纠缠在一起，虺的头部特征不明显，尾部穿凸弦纹后向上卷起穿过菱形纹。近缘处饰一周短斜线纹。宽素缘。

　　这种纹饰的布局，打破了简单的分区，三虺与菱形相接，形成整体，纹饰动感强烈，富于张力。在线条运用上开始用双线装饰，这是西汉早中期十分流行的装饰手法，在战国晚期已初见端倪了。

## 54. Mirror with design of three serpents and three rhombuses

Late Warring States Period
Diameter: 12cm, Thickness: 0.5cm, Weight: 145g
Collected in May, 2018

The mirror is round in shape. It has a small knob with design of three bow strings on a round base. The outside of the knob base is adorned with two bands of raised bow string formed by single line. The surface of the mirror is flat and straight. The decorative patterns consist of the ground motif and the major motif. The surface of the mirror is full of the fine and clear design of cloud and thunder as the ground motif. The major motif, with exquisite molding marks, is peculiar. The surface of the mirror is divided by three rhombus designs into three sections. The rhombus designs are joined to each other, one big and the other small, on the left and right sides. The serpent design is connected with the rhombus design. Each serpent has a head with indistinct features and a tail that rolls up and passes the rhombus design after crossing the design of raised bow string. A band of short slanted lines is near the rim of the mirror. The broad rim is unadorned.

The arrangement of the decoration on this mirror is a joint of the serpent design and the rhombus design as a whole, rather than the simple partition. The decoration of the mirror is vivid and powerful. The decorative patterns are formed by double lines, which prevailed in the early and middle Western Han Dynasty and appeared in the late Warring States Period.

## 55. 五山镜

战国晚期

直径 12.5 厘米，厚 0.4 厘米，重 297 克

2018 年 11 月征集入藏

圆形。小三弦钮，凹弧面宽圈带圆钮座。羽状地纹满铺镜面，五个左旋山字纹绕钮座环列。每个山字中间竖笔斜向直抵镜缘，山字的两边短竖笔向内转折呈锐角状。近缘处饰一周细线凸弦纹。镜缘宽平。此镜破损严重，所幸镶配有机托盘才能长期保存。

从现有资料看，五山镜的数量在山字镜中仅次于四山镜。目前看到的五山镜都有一共同特征，都是在圆形钮座上布局山字纹，可能是古代工匠在实践中发现，五个山字纹装饰在圆钮座外，易于布置，也更显协调、美观。安徽境内的宿州、六安、潜山都有五山镜出土，其中六安城东开发区出土的五山镜，纹饰中的草叶纹已经夸张变形，是五山镜最后阶段的产品。而本馆这面五山镜，除羽状地纹外，没有装饰花叶纹，算是五山镜中的罕见品种；从其宽平的镜缘判断，应为战国晚期的产品。

## 55. Mirror with inscription of five "*shan*" characters

Late Warring States Period
Diameter: 12.5cm, Thickness: 0.4cm, Weight: 297g
Collected in November, 2018

The mirror is round in shape. It has a small knob with design of three bow strings on a round base in a shape of a broad band with concave surface. The surface of the mirror is full of the ground motif with feather-like pattern. The inscription of five "*shan*" characters is inclined towards the left and encircles the knob base. The middle vertical strokes of "*shan*" characters are slantly stretching out to the rim of the mirror. The short vertical strokes of both sides of "*shan*" characters turn inwards and are in the shape of closed angle. A band of raised bow string formed by slender line is close to the rim of the mirror. The rim is broad and flat. This mirror was damaged heavily and has been kept with the organic tray.

According to the published articles, the mirrors with inscription of five "*shan*" characters have been found in a second number only to the mirrors with inscription of four "*shan*" characters. All mirrors with inscription of five "*shan*" characters found show a common feature of that the "*shan*" characters are arranged around a round knob base. It is inferred that the ancient craftsmen found in practice that the inscription of five "*shan*" characters is easy to be arranged symmetrically and beautifully around the round knob base. The mirrors with inscription of five "*shan*" characters were unearthed in Suzhou, Lu'an and Qianshan, Anhui Province. Of these, the mirrors unearthed in Lu'an, which are adorned with the design of exaggerated and stylized leaf, were the products of the last period of the mirrors with inscription of five "*shan*" characters. The mirror in the museum, only with feather-like pattern as ground motif and without leaf design, is the rare treasure of the mirrors with inscription of five "*shan*" characters. Based on its broad and flat rim, it is deduced to date from the late Warring States Period.

## 56. 四叶镜

战国晚期

直径 11.5 厘米，厚 0.3 厘米，重 122 克

2018 年 5 月征集入藏

圆形。小三弦钮，圆钮座。镜面平直，满铺细密的羽状地纹。羽状地纹系模印而成，由七层、每层四个方块组合而成，每个方块呈长方形状。钮座外饰四片桃形叠瓣花叶，呈"十"字形布置，叶柄之间相连，环绕钮座。卷素缘。

此镜模印精细，羽状纹线条清晰、细密，四叶纹以简单的叶片形状逐渐向相对复杂的花苞形叶片转变，是花叶纹变化过程中的产品。

## 56. Mirror with design of four leaves

Late Warring States Period
Diameter: 11.5cm, Thickness: 0.3cm, Weight: 122g
Collected in May, 2018

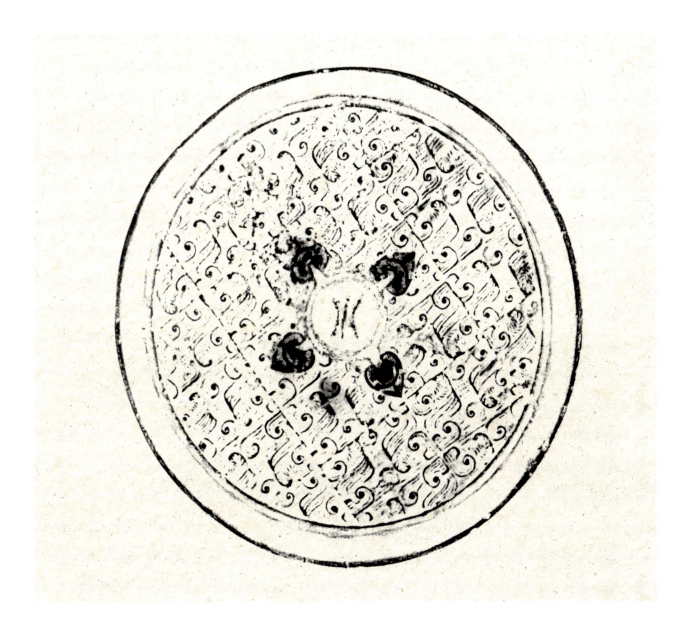

The mirror is round in shape. It has a small knob with design of three bow strings on a round base. The surface of the mirror is flat and is decorated with the elaborate ground motif of feather-like pattern. The ground motif with feather-like pattern was cast in molds and is a combination of seven layers. Each layer consists of four rectangles. The outside of the knob base is adorned with overlaid, peach-shaped leaves in each direction of cross. The petioles are connected and are arranged around the knob base. The rim rolls up and is unadorned.

This mirror, with its fine mold marks, elaborate lines of feather-like pattern and relatively complex design of leaf in a shape of bud changing from simple design of leaf, is the product of the changes of the leaf design.

## 57. 四兽四叶镜

战国晚期

直径 12 厘米，厚 0.5 厘米，重 108 克

2019 年 11 月征集入藏

圆形。三弦钮，圆钮座。钮座外饰二周单线凸弦纹，弦内饰短斜线纹。镜面中区的纹饰由地纹和主纹构成。地纹是疏朗的云雷纹。主纹是以花蕾形草叶将镜面分为四区，每区饰一兽纹，兽纹两两对称，兽的头部似犬似龙，两翼犹如龙的形态；叶纹的形态复杂，近似花苞。宽素缘。

此镜纹饰少见，造型生动活泼，风格已从楚镜装饰风格向汉代写实变化，具备战国晚期铜镜纹饰向汉代风格转变的特点。

## 57. Mirror with design of four beasts and four leaves

Late Warring States Period
Diameter: 12cm, Thickness: 0.5cm, Weight: 108g
Collected in November, 2019

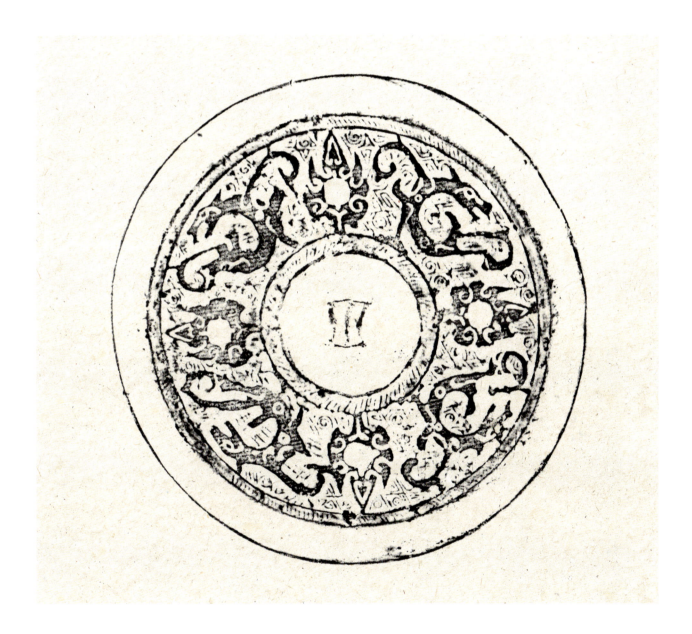

The mirror is round in shape. It has a knob with design of three bow strings on a round base. The outside of the knob base is adorned with two bands of raised bow string formed by single line. Between the bands is the design of short slanted lines. The middle of the mirror is adorned with the ground motif and the major motif. The ground motif is the clear design of cloud and thunder. The major motif is divided into four sections by the patterns of bud-shaped leaf. Each section is adorned with a beast design. The beast designs are composed symmetrically of each other. The beast has a dog-shaped or dragon-shaped head, two dragon-like wings. The leaf is in a complex shape of bud. The broad rim of the mirror is unadorned.

The decorative patterns are rarely seen and are displayed in vivid shapes. The decorative style shows a change from the style of bronze mirrors of the Chu State to the realistic style of bronze mirrors of the Han Dynasty and contains the features of the transition of bronze mirrors from the late Warring States Period to the Han Dynasty.

战国晚期

直径 14 厘米，厚 0.3 厘米，重 188 克

2017 年 12 月征集入藏

圆形。小三弦钮。钮外饰一圈凹弧面宽圈带纹。镜缘呈宽凹面，缘边上卷。

## 58. Mirror with design of broad band

Late Warring States Period
Diameter: 14cm, Thickness: 0.3cm, Weight: 188g
Collected in December, 2017

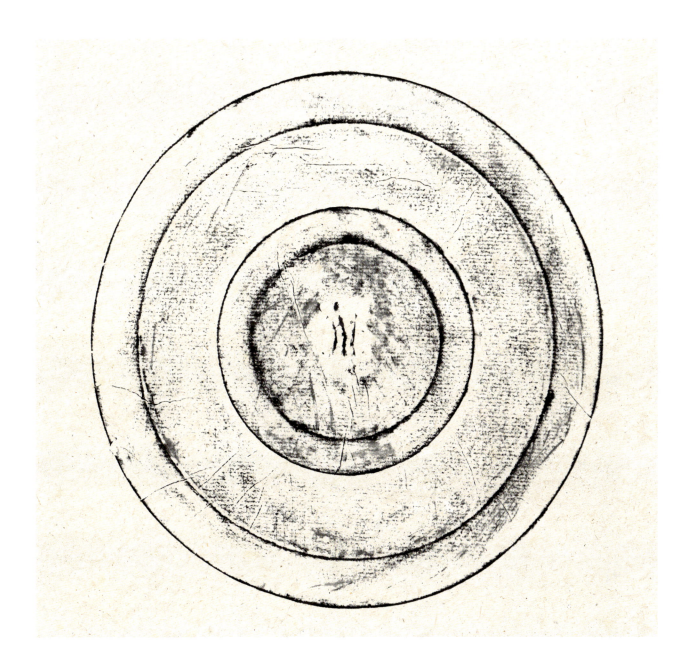

The mirror is round in shape. It has a small knob with design of three bow strings. The outside of the knob is adorned with a broad band with concave surface. The rim of the mirror has a broad concave surface and the edge of the rim rolls up.

## 59. 四叶镜

战国晚期

直径 11.1 厘米，厚 0.4 厘米，重 99 克

2018 年 5 月征集入藏

　　圆形。小三弦钮，双层圆钮座。镜面平直，满铺羽状纹，每组羽状纹有四个卷羽，每个小羽片由五道细线组成。钮座外饰呈"十"字方向布置的四小片叶纹，叶片与钮座不相连，四叶片很小，但布置精巧，地纹占纹饰的绝大部分。而后期的十二花叶镜的羽状地纹相对变少。宽素

缘。整个镜面布置的细密、清雅，十分美观。

　　此镜与本书收录的另一面也饰有四叶纹的铜镜相比，虽然尺寸相近，纹饰相同，但四个叶片不同。此镜叶片属写实的凹弧面状，另一面的叶片已经开始变化，叶片中间增横切的弧线，可能要稍晚于此镜。

## 59. Mirror with design of four leaves

Late Warring States Period
Diameter: 11.1cm, Thickness: 0.4cm, Weight: 99g
Collected in May, 2018

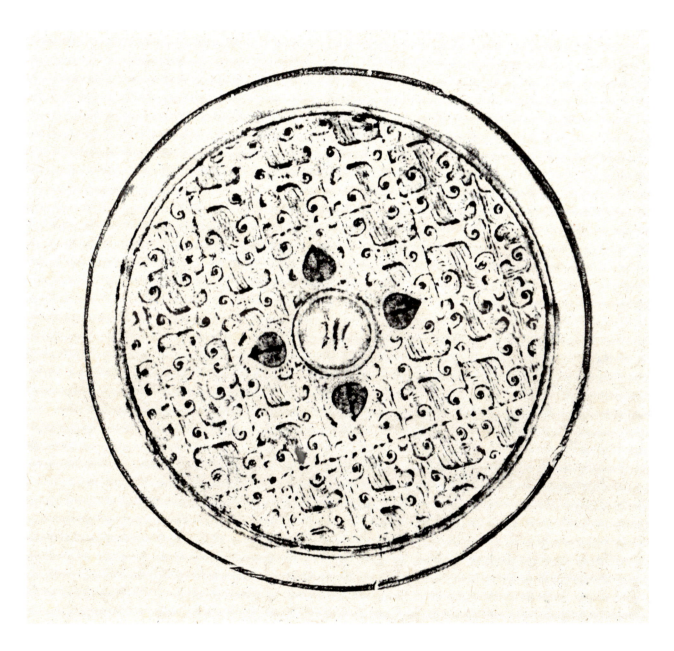

The mirror is round in shape. It has a small knob with design of three bow strings on a two-layer round base. The surface of the mirror is flat and is decorated with the elaborate ground of feather-like pattern. Each group of feather-like pattern has four rolled-up feather. Each feather is composed of five lines. The outside of the knob base is adorned with four small leaves in each direction of cross. The leaves and the knob base are not connected. Four leaves are small, but arranged with a neatness. The ground motif makes up the majority of the decorative patterns. In the late period, the feather-like pattern in the bronze mirror with design of twelve leaves possessed a small portion. The broad rim has a flat edge and is unadorned. The arrangement of the mirror is elegant and fine.

The mirror is similar in size and decorative pattern to another bronze mirror with design of four leaves in the book, but differs in the shape of the leaf. The leaf design in this mirror is in a realistic shape with concave surface. But there is a cross-cut arc in the middle of the leaf on the other mirror in the book, so the mirror appeared later.

## 60. 四虺四菱镜

战国晚期

直径 12.9 厘米，厚 0.15 厘米，重 83 克

2018 年 5 月征集入藏

　　圆形。小三弦钮，圆钮座。钮座外饰凹面宽圈带纹、短斜线纹、单线弦纹各一周。云雷地纹较粗松，模印不清。主纹中虺纹与菱形纹均分、间隔排列，双层菱纹上抵镜缘、下贴宽带纹；虺头部居中，两侧对称，身体饰鳞状涡纹。宽素缘，平沿。这种将虺纹简化成图案形状，忽略其细部特征的装饰手法，是战国晚期晚段时的风格，其模铸工艺也走向衰落。

## 60. Mirror with design of four serpents and four rhombuses

Late Warring States Period
Diameter: 12.9cm, Thickness: 0.15cm, Weight: 83g
Collected in May, 2018

The mirror is round in shape. It has a small knob with design of three bow strings on a round base. The outside of the knob base is adorned with a broad band with concave surface, a band of short slanted lines and a band of bow string formed by single line. The ground motif is the dim and coarse design of cloud and thunder. The major motif is an alternating arrangement of the serpent design and the rhombus design. The design of overlaid rhombus approaches upwards to the rim of the mirror and downwards to the broad band. Each serpent has a head in the middle and body with design of scale-shaped whorl on either side of the head. The broad rim is unadorned and has a flat edge. The decorative style of simplifying the serpent design to the shape of pattern without detailed features prevailed in the late period of the late Warring States Period, and its mold casting technique had declined.

## 61. 双宽圈带纹镜

战国晚期

直径 20.9 厘米，厚 0.2 厘米，重 407 克

2018 年 11 月征集入藏

圆形。三弦钮。钮外、镜面中区饰凹弧面宽圈带纹。镜面呈黑漆古色状。窄平缘。

此镜在同类镜中尺寸较大，有典型的秦镜风格，在荆州、长沙战国晚期晚段的墓葬中有少量出土。

## 61. Mirror with design of two broad bands

Late Warring States Period
Diameter: 20.9cm, Thickness: 0.2cm, Weight: 407g
Collected in November, 2018

The mirror is round in shape. It has a knob with design of three bow strings. The major motif is the design of broad band with concave surface. The surface of the mirror has an old-fashioned black lacquer. The rim of the mirror is narrow and flat.

The mirror is bigger in size in this kind of mirror and has the typical style of bronze mirrors of the Qin Sate. Mirrors of this kind were unearthed in small numbers in the tombs of the late period of the late Warring States Period in Jingzhou and Changsha.

Bronze Mirrors of the Warring States Period
Collected in Huainan Museum

## 62. 素面镜

战国晚期

直径 14.6 厘米，厚 0.2 厘米，重 131 克

2018 年 5 月征集入藏

圆形。小三弦钮，制作精细。素面。无缘，平沿。镜体平直，镜面光滑。

## 62. Mirror with plain ground

Late Warring States Period
Diameter: 14.6cm, Thickness: 0.2cm, Weight: 131g
Collected in May, 2018

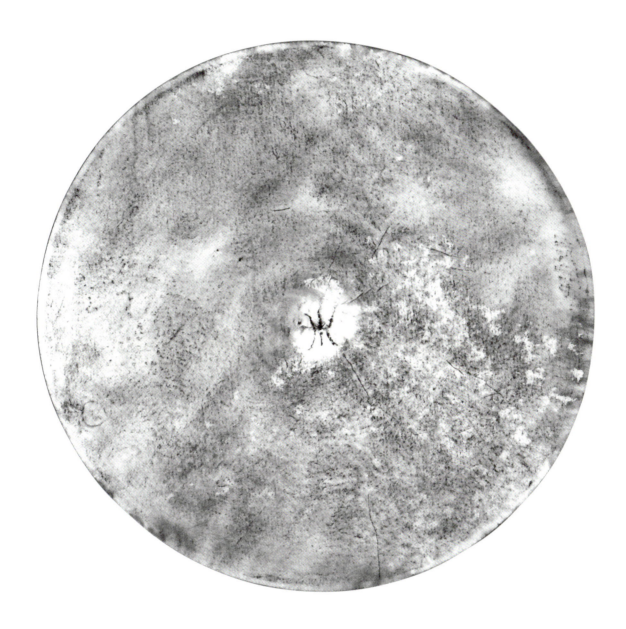

The mirror is round in shape. It has an exquisitely-cast small knob with design of three bow strings. The mirror is unadorned. The mirror is without a rim and has a flat edge. The body of the mirror is flat and straight. The surface of the mirror is smooth.

## 63. 六龙六菱镜

战国晚期

直径 16.6 厘米，厚 0.35 厘米，重 269 克

2018 年 5 月征集入藏

　　圆形。三弦钮，圆钮座。钮座外与宽带纹之间有地纹延伸的云雷纹，凹弧宽面圈带纹围绕一周，外饰凸弦纹。镜面纹饰由地纹和主纹组成，地纹是由细密的三角雷纹和云纹组成。主纹是在镜钮座上均匀布置三个菱形纹，在菱形纹之间的上方紧贴镜缘处布置一菱形纹，把镜面分为三部分，每区饰二龙纹。小龙首向上，张口，圆目，龙角与镜缘处的菱形纹相接，曲颈，腹部与翼翅弯曲成"S"型蔓枝状。近缘处饰人字形斜线纹。宽素缘上卷，平沿。

　　这种变形的龙纹镜又被称为蟠虺纹镜、蟠螭纹镜，但从其写实的头部、吻部装饰看，称之为龙纹镜更为合适。本馆藏有龙纹镜4面，此镜造型工艺、纹饰水平要明显高超一些。地纹中的金黄色疑是否为鎏金工艺，有待进一步验证。

## 63. Mirror with design of six dragons and six rhombuses

Late Warring States Period
Diameter: 16.6cm, Thickness: 0.35cm, Weight: 269g
Collected in May, 2018

The mirror is round in shape. It has a knob with design of three bow strings on a round base. The outside of the knob base is adorned with a broad band with concave surface. Between the knob base and the broad band are the design of cloud and thunder as ground motif. The outside of the broad band is adorned with the design of raised bow string. The decorative patterns consist of the ground motif and the major motif. The ground motif is a combination of the fine design of triangle-shaped thunder and the cloud design. The major motif is the design of three rhombuses around the knob base and the design of rhombus that is on the upper space between the designs of rhombuses and is close to the rim, all of which divide the surface into three sections. Each section is adorned with two dragon designs. Each dragon has a head with an upward-opening mouth, round eyes, horns that are connected with the rhombus design close to the rim, a crooked neck, feather-wings and a belly both in the shape of an S like branches. The broad rim is unadorned and rolls up. The rim has a flat edge.

The mirrors with design of stylized dragon are also known as the mirrors with design of coiled serpent or the mirrors with design of interlaced hydras. Perhaps it is proper to call them the mirrors with dragon design, from the realistic decoration of their heads and muzzles. The four mirrors with dragon design are in the collection of the museum. But this mirror is better in shape and decoration than the others. Further research is needed to confirm that the golden yellow color on the ground motif was produced by gold-plating.

## 64. 七宽带连弧纹镜

战国晚期

直径 15.4 厘米，厚 0.2 厘米，重 174 克

2018 年 11 月征集入藏

　　圆形。三弦钮，圆钮座。钮座外饰凹面宽圈带纹，镜中区饰七凹面宽带连弧纹。窄平缘。已发现的连弧纹铜镜，按地纹分类主要有素地单线连弧纹、素地凹面宽带连弧纹、云纹地宽带连弧纹和云雷纹地宽带连弧纹等四类。单线连弧纹所处时代较早。此镜云纹地纹很有特色，从卷云纹的大小不一，且每个卷云纹都独立完整，没有被宽带连弧纹叠压的特征看，应该是一块整范成型，不是用事先制作好的块状模子重复戳印而成，这不同于常见的"山"字纹镜羽状地纹的四方连续布置。本书收录的同类镜有 2 面，另一件宽带连弧纹镜的云雷纹地纹，是被宽带连弧纹叠压，地纹是断续相连，与此镜在模制方法上有明显区别。

## 64. Mirror with design of seven linked arcs formed by broad band

Late Warring States Period
Diameter: 15.4cm, Thickness: 0.2cm, Weight: 174g
Collected in November, 2018

The mirror is round in shape. It has a knob with design of three bow strings on a round base. The outside of the knob is adorned with a broad band with concave surface. The major motif is the design of seven linked arcs formed by broad band with concave surface. The rim of the mirror is narrow and flat. The bronze mirrors with design of linked arcs found, based on its ground motif, can be classified into four types, the mirror with plain ground and design of linked arcs formed by single line, the mirror with plain ground and design of linked arcs formed by broad band with concave surface, the mirror design of cloud as ground motif and design of linked arcs formed by broad band and the mirror with design of cloud and thunder as ground motif and design of linked arcs formed by broad band. The mirror with design of linked arcs formed by single line appeared earlier. On this mirror, the ground motif of cloud patterns is quite distinctive. The patterns of cirrus cloud are not of uniform size and each pattern is taken as a whole and is not overlaid by the pattern of linked arcs formed by broad band. All evidence indicates that the ground motif was cast with a whole mold, rather than was stamped repeatedly with a cast mold, which is distinguished from that the mirror with feather-like pattern as ground motif and inscription of "*shan*" character is arranged consecutively and repeatedly toward four directions. In total, there are two mirrors of this kind in the book. The other differs in molding from this mirror, and its ground motif of patterns of cloud and thunder are overlaid by the linked arcs formed by broad band and is connected interruptedly.

## 65. 四龙三凤四叶镜

战国晚期
直径 24.3 厘米, 厚 0.9 厘米, 重 894 克
2019 年 12 月征集入藏

　　圆形。三弦钮, 圆钮座。钮座外凹弧面宽圈带纹环绕一周。环带内饰右向三凤纹, 三凤首同向, 凤口大张, 凤冠向后下飘起, 前足贴圈带翘起, 腹部与尾部呈 "S" 状卷起, 三凤首尾相连。宽圈带外由四个花苞形草叶均匀四分, 叶柄下部相接, 形成一周凸弦纹。花叶之间各饰一变形龙纹。龙首居于中部上方, 紧贴镜缘, 龙首向下张口, 贴于龙身之上, 龙首前部伸出弯曲的角, 颈下伸出前足,

蹬踏镜缘, 龙的两翼在前后卷曲成涡纹状, 与相邻的龙尾环抱花叶。镜面满铺细密的云雷纹。宽素缘, 缘边卷起, 窄平。

　　在钮座外围饰以细线构成环钮座装饰的三凤纹, 与镜面以实线构成的主体龙纹形成对比, 这显示出战国晚期晚段铜镜装饰风格的演化, 在一面铜镜上看到了两种不同的装饰手法, 也是龙纹镜的最后绝唱。

## 65. Mirror with design of four dragons, three phoenixes and four leaves

Late Warring States Period
Diameter: 24.3cm, Thickness: 0.9cm, Weight: 894g
Collected in December, 2019

The mirror is round in shape. It has a knob with design of three bow strings on a round base. The outside of the knob base is adorned with a broad band with concave surface. The inside of the broad band is adorned with the design of three phoenixes. The head of each phoenix is connected with the tail of the other. The heads of three phoenixes are towards the right. Each phoenix has an opening mouth, a phoenix comb flying backwards and downwards, a foreleg lifting near the broad band, a belly and a tail both of which roll in the shape of an S. The outside of the broad band is divided into four sections by four bud-shaped leaves. The bottoms of the petioles are joined to form a band of raised bow string. Between the leaves is the design of stylized dragon. Each dragon has a head downwards in the middle and close to the rim with an opening mouth clinging to the body of the dragon, crooked horns extending from the front part of the head, the front leg protruding from the neck and stepping on the rim of the mirror, front and back wings that roll in the shape of whorl and surround the leaf with its adjacent dragon's tail. The surface of the mirror is full of the fine design of cloud and thunder. The broad rim is unadorned. The edge of the rim rolls and is narrow and flat.

The contrast of the design of three phoenixes formed by thin lines around the knob base and on the outside of the knob base and the design of dragon formed by solid lines on the main part of the surface of the mirror, indicates the changes of the decorative style of the bronze mirrors in the late Warring States Period. The two decorative styles on a single mirror show the last glory of the mirrors with dragon design.

## 66.八宽带连弧纹镜

战国晚期

直径 23.5 厘米，厚 0.2 厘米，重 674 克

2018 年 11 月征集入藏

　　圆形。三弦钮。钮外饰凹面宽圈带纹。中区饰八个内向凹面宽带连弧纹，结合处的尖角触抵镜缘。窄平缘。连弧纹布局疏朗、均匀。凹面宽带连弧纹镜较单线连弧纹镜发现的要多，且镜体形制较大，使用时间较长，在西汉墓葬中时有发现，尤其是这类形制硕大的铜镜，时代要更晚一些，下限可到西汉中期。

# 66. Mirror with design of eight linked arcs formed by broad band

Late Warring States Period
Diameter: 23.5cm, Thickness: 0.2cm, Weight: 674g
Collected in November, 2018

The mirror is round in shape. It has a knob with design of three bow strings. The outside of the knob is adorned with a broad band with concave surface. The middle of the mirror is adorned with eight linked arcs formed by broad band with concave surface and oriented inwards. The sharp joints of the linked arcs are against the rim of the mirror. The rim is narrow and flat. The patterns of linked arcs are well arranged.

The mirrors with design of linked arcs formed by broad band with concave surface were found more than those with design of linked arcs formed by single line. The mirrors of this kind are big in size and were in use for a longer time. The mirrors were often unearthed in the tombs of the Western Han Dynasty. The mirrors of this kind, with a big size, appeared later and ended in the middle Western Han Dynasty.

# 67. 单线连弧纹镜

战国晚期

直径 16 厘米，厚 0.3 厘米，重 278 克

2018 年 1 月征集入藏

圆形。小三弦钮，钮下有方形模印痕，疑为将预先铸好的钮座嵌入镜模中再浇铸成型。在本书收录的另一件同类镜上也有这种现象。钮座外饰凹面宽圈带纹，外饰内向的 11 个单细线连弧纹，弧度平缓。窄平缘。

单线连弧纹镜发现的较少，常见的是宽带连弧纹镜，

单线连弧纹镜在长沙楚墓中出土有 3 件，与本馆所藏同类镜在尺寸、形制、特征上相近，时代在战国晚期早段。这类铜镜总量不多，可能是与单线连弧镜的出现后不久被宽带连弧纹镜取代有关。

## 67. Mirror with design of linked arcs formed by single line

Late Warring States Period
Diameter: 16cm, Thickness: 0.3cm, Weight: 278g
Collected in January, 2018

The mirror is round in shape. It has a small knob with design of three bow strings. There is a square mold mark under the knob, and it is suspected that the mirror was cast after the cast knob base was inserted into the mirror mold. This kind of mold mark is also found on the mirror with the same shape in the book. The outside of the knob base is adorned with a broad band with concave surface. The outside of the broad band has eleven linked gentle arcs that are formed by single line and turn inwards. The rim is narrow and flat.

The mirrors with design of linked arcs formed by single line were rarely found, while the mirrors with design of linked arcs formed by broad band are often seen. Three mirrors with design of linked arcs formed by single line were unearthed in the tombs of the Chu State in Changsha, and are similar in size, shape and features to the mirrors of the early period of the late Warring States Period collected in the museum. The number of such mirrors is small in total. This may be explained by the fact that mirrors with design of linked arcs formed by single line were soon replaced by the mirrors with design of linked arcs formed by broad band.

## 68. 三龙三菱镜

战国晚期

直径 16 厘米，厚 0.3 厘米，重 204 克

2018 年 11 月淮南市谢家集公安分局移交

　　圆形。小桥钮，双层圆钮座。钮座外有一周凹弧面宽圈带纹，宽圈带纹内外饰一周细线凸弦纹。云雷纹为地，主纹为三条龙纹间隔三菱形纹。小龙头，回首，怒目，张口吐舌，龙首后上部有弯曲的短角顶托钮座外围的细线凸弦纹，长曲颈，前足蹬踏镜缘，前后羽翅与相邻的菱纹勾连呈"S"状，枝蔓卷曲。宽素缘，缘边卷起，窄平。

　　龙纹镜中龙的形态千变万化，三龙、四龙多以叶纹或菱形纹分隔，但工匠在处理龙纹与间隔的叶纹、菱形纹时，能够将其融为一体，通过勾连、拱卫、烘托等手法达到镜面纹饰布置均衡、疏朗的效果，这其中包含了战国晚期青铜工匠的高超技艺和超乎今人想象的审美情趣。

## 68. Mirror with design of three dragons and three rhombuses

Late Warring States Period

Diameter: 16cm, Thickness: 0.3cm, Weight: 204g

Transferred by Xiejiaji District Public Security Bureau in Huainan City in November, 2018

The mirror is round in shape. It has a bridge-shaped knob on an overlaid round base. The outside of the knob base is adorned with a broad band with concave surface. The outside of the broad band is adorned with a band of raised bow string formed by slender line. The ground motif is the design of cloud and thunder. The major motif is the decorative patterns of three dragons spaced in three rhombuses. Each dragon has a small head turning, angry eyes, an open mouth with a protruding tongue, short horns on the upper part of the head that approach the band of raised bow string on the outside of the knob base, a long crooked neck, a foreleg stepping on the rim of the mirror and the wings on the front and back that interlace with the adjacent design of rhombus in the shape of an S. The broad rim is unadorned and is narrow and flat. The edge of the rim rolls.

The dragon design on the mirrors with dragon design come in a variety of shapes. The patterns of three dragons or four dragons are often divided with the leaf design or the rhombus design. But the fact that the spaced design of leaf or rhombus can be combined by interlacing, surrounding and contrasting with the dragon design as a well-arranged whole, all point to the high skill and amazing aesthetic of the ancient craftsmen of the bronzes in the late Warring States Period.

## 69. 单线连弧纹镜

战国晚期
直径 14.4 厘米，厚 0.3 厘米，重 230 克
本馆旧藏

圆形。三弦钮，圆钮座。钮座外饰宽带纹。主区饰 11 个单线隆起的内向连弧纹。宽缘，卷沿。镜残有修。直径

较本馆藏另一面同类镜直径稍大，两镜时代大致相同。

## 69. Mirror with design of linked arcs formed by single line

Late Warring States Period
Diameter: 14.4cm, Thickness: 0.3cm, Weight: 230g
Collection of Huainan Museum

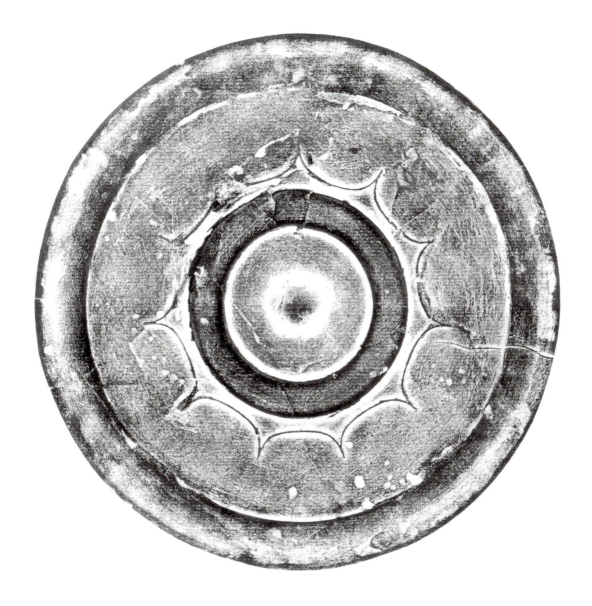

The mirror is round in shape. It has a knob with design of three bow strings on a round base. A broad band adorns the outside of the base. The major motif is eleven linked arcs inward formed by single line. It has a broad rim rolling upward. The mirror was once broken and repaired. The mirror is bigger in diameter than the mirror with the same design collected in Huainan Museum and is of the same date.

## 70. 羽状纹镜

战国

直径 8.2 厘米，厚 0.15 厘米，重 46 克

2018 年 11 月征集入藏

圆形。小弦钮，方钮座，钮座呈双层凹弧面方框。镜面满饰羽状纹。近缘处饰一周细弦纹。宽平缘。

此镜的宽平缘很少见，模印的羽状纹造型粗壮，具有早期羽状纹的特点。纯羽状纹镜发现的很少，长沙楚墓出土的铜镜（M1678:1）❶与此镜相似，时代应在战国中期晚段。

❶ 湖南省博物馆、湖南省文物考古研究所、长沙市博物馆、长沙市文物考古研究所：《长沙楚墓》，文物出版社，2000年。

## 70. Mirror with feather-like design

Warring States Period
Diameter: 8.2cm, Thickness: 0.15cm, Weight: 46g
Collected in November, 2018

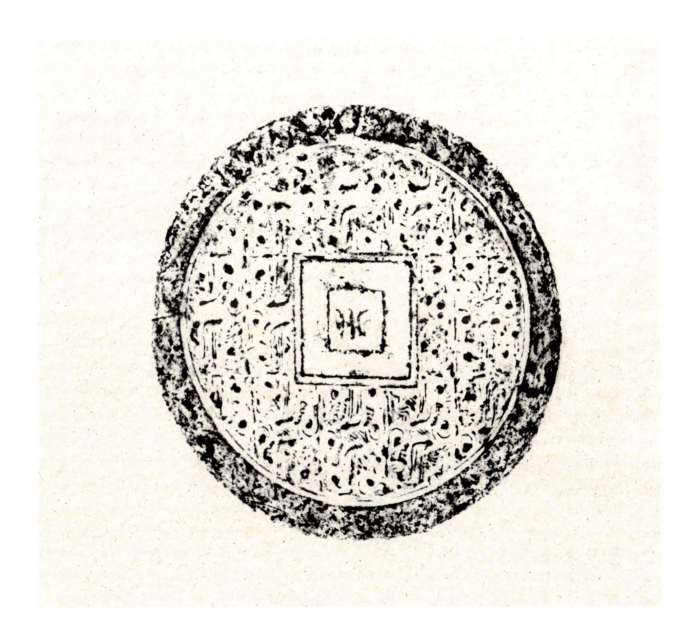

The mirror is round in shape. It has a small knob with design of three bow strings on a square base with two-layer concave surface. The surface of the mirror is full of feather-like patterns. A band of slender bow string approaches the rim of the mirror. The rim is broad and flat.

The broad and flat rim on this mirror is rarely seen. The feather-like pattern molded is in a strong shape and shares the features of the early feather-like pattern. The mirrors with only feather-like pattern were found in small numbers. The bronze mirror with number M1678:1[1], similar to this one, dating from the late period of the middle Warring States Period, was unearthed in the tomb of the Chu ·State in Changsha.

❶ Hunan Museum, Hunan Province Institute of Cultural Relics and Historical Relics and Archaeology, Changsha Museum. (Eds.), Tombs of the Chu State in Changsha City. Cultural Relics Press, 2000.

## 71. 八宽带连弧纹镜

战国晚期

直径 16.8 厘米，厚 0.1 厘米，重 243 克

2018 年 11 月征集入藏

圆形。三弦钮。钮外饰凹面宽圈带纹，卷云纹地上饰八凹面宽带连弧纹。窄平缘。卷云纹大小不一，不甚规整，八连弧纹没有叠压在卷云纹上，故每个卷云纹图案均是完整的，由此判断该镜是整模制范，而非拼范，同类镜馆藏中有 2 面。此镜的宽圈带纹和连弧纹的凹弧面上有蓝色残留物，疑为当时的填彩。

## 71. Mirror with design of eight linked arcs formed by broad band

Late Warring States Period
Diameter: 16.8cm, Thickness: 0.1cm, Weight: 243g
Collected in November, 2018

The mirror is round in shape. It has a knob with design of three bow strings. The outside of the knob is adorned with a broad band with concave surface. There is the design of eight linked arcs formed by broad band with concave surface on the ground motif of patterns of cirrus cloud. The rim is narrow and flat. The patterns of cirrus cloud are not of uniform size and are not neat. Each pattern of cirrus cloud is taken as a whole, for the design of eight linked arcs are not overlaid on the patterns of cirrus cloud. It is deduced that the mirror was cast in the whole mold rather than in pieces. There are two mirrors of this kind in the museum. Some remains of blue can be seen on the concave surfaces of the broad band and the design of linked arcs of this mirror and they may be the pigments fillings on the mirror.

## 72. 变形兽纹镜

战国晚期
直径 12.9 厘米，厚 0.3 厘米，重 130 克
本馆旧藏

　　圆形。三弦钮，圆钮座。钮座外饰一周凹弧面宽带纹和一周弦纹。主区以羽状纹为地，上饰五个变形兽纹。兽纹呈几何图案状，尾部成如意云头，身部呈"C"形弯曲。缘处以弦纹为栏，宽素缘上卷。

　　此类变形兽纹镜发现较少，湖南常德德山楚墓出土一面，比此镜略大。这种变形兽纹十分夸张，几乎看不到兽纹的特征，已经变成几何纹和花草纹，十分耐人寻味。

## 72. Mirror with design of stylized beasts

Late Warring States Period
Diameter: 12.9cm, Thickness: 0.3cm, Weight: 130g
Collection of Huainan Museum

The mirror is round in shape. It has a knob with design of three bow strings on a round base. Outside the base are a broad band with concave surface and a band of string pattern. The ground is decorated with feather-like pattern as ground motif and five stylized animal patterns. The animal pattern has a geometry-shaped head, a tail with S-shaped cloud design and a C-shaped body. The edge of the mirror is adorned with a band of string design that serves as a fence. The mirror has a broad rim without design rolling upward.

It is rare to find the mirrors with design of stylized beasts. The mirror with the same design, but a little bigger, was once unearthed in the tomb of the Chu State in Deshan, Changde City, Hunan Province. The exaggerated pattern of stylized beasts holds no features of animal pattern and is in the shape of geometric pattern and the design of flower and leaf, which is very interesting.

## 73. 变形四兽四叶镜

战国晚期
直径 14.1 厘米，厚 0.4 厘米，重 89 克
2018 年 11 月征集入藏

圆形。小三弦钮，双层凹弧面宽圈带钮座。羽状地纹上环绕钮座饰四只变形动物纹，夸张变形，几乎看不出动物本身的细部特征，兽首仅有一个长方形的圆弧面，兽首伸向镜缘，圆涡状的身体贴于圆形钮座，细长尾内卷，尾内有羽毛状绳纹，尾端生出一扁叶状花纹。宽素缘上卷，平沿。

变形兽纹是战国晚期铜镜中出现的新品种，把动物变形成图案式的抽象形象，似乎反映了古人审美中精神层面的取向。这种变形动物纹由何种纹饰演化而来，有螭纹变形、鸟纹变形、狐纹变形等各种观点，从已发表的资料看，变形兽纹不是某一种动物演化而来，有些变形兽纹保留了龙首、狐首的简单特征。

## 73. Mirror with design of four stylized beasts and four leaves

Late Warring States Period
Diameter: 14.1cm, Thickness: 0.4cm, Weight: 89g
Collected in November, 2018

The mirror is round in shape. It has a small knob with design of three bow strings on a base in a shape of overlaid broad bands with concave surface. On the ground motif with feather-like pattern is four exaggeratedly stylized beasts encircling the knob base. The features of the beasts could not be identified in detail. Each beast has a head that is only a rectangle arc and extends to the rim of the mirror, a body that is whorl-shaped against the round knob base and a long thin tail that rolls inwards. Its tail is adorned with design of feather-like rope and at the end of the tail is a leaf design. The broad rim of the mirror, with a flat edge, is unadorned and rolls up.

The design of stylized beast was a new decorative pattern of bronze mirrors of the late Warring States Period. It should reflect the spiritual orientation of the ancient aesthetic that the beast pattern was stylized to the abstract pattern. But what did the design of stylized beast change from? There are various viewpoints, including the design of stylized hornless dragon, the design of stylized bird and the design of stylized fox. Based on the published articles, the design of stylized beast was not changed from a particular animal. Some designs of stylized beasts hold the simple features of a dragon head or a fox head.

## 74. 宽圈带纹镜

战国晚期

直径 18.3 厘米，厚 0.4 厘米，重 367 克

2018 年 11 月征集入藏

　　圆形。三弦钮，方钮座。钮外饰凹弧面宽圈带纹。三弦钮制作精细，圈带纹模制清晰。方钮座似预先模制好嵌入镜模，浇铸成整体。窄平缘。

　　此类镜的定名有宽圈带纹、重圈带纹等，以区别细线弦纹，本书收录的同类铜镜，还是习惯上以宽圈带纹命名。

## 74. Mirror with design of broad band

Late Warring States Period
Diameter: 18.3cm, Thickness: 0.4cm, Weight: 367g
Collected in November, 2018

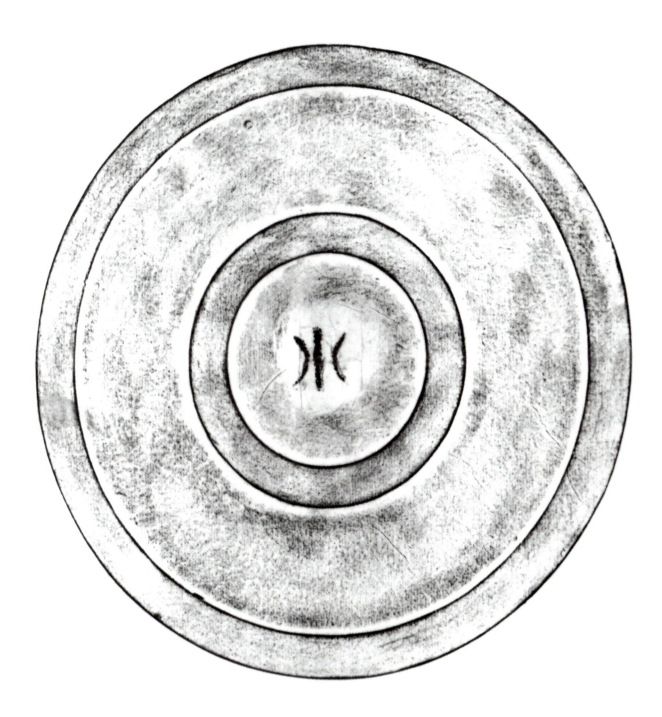

The mirror is round in shape. It has a knob with design of three bow strings. The outside of the knob is adorned with a broad band with concave surface. The rim is narrow and flat. The knob with design of three bow strings is exquisitely cast and the band design is clearly molded. It is suspected that the mirror was cast after the cast square base was inserted into the mirror mold.

The design of broad band is also known as the design of string formed by broad band or the design of duplicate broad band, to distinguish it from the design of string formed by thin line. This kind of mirror in the book still follows the name of the design of broad band.

**75. 三龙镜**

战国晚期

直径 16.3 厘米，厚 0.7 厘米，重 305 克

2010 年 9 月淮南市谢家集公安分局移交

　　圆形。三弦钮，云雷纹圆钮座。钮座。外饰绞索纹和凹弧面宽圈带纹各一周。主区纹饰以云雷纹铺地，三条龙环绕钮座均匀分布，龙头部靠近镜缘，头顶后部伸出长弯角，大眼，张口吐舌，长舌下勾，作回首反顾状，身躯右旋，两足前后伸张，前足踏于镜缘，后足勾缠于菱形纹中。身躯动感极强，与菱形纹勾连交错。主纹两侧以高凸弦纹和栉齿纹为廓。镜缘略凹弧，卷缘。

## 75. Mirror with design of three dragons

Late Warring States period

Diameter: 16.3cm, Thickness: 0.7cm, Weight: 305g

Transferred by Xiejiaji District Public Security Bureau in Huainan City in September, 2010

The mirror is round in shape. It has a knob with design of three bow strings on a round base with design of cloud and thunder. The outside of the knob base is adorned with a band of twisted rope pattern and a broad band with concave surface. The mirror is decorated with the design of cloud and thunder as ground motif and design of three dragons around the knob base. The dragons look backward, with their heads near the rim, their mouths open and their tongues protruding. Their bodies turn vividly to the right. Their forefeet step on the rim and their hindfeet interlock with the rhombus patterns. The dragons have big eyes and long horns. The dragons are interlocked vividly with the rhombus patterns. The design of raised bow string and the fine-toothed design are served as a fence on either side of the main decorative pattern. The rim with slightly concave surface rolls up.

## 76. 双宽圈带纹镜

战国晚期

直径 21.9 厘米，厚 0.4 厘米，重 471 克

2018 年 11 月淮南市谢家集公安分局移交

圆形。三弦钮。钮及钮座似预先铸好后嵌入镜模浇铸而成。钮外、镜面中区饰凹弧面宽圈带纹。素地上残留有朱砂颜料，可能是有意装饰覆盖上去的，不像是包裹铜镜的残留物，宽圈带弦纹上没有残留颜料。窄平缘。

此镜形制较大，本书收录的同类镜有 6 面，其中直径逾 20 厘米的有 2 面。长沙战国墓出土了一面直径 17.8 厘米的同类镜，根据同墓出土的遗物判断是秦将白起拔郢后的秦墓。其镜的钮座上也有小方座印痕，也似为预先制后嵌入，与本书收录的同类镜在制作工艺上相同。

## 76. Mirror with design of two broad bands

Late Warring States Period
Diameter: 21.9cm, Thickness: 0.4cm, Weight: 471g
Transferred by Xiejiaji District Public Security Bureau in Huainan City in November, 2018

The mirror is round in shape. It has a knob with design of three bow strings. The outside of the knob and the middle of the mirror are adorned with the design of broad band with concave surface. It is suspected that the mirror was cast after the cast knob and knob base were inserted into the mirror mold. It is found that some zinnober pigments remain on the plain ground and it is suspected that the pigments were painted on the plain ground, not that they were left from the parcel of the mirror. No remaining pigments are found on the design of string formed by broad band. The rim is narrow and flat.

This mirror is bigger in size. Of the six mirrors of this kind in the book, two have a diameter over 20cm. In Changsha, one mirror of this kind was unearthed in the tomb of the Warring States Period that is deduced to be the tomb of the Qin State in the period after when Bai Qi, a general of the Qin State, conquered Ying City, the capital of the Chu State according to the relics unearthed in the tomb. A small square mold mark is also found on the knob base of the mirror and it is suspected that it was inserted after the casting. The mirror was cast by a similar casting technique to that used for the mirrors of this kind in the book.

## 77. 四凤四叶镜

战国晚期

直径 8.7 厘米，厚 0.2 厘米，重 47 克

2018 年 5 月征集入藏

圆形。小双弦钮，方钮座，钮座呈凹面方格状。纹饰由地纹和主纹构成。地纹由谷纹和三角雷纹、卷云纹组成，十分细密。四凤栖于方形钮座的四角，凤首曲颈回顾，小凤冠直立，振翅，尾部高高翘起，姿态轻盈，造型生动。四凤间近镜缘处各饰一长桃形双层叶片，使整个镜面的纹饰布局均衡、匀称。窄素缘。

四凤四叶镜发现的很少，目前未见著录。此镜虽然不大，却十分精美，惜镜面稍有锈蚀。

## 77. Mirror with design of four phoenixes and four leaves

Late Warring States Period
Diameter: 8.7cm, Thickness: 0.2cm, Weight: 47g
Collected in May, 2018

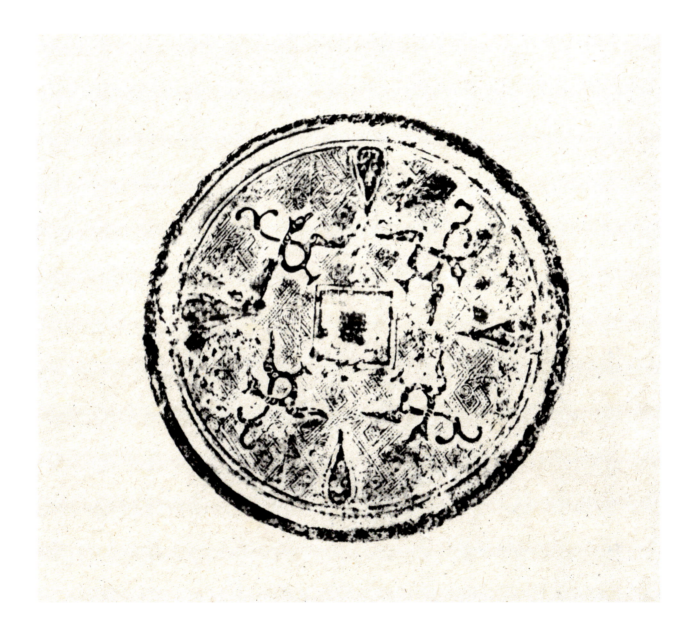

The mirror is round in shape. It has a small knob with design of two bow strings on a square base with concave surface. The decorative patterns consist of the ground motif and the major motif. The fine ground motif is formed with the design of unhusked rice, the design of triangle-shaped thunder and the design of cirrus cloud. The four phoenixes stand at each corner of the square knob base. Each phoenix is in a graceful and vivid shape of its looking back and has a crooked neck, an upturned phoenix comb, flapping wings and a high tail. An overlaid peach-shaped leaf, close to the rim of the mirror, adorns among the phoenixes, which makes the decorative patterns of the mirror show a well-arranged arrangement. The narrow rim of the mirror is unadorned.

The mirrors with design of four phoenixes and four leaves have been found in small numbers and have not been recorded in any book to this day. This mirror, though of small size, was cast exquisitely, but the surface of the mirror was slightly rusted.

## 78. 单线连弧纹镜

战国晚期

直径 14 厘米，厚 0.3 厘米，重 195 克

1972 年 4 月淮南市谢家集区红卫轮窑厂 M4 出土

　　圆形。三弦钮，圆钮座。钮座外饰凹弧面宽圈带纹。主区纹饰是在素地上以镜钮为中心，环绕单线隆起的十一个内向连弧纹，连弧纹线条纤细，弧的曲度平缓。缘边上卷。镜面有铁状锈蚀物，应是镜的附着物所致，在镜缘未锈蚀处可见光亮的镜体。

　　素地单线连弧纹铜镜发现较少。长沙楚墓发现 2 面，其 M838 出土的一面与此镜尺寸、布局基本相同，其时代定在战国楚国晚期早段，即公元前 300 年至公元前 278 年，在白起拔郢之前。淮南这面铜镜镜体轻薄，有明显的早期特征，是本地区所见最早的楚式镜，该镜出土地点是淮南地区出土铜镜数量最多也最集中的区域，由此也证明，该地区在楚国迁都寿春城之前，已经是楚国人活动的区域。

## 78. Mirror with design of linked arcs formed by single line

Late Warring States Period
Diameter: 14cm, Thickness: 0.3cm, Weight: 195g
Unearthed from the Tomb M4 of Hongwei Annular Kiln Works, in Xiejiaji District, Huainan City in April, 1972

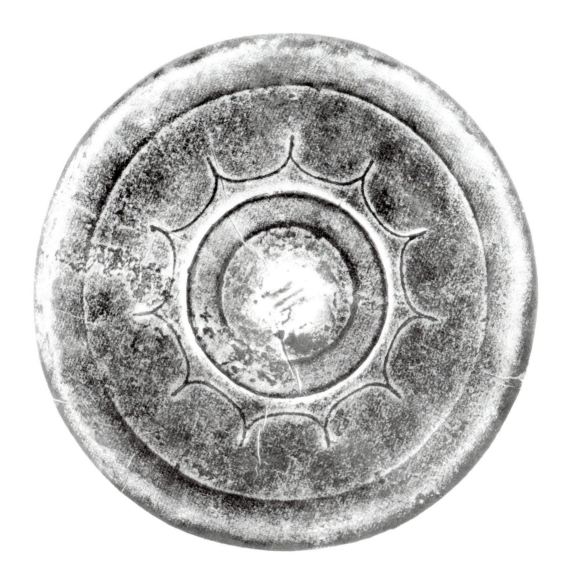

The mirror is round in shape. It has a knob with design of three bow strings on a round base. A broad band with concave surface adorns the outside of the knob. The major motif on the plain ground is eleven linked arcs inward formed by single line around the knob. The line is slender and smooth and the arcs are gently curved. The rim of the mirror rolls upward. Iron-like rust can be seen on the surface of the mirror, and it should be produced by the attachment of the mirror. The gleaming body of the mirror is visible at the unrusted rim.

The mirrors with plain ground and design of linked arcs formed by single line are rarely found. The two mirrors with the same design unearthed in the tombs of Chu State in Changsha City, one of which, unearthed from the tomb M838, is similar to this mirror in size and design and is inferred as the mirror of the early part of the late Chu State in the Warring States Period, the period from 300BC to 278BC before Bai Qi, a general of the Qin State, conquered Ying City, the capital city of the Chu State. The thin-bodied mirror bears the distinctive features of the Chu mirror in early period and is the earliest mirror of the Chu mirror found in Huainan. The area from which the mirror was unearthed, has found bronze mirrors in great numbers. All the evidence proves that the Chu State had conducted activity in this area before moving its capital to Shouchun town.

## 79. 三龙镜

战国晚期
直径 11.7 厘米，厚 0.4 厘米，重 144 克
2018 年 11 月征集入藏

　　圆形。三弦钮，圆钮座。钮座外饰二周单线凸弦纹，弦纹间各饰短斜线纹一周，呈"人"字状排列。纹饰由主纹和地纹组成。地纹由细密的云雷纹和碎粒点状纹组成，模印清晰。主纹是布局均匀的三条龙。龙首上吻部抵钮座外弦纹，小圆目，后角上扬，张口曲颈，腹部向上鼓起，一足蹬踏镜缘，下腹部翻卷盘曲，尾部上卷与相邻的龙勾连，前羽如同尾部一样与相邻的龙尾穿插勾连。宽素缘，卷沿。

　　此镜改变了同期常见的用凹弧面宽圈带纹装饰的做法，仅用弦纹装饰，反映出战国晚期铜镜装饰方法的逐渐改变。此类风格的铜镜，在战国晚期流行区域很广泛，长沙、南阳等地都有较多发现。这也反映出此时的铜镜铸造技术十分普遍，使用人群也同样日趋广泛。

## 79. Mirror with design of three dragons

Late Warring States Period
Diameter: 11.7cm, Thickness: 0.4cm, Weight: 144g
Collected in November, 2018

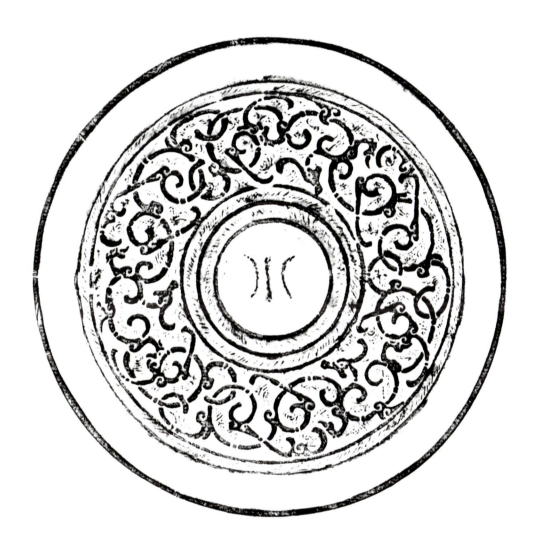

The mirror is round in shape. It has a knob with design of three bow strings on a round base. The outside of the knob base is adorned with two bands of raised bow string design formed by single line. A band of short slanted lines, which is arranged in a shape of "*ren* (man)" character, is spaced between the bands. The decorative patterns consist of the ground motif and the major motif. The ground motif, with clear mold masks, is composed of the fine design of cloud and thunder and the design of tiny spots. The major motif is the well-arranged design of three dragons. The dragons have upper lips close to the string design on the outside of the knob base, small round eyes, horns raising, open mouths, crooked necks, bellies ballooned upwards, one foot stepping on the rim of the mirror, the back part of the body coiled, tails rolled upwards and interlaced with the adjacent dragon and feather at the front part of the body interlaced with the tail of the adjacent dragon. The broad rim is unadorned and rolls up.

This mirror is decorated only with bow string design, rather than the broad band with concave surface of the same period. This mirror shows changes in the decoration of bronze mirrors in the late Warring States Period. Mirrors with the same decorative patterns were in a widespread use in the late Warring States Period and were found in large numbers in Changshang and Nanyang. It tells that the casting technique of bronze mirrors prevailed in that period and the bronze mirrors were in general use.

## 80. 宽圈带纹镜

战国晚期

直径 13.1 厘米，厚 0.3 厘米，重 172 克

2017 年 12 月征集入藏

圆形。小三弦钮。钮外饰一圈凹弧面宽带纹。窄缘，缘边上卷。

## 80. Mirror with design of broad band

Late Warring States Period
Diameter: 13.1cm, Thickness: 0.3cm, Weight: 172g
Collected in December, 2017

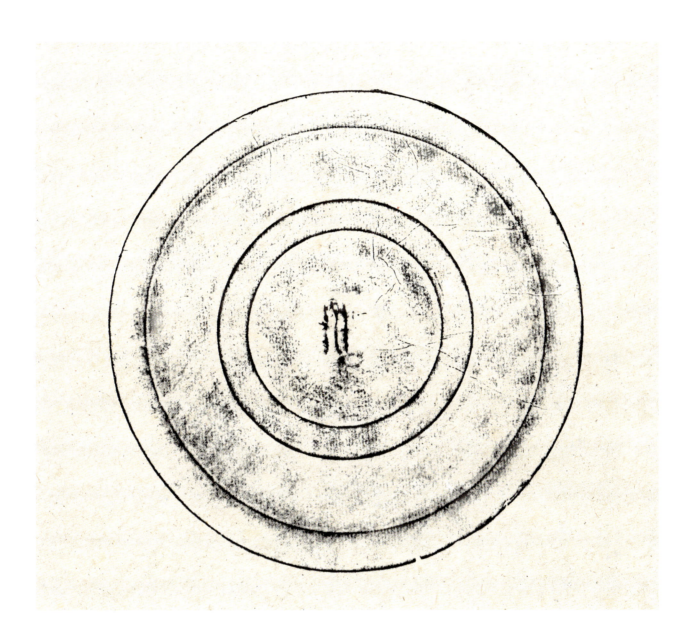

The mirror is round in shape. It has a small knob with design of three bow strings. The outside of the knob is adorned with a broad band with concave surface. The rim of the mirror is narrow and the edge of the rim rolls up.

## 81. 四龙镜

战国晚期

直径 11.6 厘米，厚 0.25 厘米，重 97 克

1982 年 8 月淮南市赖山公社莲花大队出土

　　圆形。三弦钮，圆钮座。钮座外环两周凸弦纹。主区纹饰以云锦纹铺地，地纹上均匀分布四龙纹。龙首靠近缘部，腹部呈"S"形弯曲，作张牙舞爪状，缠绕环转，动感十足。宽素缘，卷沿。此镜地纹与主纹层次分明，四龙造型简洁，为战国楚国晚期典型的龙纹镜。

## 81. Mirror with design of four dragons

Late Warring States Period
Diameter: 11.6cm, Thickness: 0.25cm, Weight: 97g
Unearthed at Lianhua Brigade, Laishan Commune, Huainan City in August, 1982

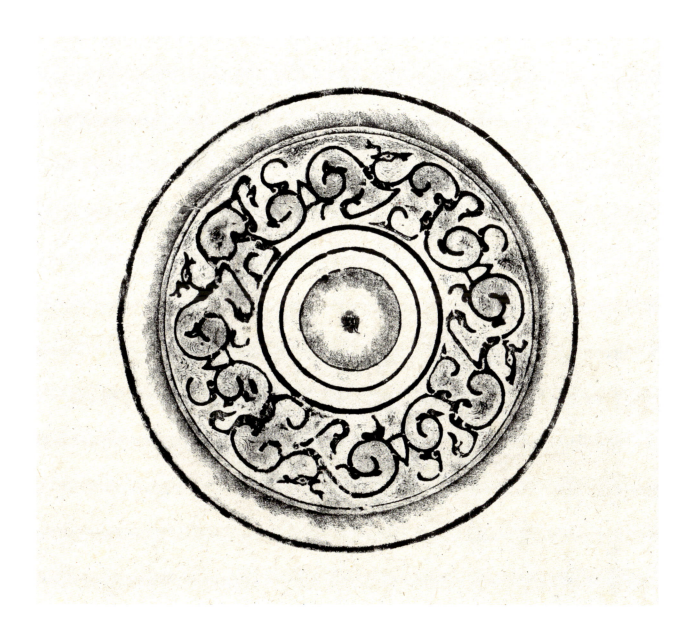

The mirror is round in shape. It has a knob with design of three bow strings on a round base. On the outside of the base are two bands of raised string design. The main decoration is adorned with pattern of Yun Brocade as the ground motif and design of four dragons. The dragon has a head near the rim and an S-shaped body, and makes a threatening gesture. The four dragons are vividly intertwined in a circle. A broad rim is unadorned and rolls. The mirror, with its distinction between ground motif and major motif and simple pattern of four dragons, is inferred to be a typical mirror with dragon design of the late Chu State in the Warring States Period.

## 82. 八虺纹镜

战国晚期
直径 12.1 厘米，厚 0.3 厘米，重 103 克
2018 年 11 月征集入藏

　　圆形。三弦钮，圆钮座。钮座外饰宽圈带纹、单线凸弦纹各一周。镜面满铺云雷地纹。主纹为变形虺纹，虺纹结构复杂，身体盘曲错结，如蔓枝状相互勾连。八虺纹分二层，靠镜缘处的四虺首如蝌蚪状向下伸出，靠近钮座的四虺首向上伸出；八虺的身躯相互勾连，但基本分区是明确的。近缘处饰二周单线凸弦纹。宽素缘上卷。

　　此镜的纹饰造型十分少见，虺纹身体短粗，风格上近似龙纹的造型和布局，只是结构更加复杂。

## 82. Mirror with design of eight serpents

Late Warring States Period
Diameter: 12.1cm, Thickness: 0.3 cm, Weight: 103g
Collected in November, 2018

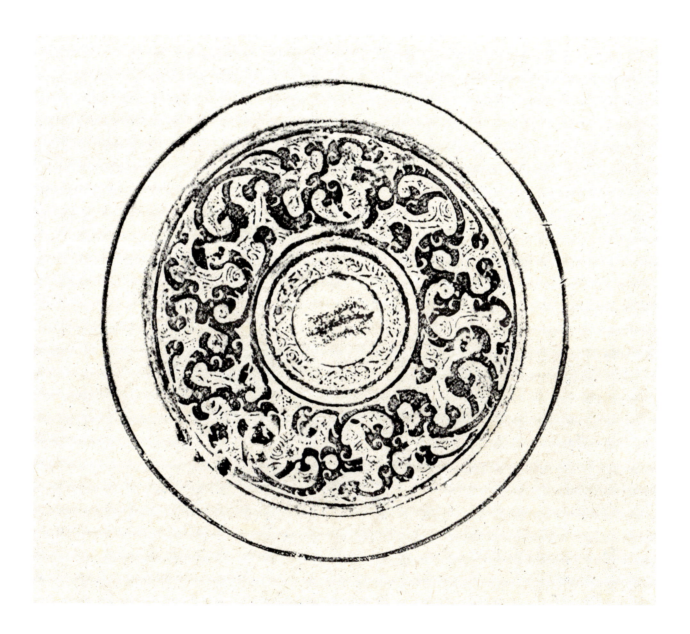

The mirror is round in shape. It has a knob with design of three bow strings on a round base. The outside of the knob base is adorned with a broad band and a band of raised bow string formed by single line. The back of the mirror is decorated with the ground motif with design of cloud and thunder. The major motif is the design of stylized serpent. The decorative patterns of serpent are in the complex shape of twisted and interlaced branches. The eight serpents are divided into two layers, the heads of the four close to the rim of the mirror extending downwards as tadpoles and the heads of the other four close to the knob base extending upwards. The bodies of the eight serpents are connected to each other, but the section is clearly visible. Two bands of raised bow string design formed by single line are near the rim of the mirror. The broad rim is unadorned and rolls up.

The decorative patterns of this mirror are rarely seen. The design of serpent, with a short and strong body, is similar in shape and arrangement to the design of dragon, but more complicated in structure.

## 83. 四山十二叶镜

战国晚期

直径9.7厘米，厚0.25厘米，重46克

2018年11月征集入藏

　　圆形。小三弦钮，方钮座，钮座呈凹弧面双层方框。纹饰由地纹和主纹组成。羽状地纹造型和线条粗犷。方形钮座四角各伸出一组叶片，呈十字交叉分布，每组叶片间以绚带纹枝条连接。在四个山字中间一竖的右上侧，各饰一叶片，枝干在山字底下斜向与钮座角处的叶片相连接，形成四角星状。四个左旋的山字纹底部与钮座平行，山字

二边竖笔顶部向内呈锐角伸出。沿口弧起，窄平。

　　此镜的钮和钮座都很小，地纹的装饰非常自然随意，有早期山字纹铜镜的特征。从已公开的资料看，潜山战国墓出土的同类型山字镜，其山字纹右旋，直径12.9厘米，从特征上看要晚于此镜。此镜是已知的十二叶山字纹镜中，直径最小的一面。

## 83. Mirror with inscription of four *"shan"* characters and design of twelve leaves

Late Warring States Period

Diameter: 9.7cm, Thickness: 0.25cm, Weight: 46g

Collected in November, 2018

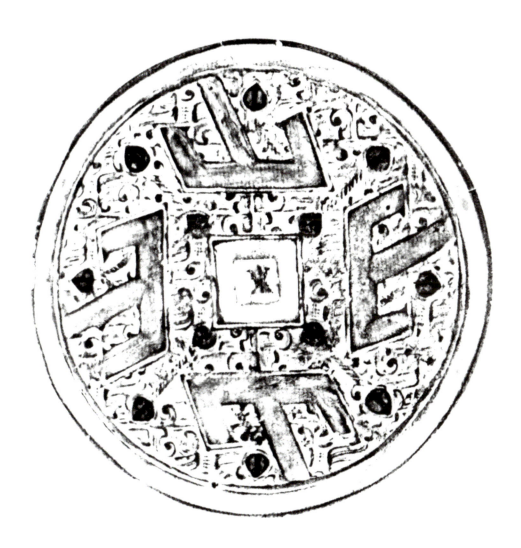

The mirror is round in shape. It has a small knob with design of three bow strings on an overlaid square base formed by broad band with concave surface. The decorative patterns consist of the ground motif and the major motif. The ground motif of feather-like patterns are rough in shape and formed by coarse lines. A group of leaves extends out from each corner of the square knob base in each direction of cross. Each group of leaves are joined by the branches with rope design. On the upper right side of the middle vertical stroke of each character is a leaf design. The branches below the characters are slanted to meet the leaves on the corners of the knob base, which is shown in the shape of four-pointed star. The inscription of four *"shan"* characters is inclined towards the left and their bottom sides are parallel to the bottom sides of the knob base. The vertical strokes of both sides of the characters turn inwards at the top and extend in the shape of closed angle. The rim of the mirror has an arc and is narrow and flat.

The mirror has a small knob and a small knob base. It is adorned with the natural ground motif. The mirror holds the features of the early bronze mirrors with inscription of *"shan"* characters. According to the published articles, there is the mirror with the same decorative patterns unearthed in the tomb of the Warring States Period in Qianshan. The mirror is in diameter of 12.9cm and is adorned with the inscription of *"shan"* characters inclined towards the right. Based on the features, that mirror is dated later than this one. This mirror has the smallest diameter among all the mirrors with inscription of *"shan"* characters and design of twelve leaves.

圆形。小三弦钮，圆钮座。钮座外饰一圈凹弧面宽圈带纹。宽缘，缘边上卷。

## 84. Mirror with design of broad band

Late Warring States Period
Diameter: 11.9cm, Thickness: 0.2cm, Weight: 89g
Transferred by Xiejiaji District Public Security Bureau in Huainan City in November, 2018

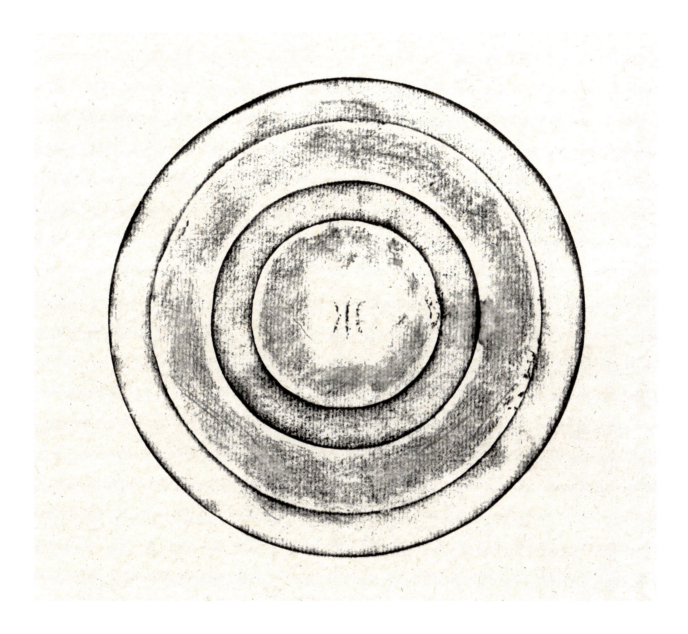

The mirror is round in shape. It has a small knob with design of three bow strings on a round base. The outside of the knob base is adorned with a broad band with concave surface. The rim of the mirror is broad and the rim rolls up at the edge.

## 85. 四山八叶镜

战国晚期
直径 11.2 厘米，厚 0.45 厘米，重 105 克
2018 年 2 月征集入藏

圆形。小三弦钮，钮座为双层凹弧面宽带围成的方框。地纹为羽状纹，主纹是四山字纹与四组连贯式的两叶相间环列。方形钮座四角处伸出十字形排列的双层花叶片，山字左旋，底边与钮座边平行。素卷缘，微弧，短平沿。

四山八叶镜是山字镜类当中发现数量最多的品种，从长江南部到北端的吉林市都有出土，说明此类镜的铸造、使用、流传，都很广泛。

## 85. Mirror with inscription of four "*shan*" characters and design of eight leaves

Late Warring States Period
Diameter: 11.2cm, Thickness: 0.45cm, Weight: 105g
Collected in February, 2018

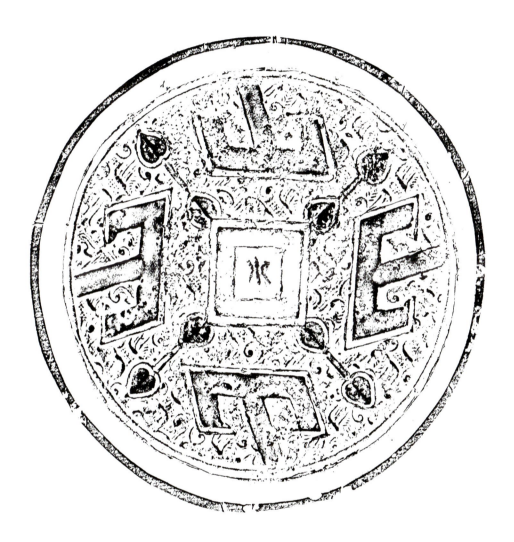

The mirror is round in shape. It has a small knob with design of three bow strings on a square base formed by broad band with concave surface. The ground motif is the feather-like patterns. The major motif is an alternate arrangement of four "*shan*" characters and four groups of two coherent leaves. The overlaid leaves extend from each corner of the square knob base in each direction of cross. The inscription of "*shan*" characters is inclined towards the left and their bottom sides are parallel to the bottom sides of the knob base. The rim rolls and is unadorned. The rim has a slight arc and the edge of the rim is short and flat.

The mirrors with inscription of four "*shan*" characters and design of eight leaves have been found in large numbers among the mirrors with inscription of "*shan*" characters. They were unearthed from the south of the Changjiang River to Jilin City in northern China. All indicate that the mirrors of this kind were cast and in use over a wide area.

　　圆形。弦钮，圆钮座。钮有修。钮座外饰一周凹面宽带纹。纹饰由地纹和主纹组合而成。地纹为云雷纹。地纹之上饰八个内向宽带连弧纹，将镜面分成内外两区，两区各饰四龙纹：内区龙向右运动，外区龙向左运动，内外区龙上下勾连。龙口大张，小圆目，前足伸，后足踏镜缘或连弧纹，尾部翻卷。此镜以三层纹饰构成了一幅细密繁缛的浅浮雕图案，是战国晚期楚镜之佳品。

## 86. Mirror with design of eight dragons and eight linked arcs

Late Warring States Period
Diameter: 16.3cm, Thickness: 0.5cm, Weight: 326g
Collection of Huainan Museum

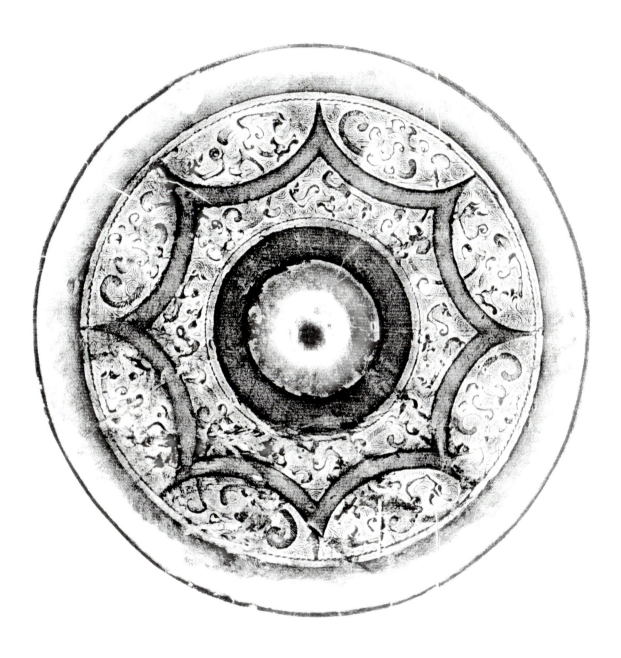

The mirror is round in shape. It has a repaired knob with string design on a round base. On the outside of the base is a broad band with concave surface. The decorative patterns contain the ground motif and the major motif. The ground is decorated with design of cloud and thunder as ground motif. The surface is divided by the broad band of eight linked arcs oriented inwards into two parts: the inner and the outer. Each section is adorned with design of four dragons, moving to the right in the inner part and moving to the left in the outer part. The dragons in both sections are interlaced. The dragons, with open mouths, small round eyes and a rolling tails, extend their front paws outward and keep their back paws at the rim or arc pattern. The mirror, with its exquisite decoration of a three-layer bas relief, is a treasure of bronze mirrors of the Chu State in the late Warring States Period.

　　圆形。小三弦钮，方钮座，钮座是以宽带凹弧面围成双层方框。纹饰由主纹和地纹组成。羽状地纹模印精细，几乎看不到拼接痕；卷羽纹和长羽纹、谷纹组合成一个单元，线条纤细。方形钮座四角各伸出两片由绹带纹连接的叶片，叶片被绹带纹环绕，叶面出筋，成凹弧面，十分精致。四个左旋山字纹，底边平行于方形钮座，山字外廓各边为双层，中间一竖为单层，这种装饰风格在战国晚期山字纹镜中被普遍使用，为什么中间一竖用单层？是工匠便于制模形成的，还是审美的要求？需要进一步理解。近缘处饰一周单线弦纹。窄缘，微弧。

　　此镜纹饰布局均衡对称，纹饰的模印、浇铸精细，是山字纹镜中的上乘之作。

## 87. Mirror with inscription of four "*shan*" characters and design of eight leaves

Late Warring States Period
Diameter: 13.6cm, Thickness: 0.45cm, Weight: 167g
Transferred by Xiejiaji District Public Security Bureau in Huainan City in November, 2018

The mirror is round in shape. It has a small knob with design of three bow strings on an overlaid square base formed by broad band with concave surface. The decorative patterns consist of the ground motif and the major motif. The ground motif of feather-like patterns were delicately molded so that the joint marks are barely visible. Each section is composed of the long-feather-like pattern, the pattern of rolling feather and the design of unhusked rice, all formed by slender lines. Two leaves that are joined with the rope design, extend from each corner of the square knob base. Each leaf is encircled with the rope design. The exquisite leaf has raised vein and is in the shape of concave surface. The inscription of four "*shan*" characters is inclined towards the left and their bottom sides are parallel to the bottom sides of the square knob base. The middle vertical stroke of "*shan*" character is formed with single line. The vertical strokes of character on both sides are formed with double lines. The decorative style of the character was in common use on the bronze mirrors with inscription of "*shan*" character of the late Warring States Period. Why is the middle vertical stroke formed with single line? Because it is easily molded or perhaps it was taken for aesthetic reasons. The answer requires further research. A band of bow string formed by single line approaches the rim of the mirror. The rim is narrow and has a slight arc.

This mirror, with well-arranged layout and delicate casting marks of decorative patterns, is a treasure of the mirrors with inscription of "*shan*" characters.

## 88. 三凤三菱镜

战国晚期

直径 11.4 厘米，厚 0.5 厘米，重 88 克

2018 年 5 月征集入藏

　　圆形。三弦钮，圆钮座。钮座外饰云雷纹。钮座围以凹弧面宽圈带纹，宽圈带外饰一周短斜线纹、单线凸弦纹。镜面中区地纹为云纹，与钮座外的云雷纹不同，这种装饰手法比较少见，一般是满铺地纹，包括钮座区在内同样铺饰，然后在上面装饰主纹。主纹为三凤与三菱相间环列。凤立二菱纹之间，勾回首，圆目，两翼勾卷，与缠枝状菱形纹交互叠压，凤的身体占据大部分镜面。宽素缘。

　　此镜与河北省博物馆收藏的同类镜在纹饰布局上基本相同，但其纹饰已开始二线分离，向汉代风格过渡。而此镜线条遒劲，是战国晚期的上乘作品。

## 88. Mirror with design of three phoenixes and three rhombuses

Late Warring States Period
Diameter: 11.4cm, Thickness: 0.5cm, Weight: 88g
Collected in May, 2018

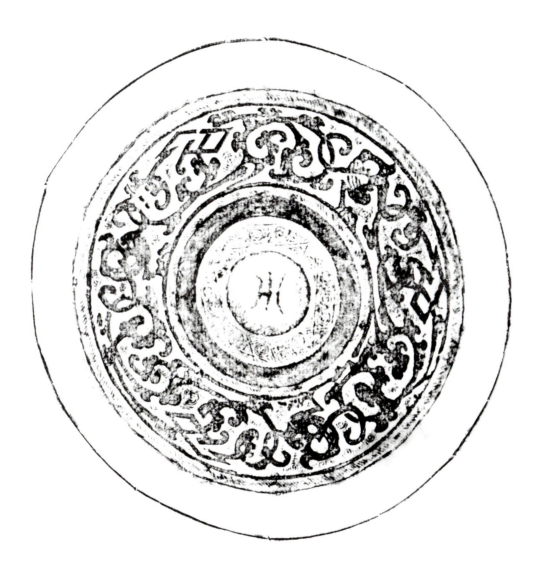

The mirror is round in shape. It has a knob with design of three bow strings on a round base. The outside of the knob base is adorned with design of cloud and thunder. On the outside of the knob base is a broad band with concave surface, a band of short slanted lines and a band of raised bow string formed by single line. The middle surface of the mirror is adorned with the ground motif of the cloud design, which differs from the design of cloud and thunder on the outside of the knob base. The decorative style of this mirror is rarely seen. It is generally seen that the surface of the mirror is full of the ground motif, including the knob base, and the major motif is on the ground motif. The major motif is an alternating arrangement of three phoenixes and three rhombuses. Each phoenix stands between the rhombuses. Each phoenix has its back turned, round eyes and two wings that roll and are interlaced and overlaid with branch-shaped rhombuses, holding most part of the surface of the mirror. The broad rim is unadorned.

This mirror is similar in decorative arrangement to the one in the Hebei Museum. But the decorative patterns of that mirror are formed by two separated lines and show the transition to the style of the Han Dynasty. This mirror, with its powerful lines, is a treasure of the bronze mirrors of the late Warring States Period.

## 89. 三虺三菱镜

战国晚期

直径 9.6 厘米，厚 0.2 厘米，重 58 克

2018 年 11 月征集入藏

　　圆形。小三弦钮，圆钮座。钮座外饰凹面宽圈带纹。云雷纹为地，主纹为三虺和三菱形相间排列。虺纹身体简化成由三个方向不一的"C"字形组成，虺首居中，下勾，身体两侧与相邻的菱形纹相勾连。宽素缘，卷沿。本馆收藏有三虺三菱镜 3 面。此镜与其他 2 面镜相比，时代最晚，虺纹和菱形纹已从单实线向双线转化，这也是战国晚期最晚段的蟠虺纹铜镜了。此类镜流行时间较长，到西汉早中期墓葬中都有出土。

## 89. Mirror with design of three serpents and three rhombuses

Late Warring States Period
Diameter: 9.6cm, Thickness: 0.2cm, Weight: 58g
Collected in November, 2018

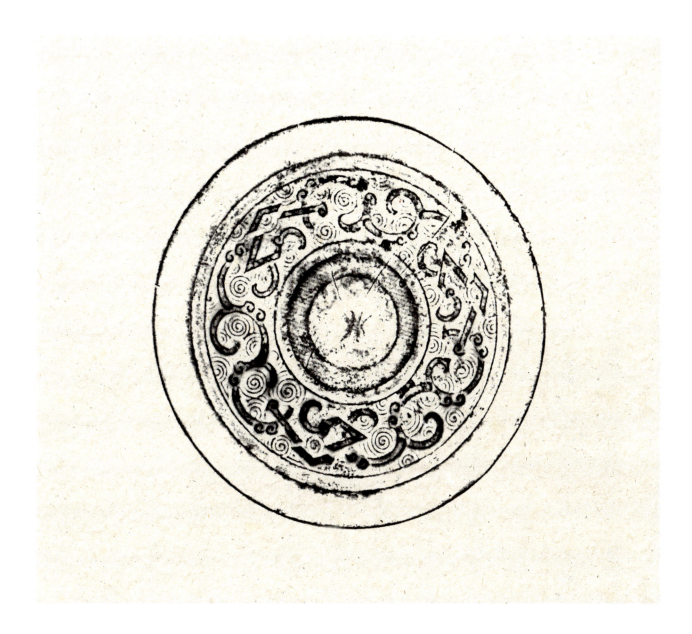

The mirror is round in shape. It has a small knob with design of three bow strings on a round base. The outside of the knob base is adorned with a broad band with concave surface. The ground motif is the design of cloud and thunder. The major motif is an alternating arrangement of three serpents and three rhombuses. Each serpent is in the shape of a combination of three C-shaped in different directions. Each serpent has a head in the middle that bends downwards and the bodies on either side of the head that are interlaced with the adjacent designs of rhombuses. The broad rim is unadorned and rolls. In all, three mirrors with design of three serpents and three rhombuses are in the museum. This mirror is later than the others. The decorative patterns of the serpent design and the rhombus design on this mirror are formed by double lines instead of single line. The mirrors of this kind dates from the late period of the late Warring States Period and prevailed for a long period. They were unearthed in the tombs of the early and middle Western Han Dynasty.

## 90. 四叶镜

战国晚期

直径 11.6 厘米，厚 0.4 厘米，重 115 克

1986 年 12 月于淮南市谢家集区施家湖乡打击盗墓收缴

圆形。三弦钮，圆钮座。钮座外饰凸弦纹一周，且与主题纹饰四叶纹相连。四叶周围满铺羽状纹，每个羽状纹呈长方形，上下左右反复排列成四方连续式。钮座外十字形方向伸出四叶，叶有粗柄，叶面分叉呈花苞形状，中间叶下有横切的弧线。羽状地近缘处以凸弦纹为栏。宽素缘，卷边。

羽状纹地叶纹镜中，四叶纹镜发现的较多，叶形的变化也最丰富。叶纹镜在战国中期出现。此镜属细涡粒状羽状纹上饰四叶，较变形粗羽状纹要早，时间在战国晚期楚国迁都寿春之前。

## 90. Mirror with design of four leaves

Late Warring States Period

Diameter: 11.6cm, Thickness: 0.4cm, Weight: 115g

Got from an operation against tomb robbers in Shijiahu Town, Xiejiaji District, Huainan City in December, 1986

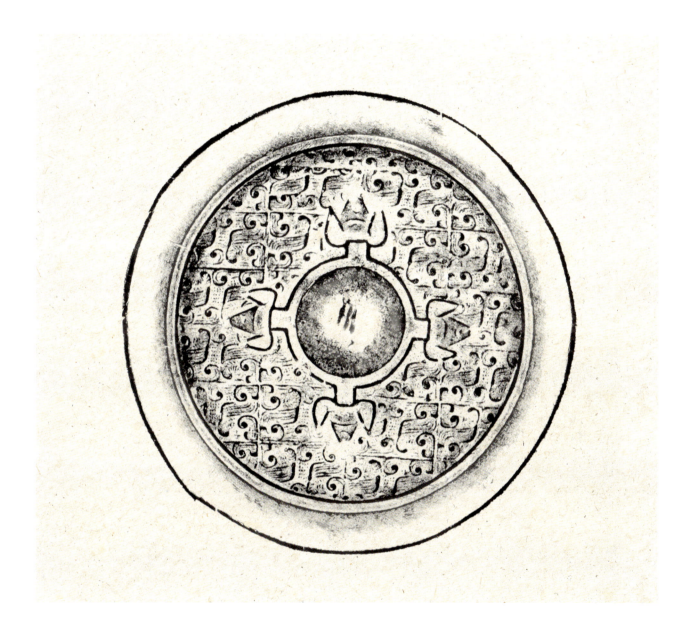

The mirror is round in shape. It has a knob with design of three bow strings on a round base. On the outside of the base is a band of raised bow string pattern, joining to the major motif of four-leaf pattern. Around four-leaf designs are feather-like patterns in a rectangle shape oriented in four directions. The four-leaf design extends out of the base in each direction of cross. Each leaf has a sturdy petiole and is in the shape of bud. Under the middle leaf is decorated with the cross-cut arc pattern. A band of raised string pattern serves as a fence between the ground motif and the rim. The mirror has a broad rim that rolls upward and is unadorned.

The mirrors with design of four leaves are commonly found in the bronze mirrors with feather-like pattern as the ground motif and leaf design, with a variety of leaf shapes. The mirrors with leaf design appeared in the middle Warring States Period. The feather-like pattern on this mirror is in the shape of granulated fine whorl and predates the mirror with stylized heavy feather-like pattern, so the mirror is inferred to be the bronze mirror of the Chu State before it moved its capital to Shouchun town in the late Warring States Period.

## 91. 三龙三叶镜

战国晚期
直径 14.3 厘米，厚 0.5 厘米，重 208 克
2019 年 12 月征集入藏

圆形。小三弦钮，圆钮座。钮座饰云雷纹和绳纹各一周，座外饰凹弧面宽圈带纹和单线凸弦纹各一周。中区纹饰由地纹和主纹组成。地纹为细密的三角云雷纹，模印清晰。主纹以三个低矮的花苞状草叶纹将镜面分隔为三区，每区饰一龙纹。龙首居中，曲颈前伸，张口獠牙，龙角很长，向后伸至镜缘，龙身卷曲得很夸张，呈"S"状翻向

镜缘，一足蹬踏镜缘，前后羽翼向两侧交叉翻转盘曲到小草叶之上。宽素缘。

此镜模印精致，纹饰布局匀称，繁而不乱，动感强烈，十分美观。以叶纹分隔的龙纹镜，在长沙和南阳都有发现，但一般草叶纹较大。此镜的草叶纹高度不及中区的一半，很少见。

## 91. Mirror with design of three dragons and three leaves

Late Warring States Period
Diameter: 14.3cm, Thickness: 0.5cm, Weight: 208g
Collected in December, 2019

The mirror is round in shape. It has a small knob with design of three bow strings on a round base. The knob base is adorned with a band of design of cloud and thunder and a band of rope design. The outside of the knob base is adorned with a broad band with concave surface and a band of raised bow string design formed by single line. The decorative patterns consist of the ground motif and the major motif. The ground motif is the fine triangle-shaped design of cloud and thunder, with clear mold marks. The major motif is divided into three sections by three short bud-like leaves. Each section is adorned with the dragon design. The dragon has a head in the middle, a crooked neck extending forward, an open mouth with buckteeth, long horns extending backwards to the rim of the mirror. The dragon is in the shape of an S with an exaggeratedly curled body, one foot stepping on the rim of the mirror and two wings turning in an interlacing gesture towards the leaves on both sides. The broad rim is unadorned.

This mirror is perfect, with its delicately molding, well-arranged and vivid decorative patterns. The bronze mirrors with dragon design, with sections divided by leaf design, were found in Changsha and Nanyang, which are decorated with big design of leaf. But this mirror is rare, with its leaf design less than half the height of the central section.

## 92. 三龙三凤三菱镜

战国晚期

直径 17.8 厘米，厚 0.45 厘米，重 313 克

2018 年 11 月征集入藏

圆形。三弦钮，圆钮座。钮座外饰斜线组成的凸弦纹和凹弧面宽圈带纹各一周，宽圈带纹外饰单线弦纹。云雷地纹满铺镜面，部分不清晰。主纹为三个双层菱形纹间隔三龙三凤纹。菱形纹饰于近宽带纹处；龙首贴镜缘处中部，腹部向上拱起，折而后卷，张口，对应斜上方的凤首；凤首居镜缘边、双层菱形纹之上，凤的长喙衔于菱形纹折角处，凤冠向后翘起，前后翼"S"状卷曲呈蔓枝状。宽素缘。

由于此镜锈蚀较为严重，仅可辨其中一组龙凤纹的形态，但仍能看出独具匠心的镜面布局。

## 92. Mirror with design of three dragons, three phoenixes and three rhombuses

Late Warring States Period
Diameter: 17.8cm, Thickness: 0.45cm, Weight: 313g
Collected in November, 2018

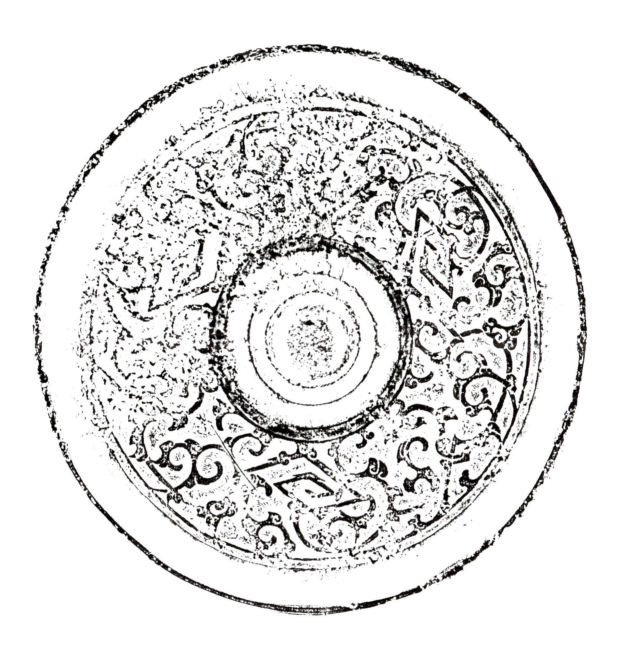

The mirror is round in shape. It has a knob with design of three bow strings on a round base. The outside of the knob base is adorned with a band of raised bow string formed by slanted lines, a broad band with concave surface and a band of bow string formed by single line. The surface of the mirror is full of the design of cloud and thunder as the ground motif. Part of the ground motif is dim. The major motif is an alternating arrangement of three overlaid rhombuses, three dragons and three phoenixes. The rhombus designs are located near the broad band. Each dragon, opposite to the head of phoenix at the inclined top, has a head in the middle that is close to the rim of the mirror, a belly arching upwards that is bent and rolled, an opening mouth. Each phoenix has a head near the rim of the mirror and on the design of overlaid rhombuses, a beak holding the breaking angle of the rhombus design, a phoenix coronet lifting backwards and front and back wings that are interlaced in the shape of a branch-like S. The broad rim is unadorned.

The mirror was rusted heavily. Only a group of the dragon design and the phoenix design can be identified. But this mirror also shows a unique decorative arrangement.

## 93. 四龙四凤宽带连弧纹镜

战国晚期

直径 21 厘米，厚 0.7 厘米，重 651 克

2020 年 11 月淮南市高新区三元孤堆楚墓出土

　　圆形。三弦钮，圆钮座。钮座外饰凹弧面宽带纹、细线弦纹各一周。近缘处饰一周短斜线纹。宽平缘。中区饰三层纹饰，地纹为云雷纹，镜面内区呈"十"字状饰四凤，凤昂首挺腹振翅，生动活泼；外区饰四龙，龙身体成"S"状向上展开，龙眼和鼻部夸张；下方的凤昂首仰视龙首，虽然凤居于镜面内区，但能够感受到是以龙为中心设计的纹饰。最上一层的八连弧纹叠压在龙的身体上。整个镜面的纹饰层次分明、分区清晰，线条饱满，十分精美。

## 93. Mirror with design of four dragons, four phoenixes and linked arcs formed by broad band

Late Warring States Period
Diameter: 21cm, Thickness: 0.7cm, Weight: 651g
Unearthed in the tomb of the Chu State at Sanyuangudui, High-tech District, Huainan City in November, 2020

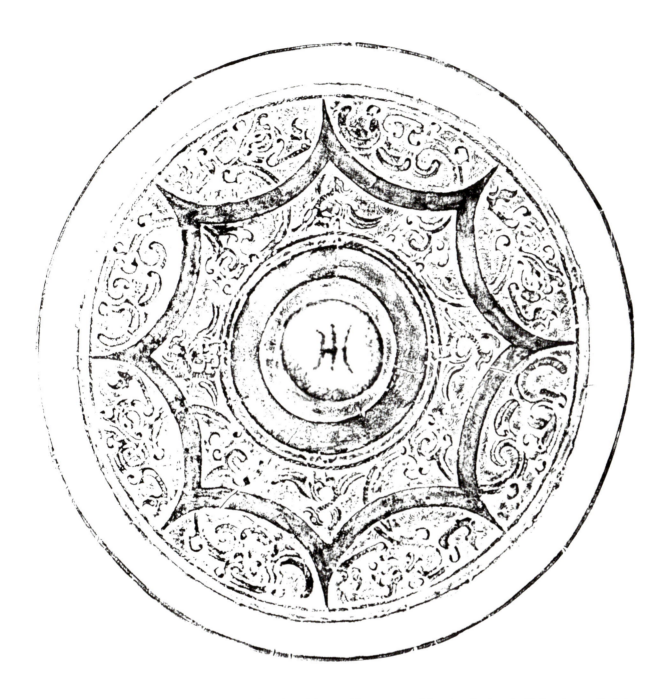

The mirror is round in shape. It has a knob with design of three bow strings on a round base. The outside of the knob base is adorned with a broad band with concave surface and a band of bow string formed by slender line. A band of short slanted line is near the rim of the mirror. The rim is broad and flat. The middle surface of the mirror is adorned with decorative patterns in three layers. The ground motif is the design of cloud and thunder. The inner part of the mirror is adorned with four phoenixes in each direction of cross. Each phoenix, in its lively and vivid shape, raises its head, squares its belly and spreads its wings.

The outer part of the mirror is adorned with four dragons. Each dragon has exaggerated eyes and an exaggerated nose, and a body extending upwards in the shape of an S. Each phoenix below looks up to the dragon. Although the phoenix design is located on the inner part of the mirror, the mirror shows a decoration with the dragon design as the center. The design of eight linked arcs at the top is overlaid on the bodies of the dragons. The mirror is so beautiful, with well-arranged decoration, clear partitions and strong lines.

## 94. 素面镜

战国晚期

直径 13 厘米，厚 0.15 厘米，重 126 克

2018 年 5 月征集入藏

圆形。小三弦钮。素面。无缘。镜体平直，镜面保存完好。

## 94. Mirror with plain ground

Late Warring States Period
Diameter: 13cm, Thickness: 0.15cm, Weight: 126g
Collected in May, 2018

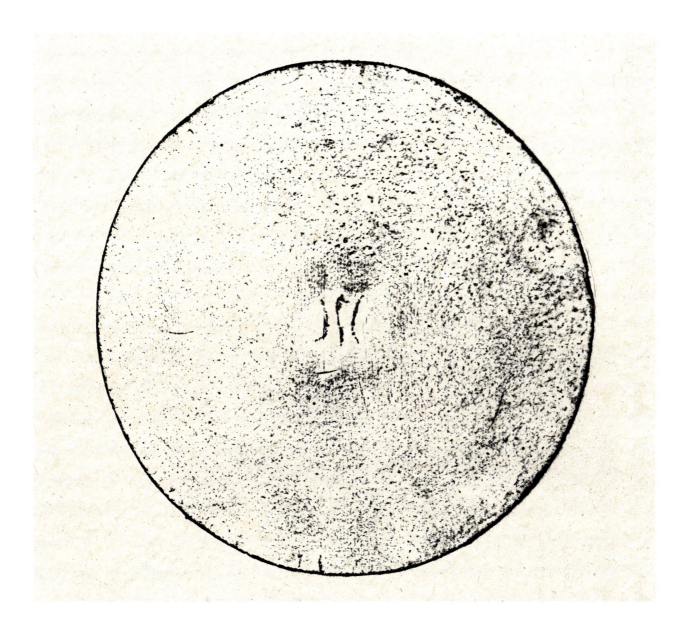

The mirror is round in shape. It has a small knob with design of three bow strings. The mirror is unadorned. The mirror has no rim. The body of the mirror is flat and straight. The mirror is kept in good condition.

## 95. 四龙四叶镜

战国晚期

直径 12.2 厘米，厚 0.2 厘米，重 101 克

2018 年 11 月征集入藏

圆形。三弦钮，圆钮座。钮座外由内及外分别饰云雷纹、凹弧面宽圈带纹、短斜线纹和单线凸弦纹各一周。镜面平整，满铺云雷地纹，不甚清晰。主纹是以四朵花苞形草叶纹将镜面中区分隔成四部分，每区饰一龙纹。龙首上抵钮座，身体后倾，前翼呈"S"状向后方盘起，依托前方的草叶，后翼卷曲拱托草叶。主纹的装饰线条十分干练、简约有致，很是美观。素缘。

此镜是战国晚期同类镜中的上乘之作。这种铜镜在湖南长沙、河南南阳都有出土，是广泛流行的镜种。

## 95. Mirror with design of four dragons and four leaves

Late Warring States Period
Diameter: 12.2cm, Thickness: 0.2cm, Weight: 101g
Collected in November, 2018

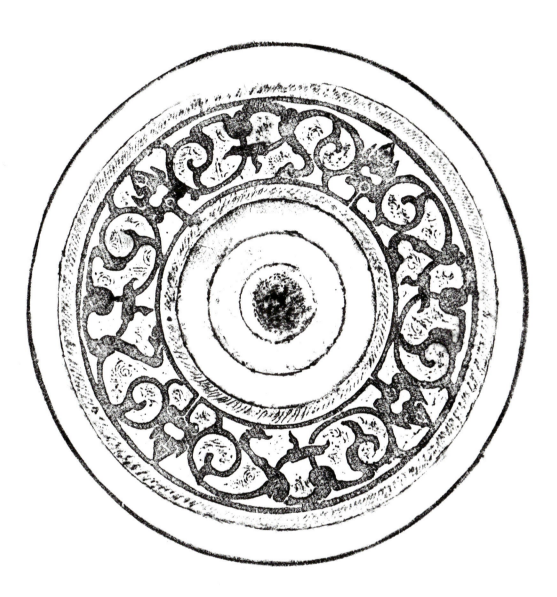

The mirror is round in shape. It has a knob with design of three bow strings on a round base. The exterior of the knob base is adorned in turn with the design of cloud and thunder, a broad band with concave surface, the design of short slanted lines and the design of raised bow string formed by single line. The flat surface of the mirror is filled up with indistinct design of cloud and thunder. The major motif is divided into four sections by four bud-like leaves. Each section is adorned with the dragon design. The dragon has a head close to the knob base, a body inverting, the front S-shaped wing twisting backwards against the front leaf and the back wing arcing against the leaf. The decorative lines of the major motif are skilful, simple and beautiful. The rim is unadorned.

This mirror is of the remarkable quality among the bronze mirrors with the same shape in the late Warring States Period. The mirrors were unearthed in Changsha, Hunan Province and Nanyang, Henan Province. It was in wide use in its day.

## 96. 四叶镜

战国晚期
直径 12.8 厘米，厚 0.6 厘米，重 270 克
1958 年淮南市唐山公社九里大队出土

　　圆形。三弦钮，方形双层钮座。钮座四边中间各伸出一单片桃形叶纹，叶片中饰对称斜线纹表现叶之脉络，向镜钮方向整齐排列，并以两个相连的短弧线横穿叶片，四叶下满铺羽状地纹。卷缘，平沿。

## 96. Mirror with design of four leaves

Late Warring States Period
Diameter: 12.8cm, Thickness: 0.6cm, Weight: 270g
Unearthed at Jiuli Brigade, Tangshan Commune, Huainan City in 1958

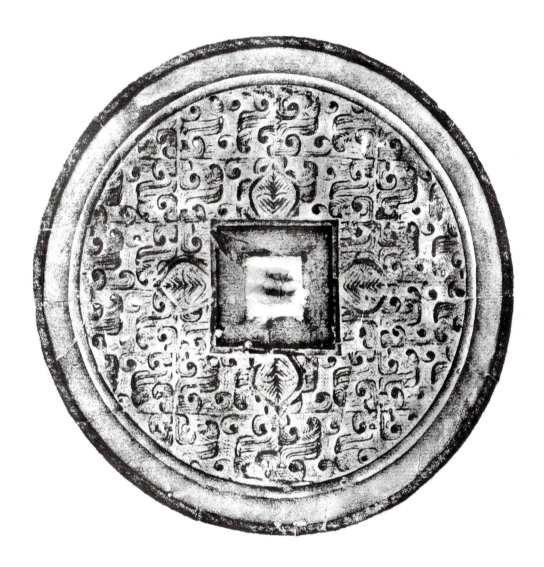

The mirror is round in shape. It has a knob with design of three bow strings on a two-layer square base. A peach-shaped leaf protrudes from the middle of each side of the knob base, and is decorated with symmetrical slanted-line patterns arranged orderly toward the knob as leaf veins and two short linked arc-like lines crossing the leaf. The feather-like pattern serves as ground motif here. The rim rolls upward and has a flat edge.

## 97. 四虺四乳镜

战国晚期—西汉

直径 10.1 厘米，厚 0.2 厘米，重 54 克

2018 年 11 月淮南市谢家集公安分局移交

　　圆形。小三弦钮，圆钮座。钮座外饰凹弧面宽圈带纹、细线凸弦纹各一周。镜面中区纹饰由地纹和主纹构成。地纹铺以疏朗的卷云纹，单个卷云纹较大，模印不清晰。主纹以四小乳丁将镜面分为四区，四虺纹极其简化，头尾不识，身体环绕乳丁，两虺之间以弧线勾连。宽素缘。

　　此镜纹饰虽具备战国晚期的小三弦钮及宽带纹特征，但已饰有西汉早期的小乳丁纹。这种铜镜使用时间的跨度很大，自战国晚期至西汉中期都有发现。河南南阳发现了一批此类铜镜。

## 97. Mirror with design of four serpents and four nipples

Late Warring States Period to Western Han Dynasty
Diameter: 10.1cm, Thickness: 0.2cm, Weight: 54g
Transferred by Xiejiaji District Public Security Bureau in Huainan City in November, 2018

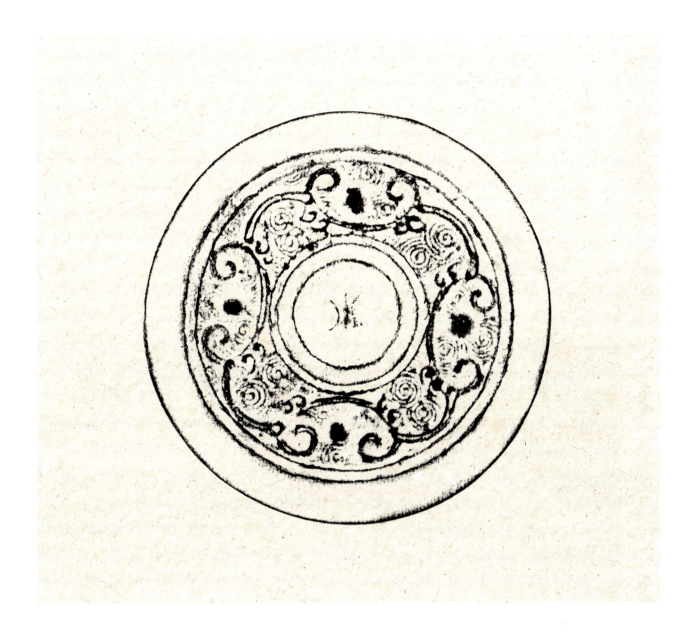

The mirror is round in shape. It has a small knob with design of three bow strings on a round base. The outside of the knob base is adorned with a broad band with concave surface and a band of raised bow string formed by slender line. The middle surface of the mirror is adorned with the ground motif and the major motif. The ground motif is the comfortable design of cirrus cloud. Each design of cirrus cloud is bigger in size and has indistinct molding marks. The major motif is divided into four sections by the design of four small nipples. The design of four serpents is adorned with simplified decoration and their heads and tails can not be identified. Four serpents encircle the nipples.

The serpents are joined with each other by the arcs. The broad rim is unadorned.

The mirror holds the features of the small knob with design of three bow strings and the broad band of the bronze mirrors in the late Warring States Period. But it is adorned with the design of small nipple which appeared in the early Western Han Dynasty. The mirrors of this kind were used over a long period from the late Warring States Period to the middle Western Han Dynasty. Some of these mirrors were unearthed in Nanyang, Henan Province.

## 98. 十二叶镜

战国晚期

直径 13.6 厘米，厚 0.5 厘米，重 148 克

1958 年淮南市唐山公社九里大队出土

　　圆形。三弦钮，方钮座。镜面满饰羽状纹。此镜采用四方连续图案方法，羽状纹两两相对应，横置排列成十行，羽翅的对应间有十分密集细小的小乳突，共三行六列，与羽状纹、主纹构成三层纹饰。主纹是从方形钮座四角向外伸出的对称长杆花叶，形如"J"形，每支杆上有两个长桃形花叶，共十二叶。宽缘卷沿。

　　羽状纹，也有学者称之为变形羽状兽纹、羽翅纹等，是截取龙纹躯体的一部分，为一个长方形，是有规律连续排列形成的四方连续图案。这种图案在装饰镜面的时候常常布满镜面，密集而整齐，有较强的装饰效果。此镜纹饰精细繁缛，但不失雅致，是特征较明显的楚式镜。

## 98. Mirror with design of twelve leaves

Late Warring states Period

Diameter: 13.6cm, Thickness: 0,5cm, Weight: 148g

Unearthed at Jiuli Brigade, Tangshan Commune, Huainan City in 1958

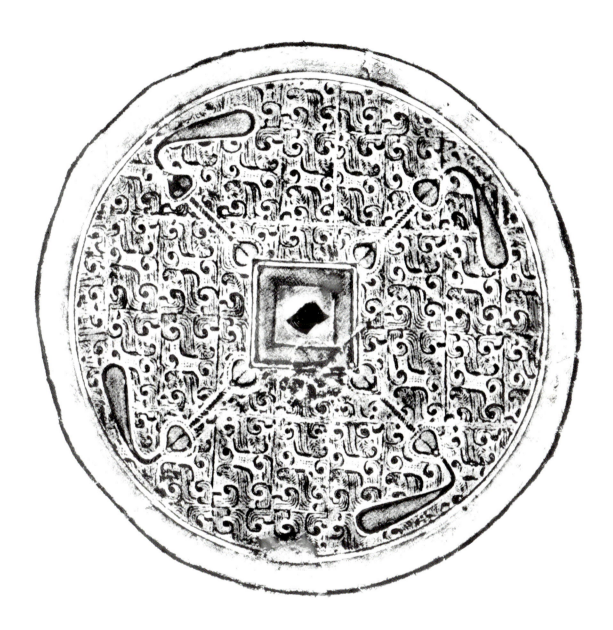

The mirror is round in shape. It has a knob with design of three bow strings on a square base. It is decorated with feather-like pattern. The decorative patterns are arranged consecutively and repeatedly toward four directions. The three-layer design of the mirror consists of feather-like pattern corresponding in twos and arranging in ten lines, nipple pattern spaced in corresponding area of feather-like pattern and arranged in three lines and six rows, and motif design. The major motif is the patterns of long J-shaped branches extending out from each corner of the square knob base. Each branch has two peach-shaped leaves and

the total number of leaves is twelve. The mirror has a broad rim that rolls up.

The feather-like pattern, also called "beast pattern in a shape of stylized feather" or "pattern of wing with feather", is the pattern of a rectangle part of dragon's body arranged symmetrically and consecutively towards the four directions. It often covers crowdedly and orderly the back surface of the mirror and has a strong decorative effect. The mirror with elaborate design is the typical of those mirrors of the Chu State.

## 99. 单线连弧纹镜

战国晚期

直径 10.6 厘米，厚 0.2 厘米，重 64 克

2018 年 11 月淮南市谢家集公安分局移交

　　圆形。三弦钮。钮外饰凹面宽圈带纹。中区在素地上　　线纤细，曲度平缓。窄缘，缘边微上卷。锈蚀较重。

饰单线连弧纹，以镜钮为中心饰七个内向单线连弧纹，弧

## 99. Mirror with design of linked arcs formed by single line

Late Warring States Period
Diameter: 10.6cm, Thickness: 0.2cm, Weight: 64g
Transferred by Xiejiaji District Public Security Bureau in Huainan City on November, 2018

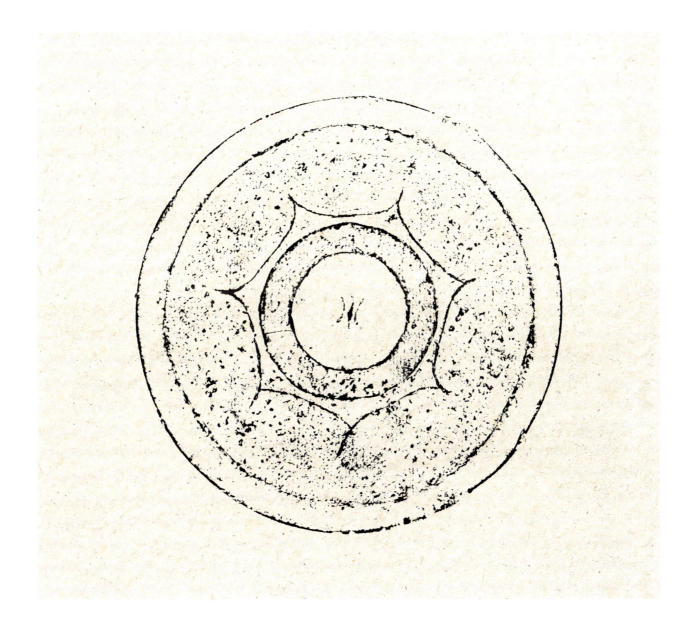

The mirror is round in shape. It has a knob with design of three bow strings. On the outside of the knob is a broad band with concave surface. The major motif is the design of seven gently linked arcs formed by thin single line and oriented inwards around the knob on the plain ground. The rim is narrow and rolls up slightly. The mirror is heavily rusted.

## 100. 四龙四叶镜

战国晚期

直径 12.2 厘米，厚 0.35 厘米，重 127 克

2017 年 12 月征集入藏

　　圆形。三弦钮，圆钮座。钮座外饰两周单线凸弦纹，弦纹间装饰"人"字形短斜线纹。地纹为云雷纹，较清晰。主纹以花苞状叶纹将镜面中区分隔成四区，每区各饰一龙纹，布局不甚对称。龙的形态为小圆目，曲颈，腹部盘曲呈"S"状，腹下二足分别蹬踏至两侧的草叶处，前二翼分别向两侧交错翻卷至草叶上。宽素缘，卷沿。

　　此镜没有战国晚期常见的凹弧面宽圈带纹，这是铜镜纹饰演化中的特征，花苞形叶纹也趋于简化，是战国晚期晚段的特点。

## 100. Mirror with design of four dragons and four leaves

Late Warring States Period
Diameter: 12.2cm, Thickness: 0.35cm, Weight: 127g
Collected in December, 2017

The mirror is round in shape. It has a knob with design of three bow strings on a round base. The outside of the knob base is adorned with two bands of raised bow string formed by single line. A band of short slanted lines, which is arranged in a shape of "*ren* (man)" character, is spaced between the bands. The ground motif is the clear design of cloud and thunder. The major motif is divided into four sections by four bud-like leaves. Each section is adorned unsymmetrically with the dragon design. The dragon has small round eyes, a crooked neck, an S-shaped belly, two feet stepping on leaves on either side and the front and back wings twisting towards both sides on the leaves. The broad rim is unadorned and rolls up.

This mirror is unadorned with the broad band with concave surface in the late Warring States Period, that is a change in the development of the decorative patterns for the bronze mirrors. And it is also a characteristic of the late period of the late Warring States Period that the bud-like leaf tends to be simplified.

## 101. 三龙三菱镜

战国晚期

直径 14.1 厘米，厚 0.3 厘米，重 177 克

2018 年 5 月征集入藏

　　圆形。三弦钮，双层圆钮座。钮座外饰凹弧面宽圈带纹和细线凸弦纹各一周，其内饰一周短斜线纹。地纹较模糊，隐约可见卷云纹。主纹为三个双层菱形纹间隔三龙纹。龙首居菱形纹左上侧，形象写实，很有特点，是少见的双圆目，大张口紧贴菱形纹斜边，勾曲颈，下羽上卷翻转，腹部及尾部向后呈"S"状卷曲拱起，羽翅勾连后面的菱形纹。宽素缘，卷平沿。

　　此镜的装饰特点在于龙首已接近于正面，两圆目一大一小，吐舌微卷，是龙纹镜中少见的品种。从龙纹的变形方式及菱形纹粗犷的风格看，铸造时间已到战国晚期晚段。

## 101. Mirror with design of three dragons and three rhombuses

Late Warring States Period
Diameter: 14.1cm, Thickness: 0.3cm, Weight: 177g
Collected in May, 2018

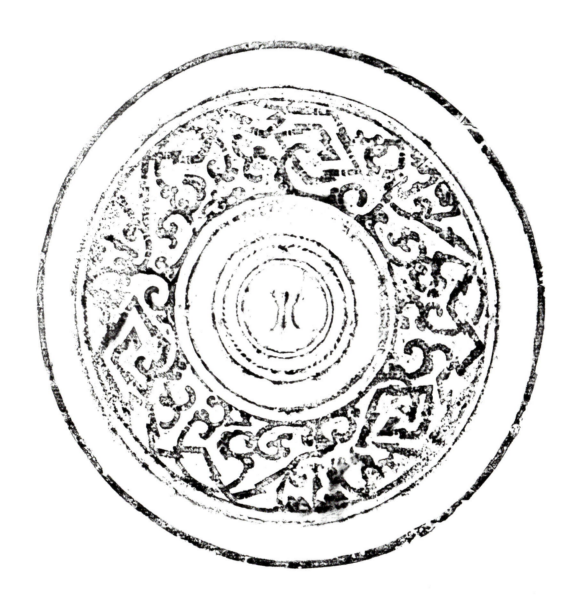

The mirror is round in shape. It has a knob with design of three bow strings on an overlaid round base. The outside of the knob base is adorned with a broad band with concave surface, a band of raised bow string formed by slender line and band of short slanted lines. The ground motif is indistinct, with the design of cirrus cloud dimly visible. The major motif is the decorative patterns of three overlaid rhombuses spaced in three dragons. Each dragon's head is located on the upper left side of the rhombus design in a realistic and special shape. Each dragon has two round eyes that are rarely seen, an open mouth that approaches the side of the rhombus, a crooked neck, feathers rolling up, a belly and a tail both which arch towards back in the shape of an S and feather-wings that interlace with the rhombus at the back. The broad rim is unadorned. The edge of the rim rolls and is flat.

This mirror is distinguished by the dragon's head on the obverse side, with two round eyes, one big and the other small, and a protruding and slightly curled tongue. The decorative style of this mirror is rarely seen in the mirrors with dragon design. Based on the deformation of the dragon and the coarse style of the rhombus design, the mirror was cast in the late period of the late Warring States Period.

## 102. 三龙三菱三叶镜

战国晚期

直径 12.1 厘米，厚 0.35 厘米，重 116 克

2018 年 11 月征集入藏

　　圆形。大三弦钮，圆钮座。钮座外饰凹弧面宽圈带纹。纹饰由地纹和主纹构成。地纹是比较疏朗的云雷纹，主纹是以三龙三菱三叶相间布置。龙纹虽简化变形，但龙首特征明显，大张口，吐舌，头上有角，身体顺时针上卷呈"C"字状；菱形纹上下三层连体折叠；草叶形似花苞。宽素缘。

　　此镜纹饰的特点是在一种纹饰中同时用单线和双线方法造型，在一面铜镜上反映出了纹饰演化的过程：龙首部分是单实线，而龙身是双线勾勒；花苞上部的尖角是双线，下部是单实线。流行于西汉早、中期的双线，在这面镜上已初步呈现。

## 102. Mirror with design of three dragons, three rhombuses and three leaves

Late Warring States Period
Diameter: 12.1cm, Thickness: 0.35cm, Weight: 116g
Collected in November, 2018

The mirror is round in shape. It has a big knob with design of three bow strings on a round base. The outside of the knob base is adorned with a broad band with concave surface. The decorative patterns consist of the ground motif and the major motif. The ground motif is the comfortable design of cloud and thunder. The major motif is an alternating arrangement of three dragons, three rhombuses and three leaves. Each dragon is in the simplified shape, with a obvious head with an opening mouth and a protruding tongue, horns on the head and a body rolling clockwise upwards in the shape of a C. The rhombus design is in the three-layer joined shape. The leaf design is in the shape of bud. The broad rim is unadorned.

This mirror is distinguished by its decorative patterns that are formed by single line and double lines at the same time, indicating the process of changing decorative patterns on one mirror. On this mirror, the head of each dragon is formed by single line, but the body of each dragon is formed by double lines; the sharp angle of each bud is formed by double lines, but the lower part of each bud is formed by single line. The decorative patterns that are formed by double lines, prevailed in the early and middle Western Han Dynasty. The preliminary changes appear on this mirror.

**103. 龙纹镜**

战国晚期

直径 12.7 厘米，厚 0.4 厘米，重 150 克

20 世纪 80 年代后期征集入藏

　　圆形。桥钮，圆钮座。钮座外环绕一周凹弧面宽带纹。主区纹饰两侧以弦纹和栉齿纹为栏，主纹在云雷纹地上饰四龙。龙首大张口，作吞钮座状，肢爪伸张，身躯弯卷，勾连交错，变化复杂。宽缘，缘边卷起。

## 103. Mirror with design of dragon

Late Warring States Period
Diameter: 12.7cm, Thickness: 0.4cm, Weight: 150g
Collected in late 1980s

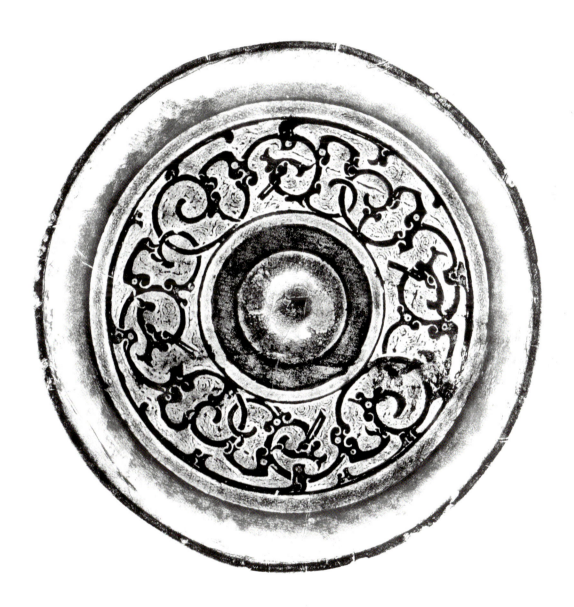

The mirror is round in shape. It has a bridge-shaped knob on a round base. The outside of the base is adorned with a broad band with concave surface. The bow string design and the fine-toothed design serve as the fence on either side of the major motif. The major motif is the pattern of four dragons on the ground motif with design of cloud and thunder. All the dragons swallow the knob, extend their paws and curve their bodies. They are interlaced one another. The mirror has a broad rim that rolls up.

## 104. 四叶镜

战国晚期

直径 11.3 厘米，厚 0.3 厘米，重 68 克

1972 年淮南市谢家集区红卫轮窑厂出土

　　圆形。三弦钮，小圆钮座。钮座饰有一周凸弦纹，四周等距伸出四桃形叶，双层叠压，外层叶由放射状短线构成，形似茸毛，叶无柄，紧贴钮座。镜面满铺细密的羽状地纹，有模印羽状地纹痕迹和范线。此镜造型规范，模范细腻。属细涡粒状羽状纹，时代较早，应不晚于战国晚期楚国迁都寿春之前。

## 104. Mirror with design of four leaves

Late Warring States Period

Diameter: 11.3cm, Thickness: 0.3cm, Weight: 68g

Unearthed at Hongwei Annular Kiln Works, Xiejiaji District, Huainan City in 1972

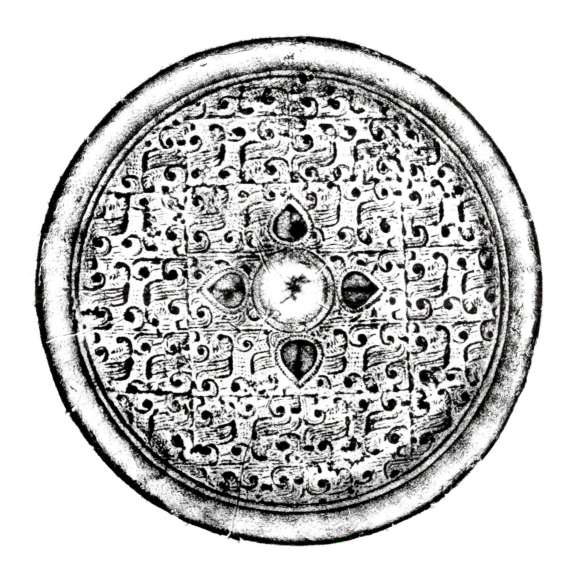

The mirror is round in shape. It has a knob with design of three bow strings on a round base. The outside of the base is adorned with a band of raised bow string pattern. Four peach-shaped leaves extend out at equally spaced intervals around the knob base. The leaves are in a two-layer shape and get close to the knob base without petiole. The outer leaves consist of short radial lines that look like fuzz. The elaborate feather-like pattern is decorated as ground motif on the back of the mirror, where mold marks can be found. This mirror has a canonical layout and an exquisite mold. The feather-like pattern is in the shape of fine granular whorl. This decorative pattern appeared in the earlier period, not later than the period before that the Chu State moved its capital to Shouchun town in the late Warring States Period.

## 105. 三龙三菱镜

战国晚期

直径 11.4 厘米，厚 0.2 厘米，重 83 克

2018 年 5 月征集入藏

　　圆形。小三弦钮，圆钮座。钮座外饰单线凸弦纹二周。地纹模糊不清，似云雷纹样。主纹是三龙间隔三菱形纹。菱形纹居近镜缘处。三龙首尾相接，龙口大张，龙首贴于镜缘，小圆目可辨，前身卷曲成涡纹状与菱形纹相接，后身呈"S"状由下向上、向内弯曲。宽缘弧起。

　　三龙三菱镜比较多见，从两湖地区到河南南阳一带都有出土，是战国晚期十分流行的铜镜纹样。

## 105. Mirror with design of three dragons and three rhombuses

Late Warring States Period
Diameter: 11.4cm, Thickness: 0.2cm, Weight: 83g
Collected in May, 2018

The mirror is round in shape. It has a small knob with design of three bow strings on a round base. The outside of the knob base is adorned with two bands of raised bow string formed by single line. The ground motif is indistinct, like the design of cloud and thunder. The major motif is the decorative patterns of three dragons spaced in three rhombuses. The rhombus designs are located near the rim of the mirror. The dragon's head is connected with another dragon's tail. Each dragon has a big open mouth, a head close to the rim, small visible round eyes, the front part of the body that is in the shape of whorl and is connected with the rhombus design and the back part of the body in a shape of an S curving from below to top inwards. The broad rim rolls in the shape of arc.

The mirrors with design of three dragons and three rhombuses are common. And they were unearthed from the Hubei and Hunan regions to Nanyang, Henan Province. The mirrors of this kind prevailed in the late Warring States Period.

## 106. 变形三虺三菱镜

战国晚期

直径 20.7 厘米，厚 0.25 厘米，重 364 克

2019 年 11 月征集入藏

　　圆形。三弦钮，圆钮座。钮座外饰一圈凹面宽圈带纹。地纹为较为粗松卷云纹。主纹以三个重叠菱形纹均分镜面，间饰三变形虺纹。虺首居两菱形纹中间，小首，小圆目，腹部向镜缘处拱起，尾部缠绕卷曲与下方的菱形纹相接，身体上有布满蔓枝状向内勾起的涡纹。虺纹简化成图案形状，难以辨识。近缘处饰一周短斜线纹。宽素缘。

　　虺纹，多认为是蛇纹的变形，但一般身体短小，又称为蟠虺纹、虺龙纹等。

## 106. Mirror with design of three stylized serpents and three rhombuses

Late Warring States Period
Diameter: 20.7cm, Thickness: 0.25cm, Weight: 364g
Collected in November, 2018

The mirror is round in shape. It has a knob with design of three bow strings on a round base. The outside of the base is adorned with a broad band with concave surface. The ground motif is the coarse design of cirrus cloud. The major motif is an alternating arrangement of the design of three overlaid rhombuses and the design of three stylized serpents and is divided by the rhombus design into three sections. Each serpent has a small head with small round eyes that is located in the middle of the two rhombuses, a belly arching towards the rim of

the mirror, a tail coiling and interlacing with the rhombus below and a body with design of whorl in the shape of branches rolling inwards. It is difficult to recognize the serpent design in the shape of the pattern. A band of short slanted lines is near the rim. The broad rim is unadorned.

The serpent design is generally considered to be the design of stylized snake. But it is also known as the design of coiled serpent or design of serpent for its short body.

## 107. 四虺四叶镜

战国晚期

直径 15.3 厘米，厚 0.3 厘米，重 172 克

2019 年 11 月征集入藏

　　圆形。三弦钮，圆钮座。钮座外饰一圈凹弧面宽圈带纹，宽圈带纹内饰有粒状碎点纹。纹饰由地纹和主纹构成。地纹是疏朗活泼的卷云纹，单个纹饰形体较大。主纹是以双线四花苞状叶纹将镜面分成四区，每区饰一简化的虺纹；虺纹用双线方法装饰，看不出头尾特征，虺身是弯曲交错的双曲线，勾连花叶。宽素缘。这种双线构成的主纹，从战国晚期开始出现，到西汉中期时十分流行。

## 107. Mirror with design of four serpents and four leaves

Late Warring States Period
Diameter: 15.3cm, Thickness: 0.3cm, Weight: 172g
Collected in November, 2019

The mirror is round in shape. It has a knob with design of three bow strings on a round base. The outside of the base is adorned with a broad band with concave surface. The broad band is adorned with the design of tiny spots. The decorative patterns consist of the ground motif and the major motif. The ground motif is the big bright design of cirrus cloud. The major motif is divided into four sections by the four-bud-like leaves design formed by double lines. Each section is adorned with the design of simplified serpent. The serpent is formed by double lines and the body of the serpent is formed by double lines that are twisted and interlaced with leaf. The serpent has no well-defined head and tail. The broad band is unadorned. The major motif, formed by double lines, appeared in the late Warring States Period and prevailed in the middle Western Han Dynasty.

## 108. 三龙三菱镜

战国晚期
直径 19.8 厘米，厚 0.7 厘米，重 404 克
2018 年 11 月淮南市谢家集公安分局移交

　　圆形。三弦钮，圆钮座。钮座外饰凹面宽圈带纹和单线凸弦纹各一周。镜面平直，满铺云雷地纹直至钮座外，可以看出主纹和宽带纹、弦纹皆饰于地纹之上。主纹为三龙纹间隔小巧的菱形纹。龙首较大，伏于钮座外围，圆目，短角，大张口中有上、下二獠牙，曲颈回首，前羽翅呈"S"状卷起，勾连小菱形纹；后羽翅展开翻卷，由上而下穿过小菱形纹，整个龙纹呈蔓枝状卷曲。近镜缘处饰二周凸弦纹，宽缘弧起，窄边。

　　此镜的纹饰模印很清晰，龙的姿态矫健有力，有很强的张力，与本馆所藏六龙三菱纹镜的装饰风格和铸造工艺上很相近，铸造时间当在战国晚期晚段。

## 108. Mirror with design of three dragons and three rhombuses

Late Warring States Period
Diameter: 19.8cm, Thickness: 0.7cm, Weight: 404g
Transferred by Xiejiaji District Public Security Bureau in Huainan City in November, 2018

The mirror is round in shape. It has a knob with design of three bow strings on a round base. The outside of the knob base is adorned with a broad band with concave surface and a band of raised bow string formed by single line. The surface of the mirror is flat and straight is full of the ground motif of the design of cloud and thunder that extend to the outside of the knob base. The major motif, the broad band and the design of bow string adorn on the ground motif. The major motif is the decorative patterns of three dragons spaced in three rhombuses. Each dragon has a bigger head bending over the outside of the knob base, round eyes, short horns, an open mouth with two buckteeth up and down, a crooked neck turning back, the front wing that rolls in the shape of an S and interlaces with the small design of rhombus and the back wing spreading and rolling that passes the small design of rhombus from top to bottom. The design of dragon is in the shape of curled branches. Two bands of raised bow string adorn near the rim of the mirror. The broad rim rolls in the shape of arc and has a narrow edge.

The decorative patterns of this mirror have clear molding marks and the dragon design on the mirror is in a powerful and vigorous shape with a strong decorative effect. The mirror, similar in decorative style and casting technique to the bronze mirror with design of six dragons and three rhombuses in the museum, was cast in the late period of the late Warring States Period.

## 109. 三凤三菱镜

战国晚期

直径 11 厘米，厚 0.6 厘米，重 136 克

2018 年 5 月征集入藏

圆形。小三弦钮，圆钮座。钮座外饰一圈卷云纹。卷云纹围钮座环绕布置，这种装饰手法比较少见。云纹外饰一凹弧面宽圈带纹，宽圈带纹内饰短斜线纹和单线细弦纹。镜面由地纹和主纹构成，地纹为云雷纹，主纹为三凤三菱纹相间环列。凤立于二菱纹中间，勾回首，口衔凤的

尾羽，单足立于钮座之上，两翼勾卷，与缠枝状菱形纹交互叠压。宽素卷缘。

此镜模印清晰，菱形纹与缠枝纹细密复杂，繁而不乱，凤的姿态生动有趣，是此类铜镜中的精品。

# 109. Mirror with design of three phoenixes and three rhombuses

Late Warring States Period
Diameter: 11cm, Thickness: 0.6cm, Weight: 136g
Collected in May, 2018

The mirror is round in shape. It has a small knob with design of three bow strings on a round base. The outside of the knob base is adorned with a band of the design of cirrus cloud. This is very rare. Out the design of cloud are a broad band with concave surface, a band of short slanted lines and a band of slender bow string formed by single line. The surface of the mirror is adorned with the ground motif and the major motif. The ground motif is the design of cloud and thunder. The major motif is an alternating arrangement of three phoenixes and three rhombuses. Each phoenix stands between the rhombuses. Each phoenix turns its back, holds its tail in its mouth, steps on the knob base with one leg and rolls its wings which are interlaced and overlaid with the design of branch-shaped rhombus. The broad rim is unadorned and rolls.

This mirror, with its clear molding marks, its exquisite and well-arranged design of rhombus and branch and the design of phoenix in a lively and interesting shape, is a treasure of its kind.

# 110. 三龙三菱镜

战国晚期

直径 14.1 厘米，厚 0.4 厘米，重 166 克

2018 年 2 月征集入藏

　　圆形。小三弦钮，圆钮座。钮座外饰四层纹饰，由内而外分别是：云雷纹、斜向短线纹、凹面宽圈带纹、斜向短线纹各一周，中间以细绚纹分隔。地纹为模印的云雷纹，主纹由三个菱形纹间三变形龙纹组成。三只龙首均左向安排，最具特点的是，龙首有双目，在镜缘处向下大张口，龙身前段下穿勾连前面的菱形纹，后段占龙纹的大部，成蔓枝状勾连卷曲，与尾部菱形纹相接，龙的姿态很有动感，十分生动有趣。宽素缘，缘边卷起，窄平。

　　龙纹镜是战国晚期铜镜中的主流，龙的形态千变万化，但龙首有双目的，接近于正面龙首的龙纹镜，十分罕见。

## 110. Mirror with design of three dragons and three rhombuses

Late Warring States Period
Diameter: 14.1cm, Thickness: 0.4cm, Weight: 166g
Collected in February, 2018

The mirror is round in shape. It has a small knob with design of three bow strings on a round base. The outside of the knob base is adorned respectively from the inside out with a band of cloud and thunder, a band of short slanted lines, a broad band with concave surface and a band of short slanted lines, all of which are divided with the rope design. The ground motif is the cast design of cloud and thunder. The major motif is the decorative patterns of three dragons spaced in three rhombuses. The heads of three dragons turn to the left in order. Each dragon is distinguished by its head with two eyes and an open mouth backward near the rim of the mirror, its body with the front part passing underneath and interlacing with the front design of rhombus and the back part that takes up a majority of the whole body and is in a shape of interlaced and curled branches that are joined with the rhombus design on the tail. The dragon design is vivid and interesting. The broad rim is unadorned. The edge of the rim rolls up and is narrow and flat.

The mirrors with dragon design are the main trend in the bronze mirrors in the late Warring States Period. The dragon comes in a variety of shapes. But the mirrors with dragon design, with the dragon's head with two eyes on the obverse side, are rarely seen.